T4-AHG-837

The Way, the Truth, and the Life

Other books by
C. George Fry

A History of Lutheranism in America, 1619–1930
The Age of Lutheran Orthodoxy, 1530–1648
Islam: A Survey of the Muslim Faith
The Middle East: Crossroads of Civilization
An Anthology of Middle Eastern Literature

Other books by
Duane W. H. Arnold and C. George Fry

A Lutheran Reader
Francis of Assisi: An Evangelical Faith for Today

The Way, the Truth, and the Life

An Introduction to Lutheran Christianity

Duane W. H. Arnold

C. George Fry

Baker Book House Grand Rapids, Michigan 49506

ISBN: 0-8010-0189-7

Library of Congress Card Catalog Number: 82-72830

Printed in the United States of America

The lithographs reproduced in this volume were prepared by Ron Knepper, a noted Lutheran artist in Fort Wayne, Indiana.

The diagrams of floor plans of various churches and the diagram of a properly vested altar are from *The Small Church* (New York: Abingdon, 1926).

Unless otherwise indicated, all Scripture references are from the King James Version of the Bible.

The cover art by Steve Bates is based on a photo by Dimitri Kessel that appeared in *Splendors of Christendom* (Lausanne: Edita S.A. Lausanne, 1954). The photo also appeared in *Life* magazine (10/21/59) and is copyrighted 1959 by Time, Inc. The drawing depicts the great nave and central mosaic of the Basilica of Sant' Apollinaire in Classe, near Ravenna, Italy. The mosaic features the transfiguration of Christ. The sanctuary dates from the sixth century, the time of an undivided church. The art reflects the centrality of cross and altar in Lutheran theology and piety.

To
His Majesty
King Olav the Fifth
of
Norway

Contents

Foreword

What is Lutheran Christianity? What do Lutherans believe? Do Lutherans have identifiable characteristics? These are important questions not only for Lutherans who may or may not feel some ambiguity about their identity, but also for non-Lutherans whose knowledge of Lutheranism often is limited to fragments and who may, themselves, be struggling to put their own beliefs in order. Since Lutheranism was the cradle of Protestantism, and as such influenced the development of virtually all Protestant denominations, Lutheran identity takes on a significance in our time that exceeds ecclesiastical bounds. Has the original witness changed, stagnated, become more relevant? Obviously, the world has altered externally, and other matters seek to displace the centrality of religion. Scholars often point to the Thirty Years' War (1618–1648) as the end of the predominance of religion in the decisions of modern man. When Pope Innocent X denounced the Treaty of Westphalia as null and void for all time, Europe in general paid little attention—as if other affairs were more important than religion. This is but one of the many signs that the modern milieu is radically different from that of the sixteenth century. Martin Luther was poignantly concerned about God's love. How could he be sure that God cared anything at all about him? Believing he should love God, but being unable to do so, Luther envisaged torment in hell as his destiny. Before his conversion experience, God and hell were for Martin Luther frightening realities. Today, the very existence of God and hell are often considered to be outmoded superstitions. Truth and reality are said to have become so relativized and subjectivized that without an agreed-upon standard of what truth and reality are, almost anything can be declared right or wrong, valid or invalid. The Humanist Manifesto of 1933 boldly asserted that God is a hypothesis no longer needed by man. In Jean-Paul Sartre's writings, there is no place for God, and human destiny is a return to unconscious being. In Samuel Beckett's dish-pot-and-death existence, God is an illusion. And for Albert Camus, the meaningless symbol of life is Sisyphus pushing a rock up the hill and watching it roll down again. Scores of writers, many of whom are the recipients of our most prestigious awards, echo this message. Of the nature of this milieu the authors of this book are keenly aware; they not only have written a lucid description of Lutheranism today but also have given a witness, a theology, a confession of what it means to be a Lutheran Christian. They take a stand and clearly state its ramifications for our lives and our hopes. It is not a stance they have invented, for Christianity is not something we ourselves imagine. Christianity is something we are given, causing us to be renewed—something we experience, live by, and pass on to others.

The authors take the revelation of God in Scripture as their base line—the same authority to which Luther appealed in his "Here I stand" speech at Worms in 1521 when he proclaimed to the assembled imperial and ecclesiastical dignitaries that he could not and would not recant what he had written unless proved wrong by Scripture interpreted by right reason. "Unless I am thus convinced, I am bound by the texts of the Bible, my conscience is captive to the Word of God, I neither can nor will recant anything, since it is neither right nor safe to act against conscience." Behind that statement was Luther's experience of justification by faith alone as a living reality within himself. In his tower experience he realized that he was justified before God not by his pious works or his status as a monk or his ability to develop a rational thesis, but by the grace of God in Christ. Luther experienced the love of God as already his, not as something he had to earn. Henceforth, he was free of innumerable rules that men had said were requirements for righteousness—which he had so vainly tried to keep in an effort to make himself pleasing to God. He was free. Good works he knew could not merit the love of God, for love is freely given, not earned: "Christ died for us while we were yet sinners." Yet, having experienced the love of God, Luther felt bound to manifest works of love to his neighbor, not because he was legally bound to do so, but because he wanted to—out of joy and gratitude for what God had done for him. He was the freest of all persons on the one hand, and on the other the most bound of all, for he was bound by God's Spirit of love to show love to others. At Worms, the Bible as such was not under dispute, but the principle by which one interprets Scripture. Reason itself was not under question, only reason untouched by the Spirit of God. Luther had discovered a living principle in Scripture, "justification by faith." In that event, the Reformation and Lutheranism began. The authors of this book honor Luther not by idolizing his every word and deed, but by drawing from the well from which he drew his strength.

The living revelation of God did not begin with Luther. It was active in heroes of the faith in the centuries before the Reformation, and its richness and meaning continue to be disclosed. To this disclosure, past and present, the authors bear a compelling witness. Their explanations and their data are not limited to the confines of Lutheranism, for Lutheranism is by no means exclusive or monolithic. They do not hesitate to appeal to other witnesses that are grounded in Scripture, thus demonstrating an ecumenism and a universalism inherent in the Lutheran communion. Nevertheless, Lutheranism is a confession—a stance for ascertaining right and wrong, validity and invalidity. In this sense the Apostles', Nicene, and Athanasian creeds are affirmed, the Holy Spirit being active in those who in the early centuries struggled to state the nature of God the Father, Son, and Holy Spirit. In this sense the authors can appropriate and affirm Irenaeus's view of the atonement as a victory over Satan, Anselm's view as a satisfaction to God, and Peter Abelard's view as a moral influence on man—alongside insights from recent history and a mutiplicity of modern disciplines. Christ is "the center and focus of all that has borne the name *Christian*," and the fullness of Christ remains unfathomable, yet daily disclosed in newness and power.

This book seeks to dispel ambiguities about Lutheranism,

and in doing so not only lucidly explains the oldest communion in Reformation Protestantism, but also speaks to other Christian groups, and to the problems that confront human beings as they attempt to understand their nature and destiny and endeavor to relate to one another and to God.

Clyde L. Manschreck
Director for the Center of
Reformation and Free Church Studies,
Chicago Theological Seminary

Preface

He who would valiant be
'Gainst all disaster,
Let him in constancy
Follow the Master.
There's no discouragement
Shall make him once relent
His first avowed intent
To be a pilgrim.

John Bunyan (1628–1688) and others

The whole church, from Catholic to Congregationalist, has seen the Christian life as one of pilgrimage. The Book of Acts refers to believers as those of the "way" (Acts 9:2). That was how Jesus described Himself in the upper room when He said, "I am the way, the truth, and the life" (John 14:6). The late Willard L. Sperry, dean of Harvard Divinity School, could state, "What is religion? It is a way. What is Christianity? It is a way. Who and what is Christ? He is the way."

Lutheranism, the world's third largest form of Christianity, is an embodiment of "the way, the truth, and the life," for the church is *corpus Christi*, the body of Christ. At its inception, Lutheranism was a way of pilgrimage. When Martin Luther first appeared on the pages of history it was at a pilgrims' festival, All Hallows Eve, when the pious had come to Wittenberg in order to venerate relics and when the indignant professor posted his Ninety-five Theses. Much of Luther's life was pilgrimage—vowing monasticism in the forest, visiting the Rome of the Renaissance, proclaiming his stance at Worms, hiding at the Wartburg, inspecting the evangelical churches of Saxony, ministering to dispersed believers, dying while on a mission of conciliation. Certainly the pilgrim spirit, so prevalent in the Christian tradition, is especially germane to Lutheranism.

Pilgrims need manuals. Lutherans produced two of the first Protestant handbooks—Philip Melanchthon's *Loci communes* and Luther's Small Catechism. Since then Lutherans have not been remiss in composing treatises on faith and life. Recently it has impressed us that there has been little written in our generation on Lutheranism as an expression of the Christian way of life. In our ministries we have searched in vain for a single volume that introduces Lutheranism in terms of its theology, liturgy, polity, and morality, and does so with a sense of vitality and destiny, relating the Lutheran community to the broader evangelical and Catholic forms of Christianity. To meet that need we wrote this book.

We are two men—one in his forties, the other in his twenties—both pilgrims, both Lutherans, both church historians, both sons of the Midwest, both with parish experience, both having traveled extensively, both knowing tragedy, both having professed Christ through conversion in our teens. We both have aspired to be able to say with Paul, "I was not disobedient unto the heavenly vision" (Acts 26:19).

Obedience, however, is conditioned by context. In writing this book, the authors recognize that they come from different generations and situations. One is a child of the fifties, the other of the sixties. Varied influences have led to our spiritual formation. Both of us can admit with author William Saroyan that there are "many places where we've done time." In each place there were people of God who ministered to us. To them we now give due recognition.

In George Fry's life there have been many such people: a grandmother, Christina Renz Ehle; a series of pastors, including the Reverend John O. Lang and the Reverend George Troutman; several professors at Capital University and Seminary, especially Edgar Ebert, Justina Eich, George Dell, Hilmar Grimm, Edward C. Fendt, Herbert Leupold, Leonhard Ludwig, and Eugene Brand; historians and philosophers at Ohio State University, particularly Harold Grimm, Francis Phelps Weisenburger, and D. Luther Evans. Others are members and friends of Our Saviour's Lutheran Church, College Station, Texas; the Lutheran Foundation, Texas

A & M University; and Saint Mark's, Martin Luther, and North Community Lutheran churches in Columbus, Ohio. Still others were associates at Wittenberg University, especially President Clarence Stoughton; Capital University, especially Presidents Harold Yochum and Tom Langevin, and Dean Frank H. Bretz; Concordia Theological Seminary, especially Dean Wil Rosin; Saint Francis College, especially Sister Joellen Scheetz, President; the Reformed Bible College, especially President Dick L. Van Halsema; the Concordia Lutheran Seminary, Brock University, especially Dean Roger J. Humann and John M. Drickamer; Damavand College, Tehran, Iran, especially President Frances Gray and Dean Mary C. Thompson. Others are connected with various churches in the Third World where I have been a visiting theologian—the Conference of the Lutheran Church in Venezuela, especially the Reverend Douglas Johnstone; the National Presbyterian Church of Mexico; the Evangelical (Presbyterian) Church in Iran; and the Episcopal Church in Iran, especially Bishop H. B. Dehqani-Tafti, confessor of Christ. To Joseph Burgess, Division of Theological Studies, Lutheran Council/USA, a special debt is due, particularly in conjunction with the Lutheran-Baptist dialogues, 1978–1981. Others are in non-Lutheran congregations that have asked me to teach in their midst, especially the First Community Church, Columbus; Tenth Presbyterian Church, Philadelphia, especially James Boice; and College Hill Presbyterian Church, Cincinnati, especially Jerry Kirk. To family and friends there is a special debt that cannot be adequately expressed—to my mother, Lena Ehle Fry; my father, Sylvan J. Fry; my brother, Jon Paul Fry; my sister, Freda Fry Hollandsworth; and, more family than friend, Harold H. Zietlow.

In Duane Arnold's life there have been many such people during a pilgrimage from Ohio to Canada, from California to Indiana. I have traveled in space. I have grown in spirit. Associating with the people of Christ, I have been ministered to by many on my pilgrimage—the members and friends of Calvary Chapel, Costa Mesa, California, and Calvary Temple, Fort Wayne, Indiana, especially the Reverend John A. Lloyd and Paul E. Paino; my former parishioners and associates at Calvary Chapel Church, Van Wert, Ohio, especially my invaluable assistant and friend, Michael G. Bell, and Stan Lenz, Steve and Cindy Jaycox, Robert Scheidt, and my colleague, the Reverend Lowell Nelson, Trinity United Methodist Church. I wish to express my gratitude to the Reverend Charles J. Evanson, Redeemer Lutheran Church, Fort Wayne, and to instructors at Concordia Theological Seminary, especially William C. Weinrich, Dean Wenthe, the Reverend Daniel Bruch, and Dean Daniel Reuning. To friends in the greater Christian community I must confess indebtedness—Brother John Michael Talbot, O. S. F., a friend of many years who has consoled me on my pilgrimage; H. H. Prince Vladimir (Chavchavadze), now a priest of the Orthodox church (Father Vladimir Christy); Robert Webber, Wheaton College, for advice and assistance, and all the signers of the Chicago Call for their courage and conviction; and the Reverend Father George Dragas, Durham University. Without the help of family, work of this sort would have been impossible. To my mother and father, Herman and Louise Arnold; my parents-in-law, George and Barbara Drew; the Right Honorable, the Lord Balerno (Alick Buchanan-Smith); and my daughter, Charity, I express affection and gratitude.

We both wish to acknowledge those who have ministered to us in very special ways—Robert Preus, President, Concordia Theological Seminary; Ron Knepper, lithographer, whose prints, from the authors' collections, grace this book; Allan Fisher and Dan Van't Kerkhoff of Baker Book House for their encouragement and counsel; and Clyde L. Manschreck, Director, The Center of Reformation and Free Church Studies, Chicago Theological Seminary, for reading the manuscript and writing the kind foreword.

These acknowledgments would be incomplete without saying thank you to Janet Drew Arnold—a great-granddaughter of Sir George Adam Smith, Old Testament scholar and moderator of the Free Church of Scotland. She ministered to the ministers in a variety of ways—in the kitchen, at the typewriter, at the desk (proofing the text), always inspiring and enabling; and in the process, Janet has honored her forebear by becoming a theologian in her own right.

With Eusebius of Caesarea, forerunner in our profession,

we plead, "I trust that kindly disposed readers will pardon the deficiencies of the work, for I confess that my powers are inadequate to do full justice to so ambitious an undertaking" (*Church History* of Eusebius, 1.1).

This book is offered to fellow pilgrims as sustenance and comfort along the Way that leads from Bethlehem to the new Jerusalem—through Wittenberg and Geneva, Canterbury and Plymouth, Rome and Constantinople—to the abundant Life and the Truth, even Christ, our Lord.

Duane W. H. Arnold
Saint Chad's College
University of Durham
England

C. George Fry
Concordia Theological Seminary
Fort Wayne, Indiana

Introduction
The Lutheran Way

Recently one of the authors was traveling in Great Britain and visiting various universities. During a stay with relatives in London, he was invited to an ecumenical meeting at Saint Basil's House. An English bishop inquired, "What do you do?" I replied, "I am studying theology." "And in what tradition?" he asked. "Lutheran," I answered. "Oh, I didn't know there were many Lutherans in America," he exclaimed. "Well, just what exactly is a Lutheran these days?"

In 1961 the other author was completing a year of seminary internship in a university town in Texas. During a graduation tea many parents were present. Noticing my clerical collar, a housewife—the mother of a member of the senior class—asked, "What church are you connected with?" "Our Saviour's Lutheran," I responded. "Lutheran?" She hesitated for a moment before asking, "Is that a new kind of Baptist?"

From London to Lubbock, Lutheranism often lacks a clear identity in the English-speaking world. To Lutherans this is puzzling. In Britain, Martin Luther's works had already been widely distributed by 1520. Henry VIII married a Lutheran princess. Cambridge University was "a hotbed of the Lutheran heresy." Many of the Anglican reformers, such as Robert Barnes (whom Luther affectionately called "Saint Robert") and Thomas Cranmer (who had a Lutheran wife), were greatly influenced by Lutheran thought. In North America, the first Lutheran service was held a year before the *Mayflower* arrived. One of the original thirteen colonies, Delaware, was settled by Lutherans. The oldest continuing Lutheran congregation in the United States was founded in

1649. Lutherans not only have a long history in Britain and America, but they also possess an easily identifiable body of theology (in *The Book of Concord* [1580]) and an easily recognizable form of worship (the Liturgy). Lutherans also are numerous in Europe, the Americas, and the Third World. Exceeded only by the Roman Catholics and the Eastern Orthodox in numbers, the Lutherans are more than 70 million strong. Of these, more than 9 million live in North America. Lutherans permeate the Atlantic community, yet often lack a sure and certain identity to those outside, be they bishop or housewife.

Why is this? One factor is the paradoxical status of Lutheranism in the Western world. In Europe, Lutheranism is often the religion of the majority of the people, if not the established church. Lutherans are insiders. Other forms of Protestanism are often unknown in these regions. In the United States, however, Lutheranism began as the religion of a minority, an immigrant faith, preached by the uprooted, practiced by the transplanted, ministering to the dislocated. Lutherans were outsiders. Other forms of Protestantism were more readily identifiable with the British sources of American society. This explains the paradox confronting American Lutherans today—they possess a clear-cut *self*-identity, yet often lack a clear-cut *social* identity.

Another factor is the paradoxical status of Lutheranism within the Christian world. Lutheranism originated as a movement for renewal within the Western church. Its founder, Luther, always regarded himself as an evangelical Catholic. Its first confession, the Augustana, was intended to precipitate reunion with Rome, not perpetuate disunion. Lutheranism aspired to become a universal current of reform within the Roman Catholic Church, comparable to Augustinianism, Franciscanism, and Thomism. Lutheranism retained this temperament for a considerable period of time. However, Lutheranism, because of the influence of nationalism and the protection afforded by certain secular princes, became a separate confessional and denominational family of churches. In many respects this phenomenon approximates the development of Anglicanism in England, Gallicanism in France, and Presbyterianism in Scotland. Lutheranism developed a distinctive theology, unique liturgies and polities, and a separate history. This also explains why Lutherans have both an ecumenical (Catholic) and an evangelical (Protestant) identity.

It seems to us that any explanation of Lutheran identity must include an overview of Lutheran history. We are all products of our past. Certainly Lutheranism is more than a heritage. It is a way of believing, a faith, as we explain in part 1. It is a way of belonging, a fellowship, as we explain in part 2. It is way of becoming, a force for good, as we explain in part 3. But before we can consider Lutheranism as a holistic way of Christian living, we need to examine its historical locus.

Lutheranism before Luther

It is hard to determine when Lutheranism was born.

There was "Lutheranism" before Luther.

Lutheranism originated as a part of a vast movement of renewal within the Western church. For more than five centuries the faithful had been seeking a "reformation in head and members" within Catholicism. Re-forming was required in three areas: community, theology, and liberty.

Christianity is a community. There was a concern with the character and quality of fellowship within the Western church. Division was rending the body of Christ. Nationalism, or at least the rise of strong territorial states, was characteristic of the time. The pope had been taken captive by agents of the king of France; the Spanish church had become virtually independent of Rome; and many a German prince boasted that "I am pope in my realm." There was the nightmare of Christendom fragmented along political lines. This territorial division was matched with pluralism in the papal office. During the great Western schism, the Latin church had two, then three, rival leaders. This inspired ecumenical councils, reminiscent of early Catholicism, convening at places such as Constance (1414–1418) and Basel (1431–1442). These congregational meetings of Western Christendom, presided over by the emperor, with clergy and laity seated by "nations," sought reunion and reform. Conciliarism was one expression of this concern for community. Another was chartism (constitutionalism); civil and canon lawyers debated the exercise of power within the community. Some, such as Marsiglio of Padua (1290?–?1343), envisioned a separation of church and state. Others thought that the church, like some of the rising national monarchies of western Europe, should evolve into a constitutional monarchy. The executive power of the pope would be limited by a constitution—either oral or written—and the pope would be responsible to a parliament or a council. Communalism was another manifestation of the desire for community. Monasticism, long a source for renewal in the church, produced amazing personalities, such as Bernard of Clairvaux (1091–1153) and Francis of Assisi (1182–1226), who released spiritual power. Lay sodalities and conventicles, such as the Brethren of the Common Life, emerged. With a passion for piety and charity, these groups had an impact on the lives of many. Intimacy with God and neighbor was a keenly felt need. Efforts to establish fellowship were both continental and congregational, both within and without the structures of the church. Christ, as the Way, appealed as never before to Europe's millions.

Christianity is a theology. There was a concern with the character and quality of belief within the Western church. The nature of saving faith and its relationship to the rest of life was a crucial issue. One approach to this concern was scholasticism. Its rise was coterminous with that of the universities. Theologians faced the challenge of reconciling faith and reason. Preeminent among the princes of the classroom was Thomas Aquinas (1225?–1274). Taught by Albertus Magnus, the only teacher ever honored with the title *Great*, Aquinas harmonized Aristotle and the Bible. The "Angelic Doctor" provided a satisfying system for many. For others his facile integration of philosophy and faith was a provocation. Intellectual ferment, symbolized by the rival positions of realism and nominalism, swept the schools. Still others felt that if the Western community was facing a major crisis, it had better recover its sources. Those roots were found in the Greco-Roman classics and in the Judeo-Christian Scriptures.

Humanism swept from Italy to the perimeters of Europe. If Aquinas had been the prince of the schoolmen, the prince of the humanists was Erasmus of Rotterdam (1466?–1536), advocate of ethics and education. He urged a new appreciation of Scripture and a reappropriation of the classics. Reform would come gradually and would be contained within the Christian commonwealth.

Intellectual candor and moral endeavor are two forms of faith. Spiritual ardor is another. Mysticism sought a direct personal relationship with Christ and was another quest for a faith sufficient for this era. Personalities as different as Thomas à Kempis (1360–1471), credited with writing *The Imitation of Christ*, and Julian of Norwich (late fourteenth century) advocated rapture with God. Not all faith could be contained within the existing structures. Dissent appeared; some renewers of church and state were rejected by both. Called heretics by some, martyrs by others, men like John Huss (1369?–1415) and Girolamo Savonarola (1452–1498) preached and perished. They had predecessors in Peter Waldo (who died c. 1217) and John Wycliffe (1320?–1384). By 1500 Europe was filled with ferment regarding faith, as people sought to appropriate Christ, the Truth.

Christianity is liberty. Fellowship and faith are matched with freedom. By 1500 there was a concern with the heritage of liberty within the church. Free spirits, though varied, were everywhere evident. Many of them were women. Catherine of Siena (1347–1380) corrected popes. Birgitta of Sweden (1303?–1373) inspired the people. Clare of Assisi (1194–1253) impressed princes. Joan of Arc (1412–1431) rallied prince and populace against foreign invaders. Martyred for her love of liberty, Joan haunted the hearts of Europeans. George Bernard Shaw, in his play, has Joan say, “If I go through the fire, I shall go through it to their hearts forever and ever.” The Maid of Orleans represented the kind of populism, personalism, and voluntarism that came to mean much to the multitudes. They anticipated the invitation of Josiah Royce: “Arise then, freeman, stand forth in thy world. It is God’s world. It is also thine.” Christ, as the Life, inspired millions.

Luther and Lutheranism

Martin Luther (1483–1546) was successful because he recapitulated the movements relating to community, theology, and liberty.

Luther embodied Christianity as a living community. To some the reformer exhibited major inconsistencies. To others the professor reconciled the paradoxes of his period. Luther was sponsored by territorial princes, yet defied pope and emperor. Luther appealed to a universal council, yet organized national churches. Luther was a product of monasticism, yet was married and at home in the secular world. Luther was nurtured by the communalism of Groote and Francis of Assisi, yet advocated a full life in secular society. Luther offered a revisioning of Christian community. His was a new synthesis. Bound by the constitution of Scripture, shaped within the context of the common tradition, open to re-formation by all believers (both clergy and laity), and filled with a sense of great expectations, the church Luther offered seemed to be a re-creation of apostolic Christianity in Renaissance Germany.

Luther embodied Christianity as a vital theology. To some the reformer lacked a doctrinal system. To others the professor provided theological insight. His beliefs reconciled for many the paradoxes inherent in Western Catholic faith. A professor at a university, Luther could appeal to the masses. Himself a product of scholasticism, Luther could burn a copy of the *Summa Theologica* on the city dump. Indebted to nominalism and humanism, Luther was the disciple of neither Duns Scotus nor Erasmus of Rotterdam, claiming he used them to discover Paul. Luther could boast, "I have more understanding than all my teachers: for thy testimonies are my meditation" (Ps. 119:99). Nurtured on mysticism, Luther practiced pragmatism, having figuratively devoured mystical literature. Luther insisted that the personal union with Jesus be expressed practically. A child of dissent, who quoted "heretics" such as Huss with approval, Luther also claimed to be a loyal son of the church, teaching only the orthodoxy of antiquity. Luther offered a revisioning of Christian theology. Founded on the Bible, centered in grace, expounded for the people, explicated by reason, appreciated through the emotions, expressed in everyday life, Lutheranism was not to be a structure, or a system, or a spirit, but a confession.

Luther embodied Christianity as liberty. To some the reformer represented either anarchy or tyranny. To others the professor was an emancipator. His life, for many, reconciled the paradoxes inherent in Western society between liberty and security. On the one hand, Luther was a free spirit. One of his earliest writings was about Christian liberty. Defying Diet and emperor at Worms, pillorying professors and pope in the press, preaching reform from the pulpit, Luther stood in the tradition of Joan or Catherine. Yet the "apostle of liberty" was also an "advocate of security." Luther condemned irresponsible revolutionaries, be they the peasants, the imperial knights, or the radical reformers. For Germany Luther has become the archetype of liberty and of security. Luther offered a revisioning of Christian liberty that was fostered by the Spirit, tested by the Scriptures, and manifested within the structures as responsible dissent.

Many Western Catholics appreciated the ministry of Luther. They received him as a doctor of the church. For them he was a reformer of the faith and a renewer of society. They hoped Luther's influence for constructive change could be contained within the ecclesiastical structure. As evangelical Catholics they would become light and leaven in Christendom, as had been the case with earlier movements. Franciscanism had renewed the community; Augustinianism had revitalized theology. Christian humanism had promised liberty. Lutheranism as "the way, the truth, and the life" of Christ would reinvigorate both Western and Eastern Catholicism (a copy of the Augustana was sent to the ecumenical patriarch at Constantinople.) Efforts were made to reconcile Lutheranism with other forms of evangelicalism (Zwinglianism, Calvinism, and Anglicanism). By 1546, the year of Luther's death, it was evident these attempts would fail. The Council of Trent (1545–1563) closed the door between Wittenberg and Rome. Various colloquies, such as that at Marburg (1529), revealed both consensus and conflict between the evangelical reformers. Zurich, Geneva, Canterbury, and Wittenberg became rival centers of reform.

Lutheranism gradually emerged as a separate confessional family of churches.

No one date marks the birth of Lutheranism. It surfaced between 1517 and 1580, between the publication of the Ninety-five Theses and the ratification of *The Book of Concord*. By the end of the sixteenth century, there was a Lutheran confession alongside those of the Roman, Orthodox, Reformed, Anglican, and Dissenting traditions. Second in size in the West only to Rome, Lutheranism was practiced primarily in the Germanies, Scandinavia, and the Baltic states (refer to Figure 1). By 1618 it numbered 15 million adherents, living under a wide variety of circumstances yet sharing the Augsburg Confession. Lutheranism, as Figure 2 illustrates, was three things: Catholic, drawing on the common tradition of the Western church; evangelical, judging that tradition by the sacred Scriptures, especially the holy Gospels; and confessional, seeking to protect its Catholic and evangelical character with a shared declaration of faith. These confessions, produced contextually, were not designed to be a Berlin Wall—a barrier to change. Rather, they were intended to be a living membrane, a body of vital faith, by which the Lutheran community could test, try, and then, if possible, incorporate new experiences into its consciousness.

Lutheranism after Luther

For almost five centuries Lutherans have sought continuing reformation, both within their own family of churches and within the broader framework of Christendom. This reforming has emphasized community, theology, and liberty. Each generation of Lutherans has both preserved and lost, recaptured and neglected crucial elements within the Lutheran synthesis.

Lutheranism worldwide, in its pilgrimage in spirit, space, and time has passed through varied ages and movements.

The first of these was the age of orthodoxy (1580–1648). Orthodoxy dominated Lutheran thought in the years between the completion of *The Book of Concord* and the conclusion of the Peace of Westphalia. It was an age of

Figure 1 **Lutherans in Reformation Europe**

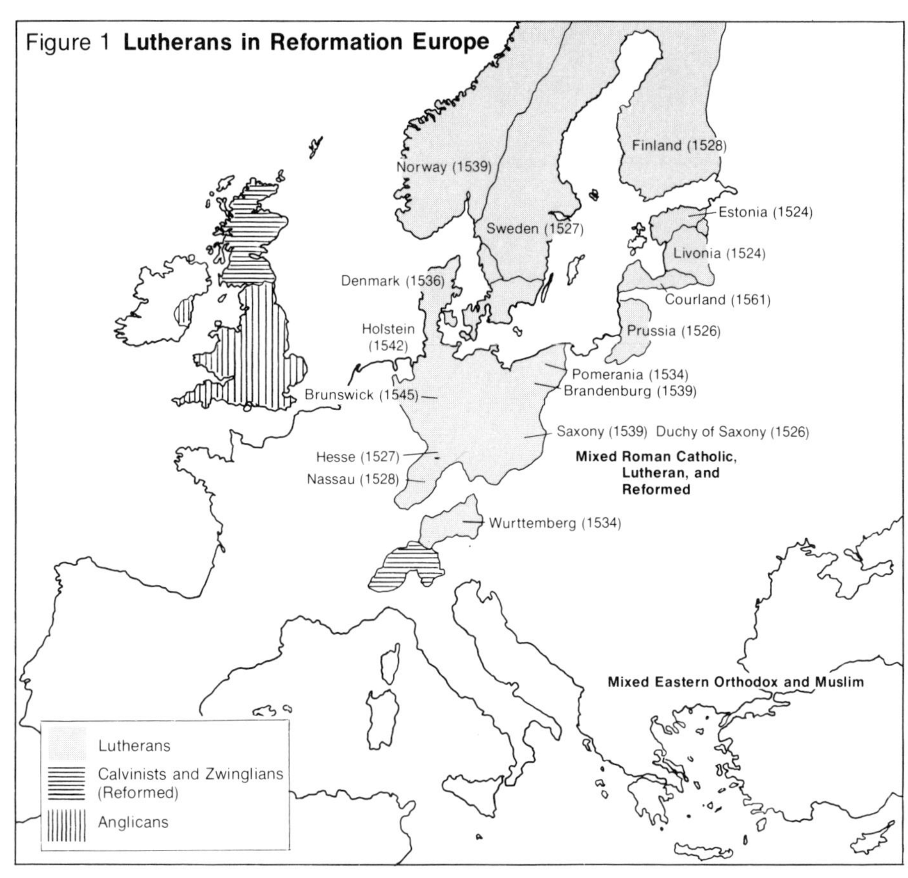

confrontation—with military warfare and confessional conflict.

The Thirty Years' War (1618–1648) saw the Lutherans struggling for political and religious survival. Confronting a revived and vibrant Roman Catholic Church, as well as Anglicanism and alternative forms of Protestantism, Lutherans often resorted to polemics. Some scholars think Lutheranism seemed to regress into mediocrity. One wit said of this period:

> We are all divided, several bodies we,
> Small in hope and doctrine, less in charity.

This indictment of the age of orthodoxy is too harsh. It tends to overlook the primary purpose of the chief personalities of

Figure 2 **The Lutheran Identity**

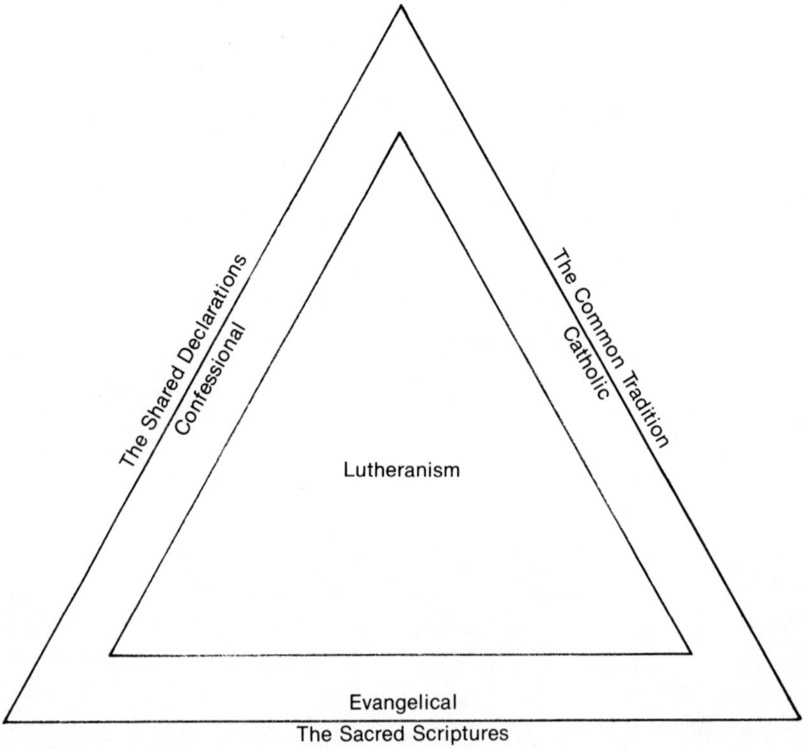

the period—the preservation of Reformation theology. The word *orthodoxy* (derived from Greek roots meaning "right praise") came to mean "right belief." For the theologians of that era, orthodoxy designated a "correct, complete, and enduring presentation of Christ as the Truth." Historian Harold J. Grimm writes,

> Orthodoxy was not necessarily synonymous with sterility [for the theologians of that age] rendered a great service to Protestantism by calling attention to the basic, dynamic Lutheran doctrine of salvation by faith alone and defending it against both syncretism and rationalism.[1]

The ambivalent attitude toward the age of orthodoxy can

1. *The Reformation Era, 1500–1650*, revised edition (New York: Macmillan, 1965), p. 537.

be explained by the ambiguities that surround its true, though often unclaimed, father, Philip Melanchthon (1497–1560). Clyde L. Manschreck, a distinguished Reformation scholar, says,

> Philip Melanchthon is one of the chief figures in the founding of Protestantism; he is also one of the most enigmatic. Because he does not fit neatly into the usual humanistic patterns of the late Renaissance nor into the patterns of the evangelical Reformation as expressed in Calvin and Luther, his role in the turbulent sixteenth century has baffled theologians and historians alike. . . . To understand Melanchthon and to assess his significance one must recognize the two historical movements which combined in him and which have never been reconciled in Protestantism—the Renaissance and the Reformation. Like the arms of a cross they join, only to separate. . . . In Melanchthon these divisions were a living unity. He cannot be explained in terms of either, for he transcended both. This is his greatness. This is his tragedy.[2]

Melanchthon was both Catholic and evangelical, humanist and Protestant, confessor and irenicist. The author of the initial Lutheran dogmatics, *Common Places* (*Loci communes*, 1521), and the first Lutheran confession, the Augustana (1530), Melanchthon also attended "almost every colloquy in Germany from 1529 to 1560." He was a close companion of Luther from 1518 until the reformer's death; orator at Luther's funeral, Melanchthon was both an interpreter and a preserver of the professor's thought. It is accurate to say that "no one knew the mind of Luther better than Melanchthon." Melanchthon also was concurrently a friend to others, such as Oecolampadius, John Calvin, Martin Bucer, and Barnes. Melanchthon was a Lutheran confessor and systematician, a founder of Lutheran orthodoxy, and an ecumenical and a Catholic Christian of universal significance.

Lutheran orthodoxy ideally maintained Luther's emphasis on salvation by faith alone, but sometimes degenerated into a Protestant caricature of scholasticism, teaching salvation by subscription to a system of abstract intellectual conceptions. *Sola fides* became *sola doctrina.*

2. *Melanchthon, the Quiet Reformer* (Nashville: Abingdon, 1958), p. 13.

The second period was the age of pietism (1648–1713). Pietism was dominant in Lutheranism in the sixty-five years between the Peace of Westphalia and the Treaty of Utrecht. This was a time of recovery. Following the ravages of the Thirty Years' War, with their devastating impact on Germany, there was a renewed concern within Lutheranism for community. Not theology, but ministry to individuals and society, was primary.

Pietism has been variously evaluated by historians. Some consider it a resurgence within Lutheranism of the spirit of medieval reform movements such as Franciscanism. Others regard it as the result of the impact of Reformed and Puritan influences upon Lutheranism. Still others interpret it as part of an international, ecumenical movement for renewal that was reflected in Moravianism, British evangelicalism and Methodism, and Roman Catholic Jansenism, as well as Lutheran and Reformed pietism. The authors consider it a reappropriation of the classic Lutheran understanding of community. At times pietism degenerated into an introspective moralism, but often was a dynamic and extroverted social expression of Christianity.

Pietism brought Lutheranism, in the person of Henry Melchior Muhlenberg (1711–1787), to America. Born in Hanover, educated at Goettingen, employed at Halle, converted to pietism, Muhlenberg aspired to be a missionary. After an initial pastorate in Germany, this desire was fulfilled. Responding to the call of three Pennsylvania parishes, Muhlenberg sailed to America, arriving in 1742. Known as "a pleasant, cordial, tactful man" and a "good organizer," Muhlenberg in the next thirty years emerged as the patriarch of colonial American Lutheranism. Isolated Lutheran congregations were knit together in a synod. A model constitution for Lutheran churches was prepared. The Savoy Liturgy from London was commended to Lutherans as a basis for common worship. Muhlenberg was an educator, a pioneer of the parochial school, a recipient of a doctor of divinity degree from the University of Pennsylvania. Patriot and ecumenist, he was a friend of both George Washington and George Whitefield. He arbitrated disputes, prepared pastors, preached in the Great Awakening, and visited congregations from New

York to Georgia. Muhlenberg's motto was said to be "The church must be planted." A representative pietist, Muhlenberg was the "apostle of community" in America.

The third era was the age of rationalism (1713–1815). Rationalism was the dominant influence in Lutheranism in the century between the Treaty of Utrecht and the Congress of Vienna. This was the age of the Anglo-American, French, and Latin American revolutions. It was the time of Napoleon. The passion of Western man was liberty. Freedom, not faith or fellowship, became the primary concern of Lutheran theologians and philosophers.

The age of the Enlightenment has been criticized by conservative Lutheran scholars. Certainly there were serious impoverishments within this period of Lutheranism. Theological certainty, liturgical integrity, sacramental frequency, and missionary intensity declined. The people of God, however, learn something from each part of their pilgrimage. The Enlightenment was concerned with liberty and tried to combine three emphases: a perception of a universe that was law-abiding; a faith that was free and open to the promptings of science and the stirrings of conscience; and a life that was founded on reason.

The eighteenth century, therefore, was a creative and a destructive one for Lutheranism. For example, it produced Johann Sebastian Bach (1685–1750) and George Frederick Handel (1685–1759) in music; Gottfried Wilhelm Leibniz (1646–1716) and G. W. F. Hegel (1770–1831) in philosophy; and Gotthold Lessing (1729–1781) and Johann C. Schiller (1759–1805) in literature. The epitome of this era of liberty was Immanuel Kant (1724–1804).

Kant, like Melanchthon, was a layman, a university professor, a controversial figure. Taught pietism as a child, transcending rationalism as a man, Kant in his advanced age sought to refute all forms of materialism and determinism and to interpret the universe as a place of spiritual liberty and moral responsiblity. Though trained for the Lutheran ministry, Kant taught a variety of subjects, including moral and metaphysical philosophy, at the University of Koenigsberg. His passion for freedom caused him to emphasize consciousness and conscience as the focal points of his world view. Though not normally considered an orthodox Lutheran, Kant's refutation of empiricism and a mechanistic view of the universe prepared the way for the nineteenth-century revival of classical Lutheranism. One conservative Lutheran said, "I had not believed had it not been for Kant. This intellectual David slew the Goliath of French Rationalism." Over Kant's grave are inscribed the words:

> The starry heavens above me
> The moral law within me.

The fourth era was the age of romanticism (1815–1871). Neoconfessionalism was prominent in Lutheranism between the closing of the Congress of Vienna and the conclusion of the Franco-Prussian War. Following the convulsions of the French Revolution and the Napoleonic wars, there was a longing for security. People sought security through a return to the classic models of Christianity: Latin and Greek, Lutheran and Reformed. A Lutheran renaissance swept Europe and America between 1817 and 1830, between the four hundredth anniversary of the posting of the Ninety-five Theses and the initial reading of the Augsburg Confession. Many pivotal personalities appeared. Two of them were especially influential for Lutheranism in North America—C. F. W. Walther and Charles Porterfield Krauth.

Carl Ferdinand Wilhelm Walther (1811–1887), though born in Saxony, was to achieve fame in Missouri. A pastor of the German state church, Walther was "awakened" through the ministry of Lutheran neoconfessionalists. An ardent student of the Bible and *The Book of Concord,* Walther became the father of the Lutheran Church-Missouri Synod (1847). The nucleus of the Synodical Conference, by 1880 this group embraced most of North America's Lutherans. Full confessional subscription to *The Book of Concord* became normative for much of Lutheranism in this period.

Walther's influence was extensive among German-speaking American Lutherans. By contrast, Charles Porterfield Krauth (1823–1883) was a native-born English-speaking Lutheran who became the first professor of systematic theology at the Philadelphia Lutheran Seminary and professor of philosophy at the University of Pennsylvania. A prolific author and a prominent controversialist, Krauth, by his preaching and writing, reintroduced much of Anglo-American Lutheranism to its confessional and Continental roots.

Romanticism in theology produced the Oxford Movement within Anglicanism, ultramontanism within Roman Catholicism, and neoconfessionalism within Lutheranism. Each identified what it regarded as crucial to its tradition—episcopacy, papacy, and theology. Each altered and enriched its community of faith. Lutheranism is incomprehensible apart from a recognition of the role of neoconfessionalism. Neoconfessionalism promoted a recovery of Lutheran theological identity, although it occasionally became a parody of Lutheranism through a tragic type of reductionism.

The fifth period was the age of liberalism (1871–1918). Liberalism was influential in Lutheranism prior to the end of World War I. The era was one of economic affluence, political enlightenment, upward social mobility, intellectual curiosity, and prior to the war, unprecedented European tranquillity. The Germany of the Second Reich, headed by a Protestant emperor, seemed to be on the path of perpetual progress. Within such a cultural and social milieu, the theologians strove to totally reinterpret Lutheranism. They desired it to be a community based on social justice, a theology committed to intellectual integrity, and a life promising more and more personal and political liberty. Confident of the capabilities of their universities and churches and their critical methodologies, and trusting fully the temper of their times, classical Lutheran liberals believed themselves to be literally on the threshold of a new era. No one person fully illustrates this influential theological movement. Even the versatile Albert Schweitzer (1875–1965)—a Lutheran Renaissance man, musician and missionary, philosopher and physician—could not quite encompass all the potential of liberalism.

Historian Adolf von Harnack (1851–1930) tried to interpret Lutheranism within the broader spectrum of worldwide Christianity. A scholar of the highest caliber, he chronicled the history of Christian dogma. Harnack analyzed the emergence of the Christian community and advocated a religion of ever-increasing liberty. From his studies of the Scriptures and the Greek and Latin fathers, Harnack felt he could offer a new Lutheran synthesis. In *What is Christianity?* (1901), which enjoyed unprecedented popularity, Harnack presented a revision of Christianity as a faith founded on the fatherhood of God, experienced in the brotherhood of man, and celebrating the infinite worth of human personality. This credo reflected the culture and conscience of its age.

The tragic inadequacies of classical Lutheran liberalism became clear on the battlefields of Verdun. Community collapsed before national, social, and class warfare. Theology was overwhelmed by pagan ideologies of East and West. Confronted with unprecedented crisis, Lutherans, in an age of apocalyptic urgency, sought to recover once more their history, theology, and identity. (Subsequent events—the bread lines of Chicago; the *Kristallnacht* of Munich; the death camps of Auschwitz and the Gulag Archipelago, where liberty perished—reconfirmed the inadequacies of liberalism.)

The sixth period is the contemporary era (1919–). Since the end of World War I no one influence has dominated Lutheranism to the exclusion of others. It is a time of pilgrimage and pluralism. Lutherans everywhere have been rethinking their identity.

Lutherans have reconsidered their theological identity. This has produced diversity, not uniformity. Existentialists and neoconfessionalists, charismatics and Luthero-Catholics, liberals and fundamentalists, conservatives and radicals, all coexist, though not without conflict, in Lutheranism today.

Lutherans have also rethought their communal identity. This has also produced diversity rather than uniformity. Some think the Lutheran community must now live in radical isolation; others think it must seek organic integration with other traditions (e.g., the Reformed in Germany, or the Anglican in India and Pakistan). For still others global association, as in the Lutheran World Federation, is an option; for certain groups, national Lutheran unification is considered essential. Some Lutherans think that interfaith cooperation and conversation are mandatory; yet others seek a renewal of the spirit of confessional confrontation, feeling that this is crucial to ensure Lutheran survival. All of these options coexist, uneasily, within Lutheranism today.

Lutherans have reexamined their legacy of liberty. For some it points to the necessity of embracing the cause of liberation; for others it means the conservation of traditional structures and institutions. For still others, moderation and amelioration through social evolution, not revolution, appear desirable. Some have rejected the heritage of freedom and have advocated repression, be it Fascist or Marxist. All of these attitudes coexist, albeit uneasily, within Lutheranism today.

No one of these approaches, in spite of each one's respective merits, combines the intellectual splendor, the moral majesty, the evangelical intensity, the biblical certainty, and the catholic quality of charity that Lutherans have come to expect as part of their identity. Lutheranism today is a mosaic, combining many different elements—some ancient, some modern; some of lasting worth, others of passing value. No wonder non-Lutherans are puzzled when they try to examine this entity called Lutheranism.

In our travels we once saw an ancient ruin containing a mosaic, initially detailed and stunning, now partially destroyed by circumstances and human carelessness. The mosiac portrays a messenger sent from God to man. The messenger's hands are extended in benediction, bearing within the palms a gift of great import. The mosaic, however, is blurred. It is hard to determine the nature of the gift. From this a local legend arose. Some people, we were told, think that the gift of God was a jewel of great price. Others insist that the divine benefaction was a simple seed.

This mosaic presents the paradox of Lutheran identity and ministry today. Some view Lutheranism as a precious stone, a jewel, to be preserved unaltered, encased in an intricately designed setting of theology and tradition. It is to be guarded, admired, and displayed to an awestruck and onlooking world. Others view Lutheranism as a seed, mysteriously valuable, filled with yet unknown potential. If planted in the soil of contemporary society and nurtured by trusting toil, it could produce fruit of unimagined variety, providing sustenance for many.

Perhaps the ancient mosiac, like Lutheranism today, has

been blurred by divine providence so that each person by faith must decide what he sees, and live accordingly. For a generation that needs both precious stones and living seed, we offer this book: an introduction to Lutheranism as a theology, a community, and a life of liberty and destiny.

Thou art the Way, the Truth, the Life:
Grant us that Way to know,
That Truth to keep, that Life to win,
Whose joys eternal flow.

George W. Doane

PART ONE

A Way of Believing

Thou art the Truth:
Thy Word alone true wisdom can impart;
Thou only canst inform the mind,
  And purify the heart.

George W. Doane

CHAPTER 1

The God of Creation

I believe in one God, the Father Almighty, Maker of heaven and earth, and of all things visible and invisible.

"In the beginning God. . . ." That's how the Bible begins.

"I believe in one God. . . ." That's how the Nicene Creed commences.

"In the Name of the Father, and of the Son, and of the Holy Ghost. . . ." That's how the service opens.

"I am the LORD thy God. . . ." That's how the Decalogue begins.

Canon and creed, cultus and code all make this initial affirmation: God!

This book about Lutheran faith and life also begins with God. There is precedent for this procedure. When Martin Luther wrote the Small Catechism, he began with this explanation of the first commandment: "We should fear, love, and trust in God above all things." In keeping with that tradition, this text begins with God: discussing knowledge of God, the existence of God, the attributes of God, and the work of God.

Knowledge of God

"Canst thou by searching find out God?" (Job 11:7). That question is as ancient as the Book of Job. From time immemorial men have believed, in the words of the author of the Epistle to the Hebrews, that God "is a rewarder of them that diligently seek him" (Heb. 11:6).

"How can I know God?" That question is as modern as a

Martin Luther

(1483–1546)
Reformer of the Church

Midwest college classroom. At Ohio State University, in a course about the philosophy of religion, taught by D. Luther Evans, a student asked, "Can I know God?" To this Evans replied, "God is the great self-evident fact of the universe. His works and His words reveal Him."

Lutherans agree with Evans's statement. They believe that God can be known through nature and Scripture.

God can be known through nature. Theologians call this knowledge natural (general or universal) revelation. It is available to all persons, regardless of creed or culture, country or condition. This is what Thomas Jefferson called "the Laws of Nature and of Nature's God." Such knowledge of God is derived by inference from His deeds.

Natural theology stems from four sources.

There are inferences from the physical sciences. The study of the cosmos, the natural habitat of humanity, can provide us with definite impressions of the Divinity. Much can be deduced from analysis of the universe, from the sands on the seashore to galaxies spinning though space. In ancient times a poet in Israel exclaimed, "The heavens declare the glory of God; and the firmament sheweth his handiwork" (Ps. 19:1). In medieval times an Italian poet, Francis of Assisi, celebrated God in all creatures, the "burning sun," the "silver moon," "flowing water," and "fire so masterful and bright." In modern times a poet has praised God's work in "earth and all stars," "loud rushing planets," "hail, wind, and rain," and "loud blowing snowstorm," for all "sing to the Lord a new song."

There are inferences from the life sciences. Study of botany, zoology, or biology can provide us with definite impressions of the Divinity. Much can be deduced from analyzing forms of life, from the ameba to man. The psalmist exclaimed, "Praise the LORD from the earth, ye dragons, and all deeps: . . . beasts, and all cattle; creeping things, and flying fowl" (Ps. 148:7, 10). Jesus marveled at works of His Father, such as the lilies of the field and the birds of the air. Francis of Assisi praised God for

> Dear mother earth, who day by day
> Unfoldest blessings on our way,

O praise him, alleluia!
The flowers and fruits that in thee grow,
Let them his glory also show.

In modern times a Scottish poet, Walter Chalmers Smith, meditating on the mystery of life, wrote,

To all life thou givest, to both great and small;
In all life thou livest, the true life of all;
We blossom and flourish like leaves on the tree,
And wither and perish; but naught changeth thee.

There are inferences from the social sciences and the humanities. Study of history and the life of the human family in community can provide us with definite impressions of the Divinity. Much can be deduced from analysis of society. The psalmist exclaimed,

> Kings of the earth, and all people; princes, and all judges of the earth: Both young men, and maidens; old men, and children: Let them praise the name of the LORD: for his name alone is excellent; his glory is above the earth and heaven.
>
> [Ps. 148:11–13]

Francis of Assisi felt the whole human enterprise to be a symphony of praise to the Deity:

And all ye men of tender heart,
Forgiving others, take your part,
O sing ye, alleluia!
Ye who long pain and sorrow bear,
Praise God and on him cast your care.

In modern times a poet has found echoes of God in "Trumpet and pipes! Loud clashing cymbals!" and "engines and steel! Loud pounding hammers!" and "limestone and beams! Loud building workers!" for all "Sing to the Lord a new song!"

There are inferences from the reflective sciences. Study of human personality in philosophy and psychology can provide us with definite impressions of the Divinity. God is reflected in our consciousness and consciences. Man's mentality and sense of morality, if given sufficient analysis, can give us deductions about the nature of God. The psalmist identified the chief labor of God as human personality, for

> The LORD looketh from heaven; he beholdeth all the sons of men. From the place of his habitation he looketh upon all the inhabitants of the earth. He fashioneth their hearts alike. . . .
>
> [Ps. 33:13–15]

Centuries later in Anatolia, a Greek poet, Aratus, said of God, "For we are also his offspring," a line quoted approvingly still later by Paul the apostle in Athens (see Acts 17:28). Paul, in that dialogue with the philosophers on Mars Hill, also cited another classical poet, perhaps Epimenides, who testified of God, "In him we live, and move, and have our being" (see Acts 17:28). Paul then concluded that the witness of philosophy and psychology is that "we are the offspring of God" (Acts 17:29). This sentiment was reflected in the poetry of a nineteenth-century American sage, Oliver Wendell Holmes, Sr., who mused,

> Lord of all being, throned afar,
> Thy glory flames from sun and star;
> Center and soul of every sphere,
> Yet to each loving heart how near!

While natural theology is useful, Lutherans do not regard it as a sufficient basis for religion. Religion is the worship and service of God. From natural theology most peoples have derived their beliefs. From the study of nature they have concluded that there is a God or gods, to be feared, worshiped, and obeyed. Paul, himself a student of natural theology, explained this phenomenon in his discourse to the Epicureans and Stoics in Athens. The apostle remarked that the nations "seek the Lord, if haply they might feel after him, and find him, though he be not far from every one of us" (Acts 17:27). A major problem is inherent in such systems—they tend to be impersonal, for they reduce God to an object. In an impersonal system, our relationship to God is not that of friends, but of strangers. God in His very essence remains unknown.

Paul informed the Athenians that in spite of all their art, literature, science, and philosophy, they still thought "that the Godhead is like unto gold, or silver, or stone, graven by art and man's device" (Acts 17:29), or else He remains "the Unknown God" (Acts 17:23). A personal relationship with Him was impossible, for His identity remained a mystery. The explanation of this is simple: only personality can reveal personality; only a perfect Personality could reveal God perfectly. That is why Paul "preached unto them Jesus, and the resurrection" (Acts 17:18), for in Christ, God gives Himself to us personally. Lutherans teach that saving knowledge of God can come only through special (specific or particular) revelation.

The distinction between natural and revealed religion was explained one day in a dogmatics class taught by Edward C. Fendt. He was contrasting natural and special revelation. Noticing how puzzled the seminarians appeared, Fendt stated, "Gentlemen, the problem is with the word *know*. In English we have only one term that must convey two different meanings." Fendt explained that in other languages, including Greek and German, there are two separate words that mean "know." In German, for instance, the term *wissen* refers to "knowledge of things," as suggested in the noun for "science," *Wissenschaft*. This is knowledge about objects, based on experimentation and inference, which we then employ for our advantage, so that things serve us. But the Germans have another word, *kennen*, which refers to "knowledge of persons," as suggested in the verb *kennenlernen*, "to get to know someone." Such knowledge derives from conversation and sharing, and is expressed in love and friendship. Thus we are transformed, desiring to serve the other person. This knowledge leads to commitment. A primary example is that of man and wife. The Bible speaks of intimacy between Adam and Eve with the word *know* ("Adam knew Eve his wife," Gen. 4:1). This type of knowing is found in revealed religion, for the Bible describes the relationship of God and the church in terms of marriage, comparing them with husband and wife.

Lutherans believe that special revelation, which resulted in the gathering of a covenanted people, was given to Abraham. In their midst the prophets spoke and wrote the Word of God. These writings found their climax in Jesus Christ, God incarnate as Savior. The author of Hebrews observed, "God, who at sundry times and in divers manners spake in time past unto the fathers by the prophets, Hath in these last days spoken unto us by his Son, whom he hath appointed heir of all things . . ." (Heb. 1:1–2). This special revelation, recorded in sacred Scripture, is the source and norm for the believing community and its theology.[1]

The word *theology* is derived from two Greek words meaning "discourse concerning God." Once knowledge of God is obtained, it is possible to teach others about Him. Such teaching is called doctrine (from the Latin for "learning" or "teaching"). This activity is one of the main functions of the Christian community. J. A. Singmaster, professor of theology at Gettysburg Seminary, defined Christian theology as "the systematic presentation of the Christian faith, resting on the Bible, developed in the Church, and realized in Christian experience."[2] For Lutherans the context of theology is the church; the primary source is Scripture; the intended purpose is salvation.

Theodore G. Tappert, a professor of church history at Lutheran Theological Seminary in Philadelphia, reflects on how Lutherans thought theologically in the formative period of their history, the age of orthodoxy (1580–1648).[3] Tappert describes the existence of a Lutheran trilateral, a tripod for theology (see Figure 3).

The primary source for faith and practice is sacred Scripture. The Bible is the "fixed and final authority" by which all matters are tested.

The secondary sources for faith and practice are reason and experience. Reason is a method of logical thought, borrowed from philosophy, and a body of material from natural theology, the findings of the sciences. Experience is the ap-

1. See chapter 4, "The Means of Grace," for an extended discussion of the nature and function of sacred Scripture.

2. *A Handbook of Christian Theology* (Philadelphia: The United Lutheran Publication House, 1927), p. 15.

3. "Orthodoxism, Pietism, and Rationalism, 1580–1830," in *Christian Social Responsibility*, ed. Harold C. Letts (Philadelphia: Muhlenberg, 1957), vol. 2, *The Lutheran Heritage*, pp. 36–88.

Figure 3 **A Lutheran Trilateral**
(Tripod for Theology)

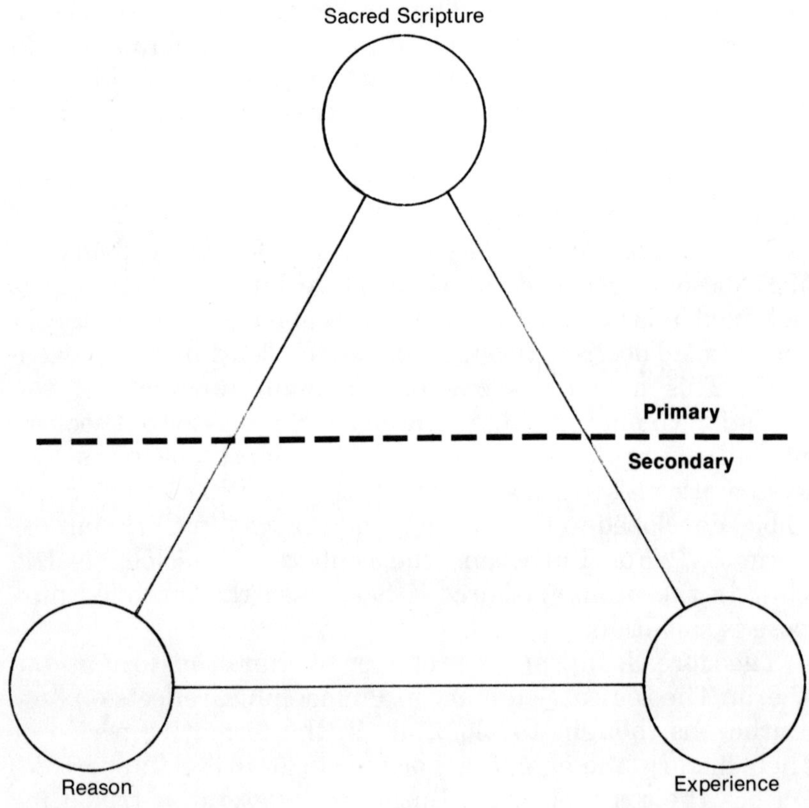

prehension of Christ in faith, both by the individual and by the community in its history (tradition).

Lutherans have never endorsed any one system or method of theology. Unlike the Reformed family of churches, which has John Calvin's *Institutes of the Christian Religion*, Lutherans lack a normative dogmatics. Lutherans do have one normative set of creeds, received almost universally, contained in *The Book of Concord.* This anthology, however, only indicates certain binding points of faith and life; it does not pretend either to present a comprehensive summary of Christian faith or to inculcate any set procedure for theology. However, the method devised in the seventeenth century has probably been the most influential paradigm among Lutherans. Perhaps the nature of Lutheran theology was best described by A. M. Fairbairn, a British Congregationalist, when he wrote,

> . . . Lutheran theology is essentially a soteriology, a science of the Redeemer's Person and work, profoundly conscious of man's sin and the grace by which he is saved. To it two things were necessary—the Scriptures, the source of all knowledge of the justifying Person—and the Sacraments, means by which His people communicate with Him, especially in the act of His passion and death.[4]

The Existence of God

Few questions in human history have been asked more often than "Does God exist?" Many answers have been offered to that question. It is not our purpose in this volume to examine all the arguments present to prove the existence of God. Five arguments do, however, seem to predominate within the Christian community.

First is the cosmological argument for proving the existence of God. This is often associated with the Greek philosopher Aristotle (384–322 B.C.). He was the son of a physician, a student of Plato, the teacher of Alexander the Great, and maintained that "the world which exists must have a First Cause. . . ." Aristotle argued from the consciousness of self-determining beings as real causes. The inference, therefore, is that the first or real cause behind the world is a Person.

Aristotle's case for proving the existence of God has been favorably viewed by most Christians. Similar thoughts are found in the Scriptures. The author of the Letter to the Hebrews stated, "Every house is builded by some man; but he that built all things is God" (Heb. 3:4). Paul, in his Letter to the Romans (in the very context where he clearly enunciated

4. Quoted by Singmaster, *A Handbook of Christian Theology*, p. 31.

his doctrine of justification by grace alone through faith), contested eloquently for the cosmological argument for God's existence, writing,

> . . . that which may be known of God is manifest in them [the Gentiles]; for God hath shewed it unto them. For the invisible things of him from the creation of the world are clearly seen, being understood by the things that are made, even his eternal power and Godhead. . . .
>
> [Rom. 1:19–20]

Thomas Aquinas, doctor of the church and a medieval Latin theologian (1225?–1274), employed the cosmological argument in his five proofs of God's existence. In popular piety this proof is often used, as is reflected in the hymn, "Holy, Holy, Holy," by the Anglican bishop, Reginald Heber (1783–1826), who sang,

> Holy, holy, holy, Lord God Almighty!
> All thy works shall praise thy Name,
> in earth and sky and sea;
> Holy, holy, holy, merciful and mighty,
> God in three Persons, blessed Trinity.

Second is the teleological argument for proving the existence of God. This is often associated with the Greek philosopher Plato (427?–347 B.C.), a native of Athens, a student of Socrates, the founder of the Academy, and a teacher of Aristotle. Plato taught that the universe is ultimately Spirit and Reason, a place of intelligence and purpose. The teleological argument is that of "the evidence of design and purpose in nature." This universe is intentional, not accidental, in its operation; rationality, not absurdity, marks its functions. Such evidence indicates a supreme Mind in control of the cosmic process.

Plato's case for proving the existence of God has also been favorably viewed by most Christians. Similar thoughts are found in the Scriptures. Often in the canonical context they are related to the teaching about providence, that is, that God is working out eternal purposes in the lives of individuals and nations. The psalmist praised God,

> which made heaven, and earth, the sea, and all that therein is: which keepeth truth for ever: Which executeth judgment for the oppressed: which giveth food to the hungry. The LORD looseth the prisoners: The LORD openeth the eyes of the blind: the LORD raiseth them that are bowed down: the LORD loveth the righteous: The LORD preserveth the strangers; he relieveth the fatherless and widow: but the way of the wicked he turneth upside down. The LORD shall reign for ever. . . .
>
> [Ps. 146:6–10]

The author of the Letter to the Hebrews simply stated that God is "upholding all things by the word of his power" (Heb. 1:3). Within the history of the church the name most commonly connected with the teleological argument is probably that of William Paley (1743–1805), a British churchman, who offered his famous analogy of the watch and the Watchmaker. For this apologist in the Age of Reason, the universe was a finely honed instrument that in its existence testified to a supreme guiding Intelligence. For ordinary Christians, a sense of God's presence and purpose permeates their lives, as it does nature and history, and they sing, with Joseph H. Gilmore, the American Baptist hymnist,

> He leadeth me: O blessed thought!
> O words with heav'nly comfort fraught!
> Whate'er I do, where'er I be,
> Still 'tis God's hand that leadeth me.

Third is the ontological argument for proving the existence of God. This is usually associated with the medieval Catholic theologian and philosopher Anselm (1033–1109), Archbishop of Canterbury (though a native of Italy), remembered as the deathbed confessor of William the Conqueror. Anselm argued that "the existence of the idea of God in the mind of man implies the actuality of his existence." If God is not, how can we explain the presence of this notion in the minds of individuals and its persistence among the peoples of the earth? Surely the belief that a God (or gods) exist has been almost universal among humans.

Anselm's case for proving the existence of God has also been favorably viewed by most Christians. Similar sentiments are found in the Scriptures. The psalmist confessed in ancient times,

> O LORD, thou hast searched me, and known me. Thou knowest my downsitting and mine uprising, thou understandest my thought afar off. Thou compassest my path and my lying down, and art acquainted with all my ways. For there is not a word in my tongue, but lo, O LORD, thou knowest it all together.
>
> [Ps. 139:1–4]

Echoes of this confession are found in the anonymous but popular German hymn, "When Morning Gilds the Skies." This song celebrates not only the God of nature, but also the Lord of consciousness, for

> To him, my highest and best,
> Sing I, when loved-possest,
> May Jesus Christ be praised.

Fourth is the ethical or moral argument for proving the existence of God. This is normally associated with the modern German philosopher, Immanuel Kant (1724–1804), a candidate for the Lutheran ministry, a professor at the University of Koenigsberg, and a pathfinder of contemporary thought. Kant placed the conception and knowledge of a supreme being upon an ethical basis and formulated his famous categorical imperative: "Act as if the maxim from which you act were to become through your will a universal law of nature."

Kant's case for proving the existence of God also has been favorably viewed by most Christians. Forerunners of this ethical argument are evident in natural theology (in the almost universal profession of the Golden Rule or the law of reciprocity in most world religions) and in the Bible. Paul, writing to the Romans, used the evidence of conscience as a compelling argument for the existence of God, stating that

> ... when the Gentiles, which have not the law, do by nature the things contained in the law, these, having not the law, are a law unto themselves: Which shew the works of the law written in their hearts, their conscience also bearing witness, and

> their thoughts the mean while accusing or else excusing one another.
>
> [Rom. 2:14–15]

The sense of moral imperative is frequently found in Christian hymnody in songs of exhortation such as the popular revival anthem, "Stand Up, Stand Up for Jesus," by the American Presbyterian, George Duffield, Jr., who called for "a brotherhood whose principle of living is the Golden Rule," and challenged, "Where duty calls or danger/Be never wanting there."

Fifth is the covenantal argument for proving the existence of God. This argument is based on three facts of history—the call, the church, and the Christ.

Blaise Pascal (1623–1662) was a Roman Catholic thinker of evangelical persuasion in the era of the French Enlightenment. Pascal's work was widely read in Lutheran circles. During Pascal's lifetime the traditional arguments for proving the existence of God were hotly debated within the European intellectual community. Pascal was persuaded that there was danger inherent in proving God in the same way as one would demonstrate a proposition in geometry. In *Pensées*, Pascal wrote,

> The God of the Christians is not a God who is simply the theory of geometric truths. This is the God of the pagans. He is not a God who crowns with blessings those who serve him. This is the God of the Jews. The God of the Christians is a God of love and consecration, a God who makes them feel their utter misery and his infinite mercy, who unites himself with the ground of their being and fills them with humility, joy, confidence, and love. He makes the soul feel that its peace lies wholly in him, and that it has no joy save to love him. To know God after this fashion one must know first one's own misery and worthlessness and the need of a mediator in order to approach God and be united with him. That knowledge of God without the recognition of our misery engenders pride. The recognition of our misery without the knowledge of Jesus Christ produces despair. But the knowledge of Christ frees us alike

> from pride and despair, because here we find conjoined God and our misery and the only way in which it can be repaired.[5]

Pascal contended that the God of the philosophers is not the God of Abraham, Isaac, and Jacob, because only in the God of the covenant, the call, the church, the Christ, and the cross is there salvation.

Pascal's contention, though not universally accepted, is helpful. Biblical religion begins with the divine initiative, the Savior-God seeking His straying people. This is the theme of the Bible from Genesis to the Revelation. Most Christians would agree with Luther's Small Catechism that they believe in God, not because of logical argumentation, but

> I believe that I cannot by my own reason or strength believe in Jesus Christ, my Lord, or come to Him; but the Holy Ghost has called me by the Gospel, enlightened me with His gifts, sanctified and kept me in the true faith. . . .

The Bible does not offer systematic arguments for proving the existence of God. Certainly it does not deny the validity of the cosmological, teleological, ontological, and ethical proofs. It does proceed, however, in a different fashion. God reveals Himself as a deliverer and men respond in faith. In the primordial days described in Genesis, God sent a pious man, Seth, to share His gospel, and "then began men to call upon the name of the LORD" (Gen. 4:26). The covenant was offered periodically and repeatedly until finally, with Abraham, the patriarch, a church was formed that continues until today. This is why Lutheran Christians sing with such enthusiasm the hymn, "The God of Abraham Praise," a paraphrase of the Hebrew *Yigdal* or doxology prepared by a Methodist minister, Thomas Olivers (1725–1799):

> The God of Abraham praise,
> Who reigns enthroned above:
> Ancient of everlasting days,
> And God of Love;

5. Quoted by Roland H. Bainton, *Christendom: A Short History of Christianity and Its Impact on Western Civilization*, 2 vols. (New York: Harper and Row, 1966), vol. 2, p. 66.

To him uplift your voice,
At whose supreme command
From earth we rise, and seek the joys
At his right hand.

The God of the covenant, unlike that of the cosmos, consciousness, and conscience, can be known personally. To us He gives His name, a revelation of His reality, identity, and accessibility. For the people of the Bible God was known by various names, such as El or Elohim ("the high and exalted one"), Yahweh ("he who causes to be"), the Lord of Sabaoth ("Lord of hosts") and Adonai ("my Lord"). To Abraham He came as the Lord of the covenant, the God who calls. To Moses He came as the great I Am ("I AM THAT I AM," Exod. 3:14). To Samuel He came by voice and vision. To Elijah He came in "a still small voice" (I Kings 19:12). To Isaiah He came "sitting upon a throne, high and lifted up, and his train filled the temple" (Isa. 6:1).

To the early Christians, Christ was the fullness of this pattern of revelation, "For God, who commanded the light to shine out of darkness, hath shined in our hearts, to give the light of the knowledge of the glory of God in the face of Jesus Christ" (II Cor. 4:6). For them it was this Jesus who revealed God as a blessed Trinity, teaching them to share with all "the name of the Father, and of the Son, and of the Holy Ghost" (Matt. 28:19).[6]

The Attributes of God

Among the many definitions of God, we prefer one offered by Christopher Ernst Luthardt, a Lutheran professor of theology at Leipzig. Luthardt defines God as "absolute personality and holy love." By this definition, the attributes of God include those of His very nature, independent of His connection with the created universe. These attributes have to do with the inner being of God.

The first of these attributes is life, for He is "the living

6. See chapter 3, "The Spirit of Conviction," for an extended discussion of the doctrine of the Trinity.

God" (Jer. 10:10) and "hath life in himself" (John 5:26). Yet the life that God possesses in Himself cannot be thought of as a process, or as relative to other life surrounding it. It is the "ground of being." This life must be thought of in its simplest terms, that of self-contained and self-sustained creative and mental energy. As Aristotle said, "Life is the energy of the mind." The life of God, however, resides not in mere consciousness, but in self-consciousness, for God is a personal being. God alone within all the universe may truthfully say, "I AM THAT I AM" (Exod. 3:14), for He alone possesses absolute personality.

Because God is a personality, He can be compared with human personality. Man is made in His "image and likeness," yet comparisons can be deceptive. God's personality, while similar to ours, retains certain important differences. Our personalities are finite, or bonded to creation. God is infinite; there are no limits or bounds, except those with which He chooses to limit Himself. Our personalities exist in bodies; God is not material, for "God is a Spirit" (John 4:24). As a spiritual personality, God is without the limits of time or space. God is unbegotten, eternal, without beginning or end, while we are created or generated spirits. As Paul said of God, He is "the King eternal, immortal, invisible" (I Tim. 1:17). As a person, God possesses rationality, which means He is without error or ignorance; volitionality, which means He is without restraint (save those limits He imposes upon Himself); feeling and emotion, but without corruption. God is immutable (without change), for He is the "uncorruptible God" (Rom. 1:23) and "the Father of lights, with whom is no variableness, neither shadow of turning" (James 1:17). God is one; He possesses an absolute unity without contradiction or division (Deut. 6:4).

Three attributes form a bridge to the creation. They are qualities of God's nature and also dictate the relationship of the Creator to the created.

God possesses in His nature absolute truth. He is "the only true God" (John 17:3), and "a God of truth and without iniquity, just and right is He" (Deut. 32:4). This attribute of truth is not one of activity, as in the creation, but is of God's essence. He is not just truthful; He is truth. Because of this, all truth found in the creation finds its source and norm in God. This attribute also guarantees the revelation of God to man as a "truth-bearing event."

God possesses in His nature absolute holiness. That the God we worship is "glorious in holiness" (Exod. 15:11) is a binding confession in the Judeo-Christian heritage. This holiness is not just the demands that God makes of His creation as a judge. The term *holiness* describes what God is. He is holy and pure in His very substance before He wills and demands purity. The holiness of God is the ground and foundation of all moral energy and movement. It is the source and norm of all that calls itself just. God's holiness forms the background for the fall of man, the administration of the law at Sinai, the Old Testament sacrificial system, and the coming of "the holy one" of God—Jesus Christ.

God possesses in His nature absolute love. That "God is love" (I John 4:8) is an ancient confession of the church. This love is not the mere goodness of God to His creation, or the manifestation of His mercy. Nor should this love be construed as a moral quality of personality or a surge of emotional affection. This attribute is of God's essence and acts in conjunction with other attributes such as truth, infinity, holiness, and immutability. God's love is the bond of the holy Trinity, in which is found the perfect object, source, and norm of love. This love forms the basis for revelation in God's giving to His creation. He is "God, that giveth" (James 1:5), yet He not only gives gifts, but also gives Himself to us in the person of Jesus Christ. This love in its essence is sacrificial, and involves a God who willingly accepts suffering and loss in the person of the Son, for the sake of mankind. This is the Good News.

We have been speaking thus far of God's nature, apart from creation, time, and space. How does this essential creative Being relate to His creation? William Law, the British author, observed, "All that which we call the attributes of God are only so many human ways of our conceiving that abysmal All which can neither be spoken nor conceived by us." We must first state that in relation to the created order God is eternal (Ps. 90:2), not temporal, in His nature. Second, God possesses immensity (I Kings 8:27), and therefore is not subject to the limitations of space, but contains in Himself the cause of space. Our God then transcends both the limits and the categories of time and space.

God is omnipresent. "Do not I fill heaven and earth?" (Jer. 23:24). This means God is everywhere in His totality. "He be not far from every one of us: For in Him we live, and move, and have our being" (Acts 17:27–28). As a poet said, "Though God extends beyond Creation's rim/Each small atom holds the whole of Him." This presence of God in all creation is not bound by necessity, as in pantheism, but is the free act of God bound only by His will.

God is omniscient, and there is no "creature that is not manifest in His sight: but all things are naked and opened unto the eyes of him with whom we have to do" (Heb. 4:13). This means that God knows all things, both actual and potential, in the past, present, and future. This omniscience, in and of itself, is not causative. It is, however, the source of the eternal wisdom of God in His revelation to man.

God is omnipotent. "I am the Almighty God" (Gen. 17:1). The Gospels state that "with God nothing shall be impossible" (Luke 1:37). It has been said that if one can accept the first verse of the Bible, "In the beginning God created the heaven and the earth" (Gen. 1:1), one will have no problem accepting the concept of the omnipotence of God. God's power is absolute and bound only by His wise and holy will. The exercise of this power is, therefore, not compulsion, but is consistent with God's nature.

God's general relationship to space and time finds its apex in the special relationship of God to man. What attributes govern this relationship? We may speak of three particular attributes extended to man which have their roots in God's nature as truth, holiness, and love.

Truth is extended to man as faithfulness. We may depend on the faithfulness and truthfulness of God above all else. Our God is a "faithful creator" (I Peter 4:19), who has "magnified [His] word above all [His] name" (Ps. 138:2). We also know that it is impossible for God to lie" (Heb. 6:18) and that "God is true" (John 3:33). This assures the believer that the promises of God may be trusted.

Holiness is extended to man as righteousness. "Be ye holy; for I am holy" (I Peter 1:16). This involves the expectation of God toward man in regard to morality and justice. It reveals its highest demands in the Sinaitic covenant, the law of Moses, and its explication by Christ in the Sermon on the Mount. Such righteousness makes God the judge of the universe who "will render to every man according to his deeds" (Rom. 2:6).

Love is extended to man as mercy. "God so loved the world" (John 3:16). This one phrase sums up all that can be said concerning the mercy and love of God toward a willful and disobedient creation. Due to His "love toward man" (Titus 3:4), God has granted "unto us all things that pertain to life and godliness" (II Peter 1:3). He has done this most clearly in the giving of the person of the Son, Jesus Christ, and placing upon Him the sin and unrighteousness of all mankind.

Only in the God of the Bible do truth, holiness, and love meet to extend themselves to mankind as faithfulness, righteousness, and mercy. As Nicholas of Cusa observed, in God there is a "coincidence of opposites." The God who demands justice fulfills this justice Himself, on man's behalf. The God whose holiness abhors sin embraces the sinner, and makes him holy. "Mercy and truth are met together; righteousness and peace have kissed each other" (Ps. 85:10). This is truly the mystery of the faith.

The Works of God

Jesus said, "My Father worketh hitherto, and I work" (John 5:17).

Lutherans accept that statement.

The God of the Bible does great works.

Lutherans, together with other Christians, speak of three mighty acts of God—creation, redemption, and sanctification. In subsequent chapters we will discuss the latter two labors; in this one, the first.

God is the Creator. Luther, in simple but profound words, explained what Christians mean when they confess, "I believe in God the Father Almighty, Maker of heaven and earth." He wrote, in the Small Catechism,

> I believe that God has made me and all creatures; that He has given me my body and soul, eyes, ears, and all my members, my reason and all my senses, and still preserves them; also clothing and shoes, meat and drink, house and home, wife and children, fields, cattle, and all my goods; that He richly and daily provides me all that I need to support this body and life; that He defends me against all danger, and guards and protects me from all evil; and all this purely out of fatherly, divine goodness and mercy, without any merit or worthiness in me; for all which it is my duty to thank and praise, to serve and obey Him. This is most certainly true.

Lutherans confess that God is the creator and preserver "of all things visible and invisible." This means four things.

God is the creator and preserver of the physical world, the area of matter and motion. Out of nothing God manufactured the elements of the universe (*creatio ex nihilo*). From atoms and energy God forged suns and moons, planets and stars, supernovae and galaxies, black holes, "rocks and rills . . . and templed hills." With compelling beauty the Book of Genesis describes the dynamic that God built into the universe, a principle of alternation and cycle, light and darkness, day and night, sky and land, earth and water. All things fit together in a symphony of creation. The conductor is God, who preserves the world He made. This universe is upheld by God, who sustains it with His power. The world functions in a uniform and objective fashion, one that is subject to sensory observation, rational explanation, aesthetic appreciation, and scientific prediction. This is a cosmos, not a chaos, and it is a universe suited to the growth of persons.

God is the creator and preserver of the biological world, the realm of flora and fauna. Redwoods and daffodils, dinosaurs and puppies, elephants and cardinals, acorns and orangutans—all the panorama of living things came from Him. Again the Book of Genesis celebrates the abundance of life, describing "all creatures great and small" in these words: "the earth brought forth grass, and herb yielding seed after his kind, and the tree yielding fruit" (Gen. 1:12) and "every beast of the field, and every fowl of the air" (Gen. 2:19) as well as "great whales, and every living creature that moveth, which the waters brought forth abundantly" (Gen. 1:21). The splendor of fish and fowl, bird and beast, has impressed generations of believers. One believer, Cecil Frances Alexander, whose husband became Anglican primate of Ireland, read the opening chapters of Genesis, repeated the first sentence of the creed, and then composed these lines:

All things bright and beautiful,
All creatures great and small,
All things wise and wonderful,
The Lord God made them all.

Each little flower that opens,
Each little bird that sings,
He made their glowing colors,
He made their tiny wings.

God is the creator and preserver of the spiritual world, the province of "angels and archangels and . . . all the company of heaven." From Genesis to the Revelation the Bible speaks of invisible yet intelligent beings. Angels guarded the gates of paradise after man's expulsion from Eden; they will welcome the saints into eternal bliss at the parousia. Angelic messengers brought good news to the Virgin Mary, to the shepherds in the fields on the night of Christ's birth, to Jesus when He was tempted in the wilderness, to the women at the empty tomb, to the disciples on the hill of ascension, to Peter in prison, and to Saint John the Divine in prayer. Of this world Athelstan Riley wrote,

Ye watchers and ye holy ones.
Bright seraphs, cherubim and thrones,
Raise the glad strain, Alleluia!
Cry out, dominions, princedoms, powers,
Virtues, archangels, angels' choirs,
Alleluia! Alleluia! Alleluia! Alleluia! Alleluia!

God is the creator and preserver of humanity, that point in the universe where the physical, biological, and spiritual realms intersect to create embodied personality. Male and female, white, black, brown, yellow, red, and bronze, short and tall, with hair fair or dark, eyes a rainbow of colors—God made humankind. In stark simplicity the Book of Genesis reports that "God created man in his own image, in the image of God created he him; male and female created he them" (Gen. 1:27). This sentiment is repeated and amplified in the Psalter, in which the poet asks,

> What is man, that thou art mindful of him? and the son of man, that thou visitest him? For thou hast made him a little lower than the angels, and hast crowned him with glory and honour. Thou madest him to have dominion over the works of thy hands; thou hast put all things under his feet.
>
> [Ps. 8:4–6]

According to the Scriptures, humans are unique in four ways.

God has created and preserved humans with unique physical features. As the psalmist observed, "I am fearfully and wonderfully made" (Ps. 139:14). Or, as Luther confessed, "I believe that God . . . has given me my body . . . eyes, ears, and all my members . . . and all my senses. . . ." God endowed humans with several unique physical traits that make it possible for us to "have dominion over the fish . . . the fowl . . . the cattle, and over all the earth" (Gen. 1:26). One of these traits is our erect posture, with the head held high, free to swivel on the neck, and look in three of the four directions as well as up and down. By nature man's eyes look forward and upward. This means we need only two of our four limbs for walking, which frees our arms and hands for exploration. Other animals must smell, scratch, taste, or bite objects. Man can handle them, feel them, weigh them.

There is also the hand, formed with four fingers and an opposing thumb. Imagine the versatility of the human hand—a pointer, the first sign; a counter, the first adding machine; closed it is a fist, the earliest hammer or club. No wonder the English word *manufacture* comes from *manus*, the Latin word for "hand." This amazing instrument is attached to the wrist, whose flexibility is unmatched by anything man ever made. Connect that wrist to the arm, and it is possible to rotate the entire limb.

Then, of course, there is the brain. This is the first computer, a complex nervous system, a highway along which messages travel at the rate of 200 miles per minute. In the brain is the physical basis for the mind, which is able to transcend time and space.

God has created and preserved humans with unique social patterns. Man's physical uniqueness makes possible his distinctive social behavior. Man is "the social animal," or as Paul said, "We are members one of another." Language is one mark of our social solidarity. Other animals, such as the bees and the porpoises, communicate. But only man has developed language and literature. We communicate to build a human community. We care and share. Animals know association—as in an anthill, a beehive, or a pride of lions. These associations, however, are not so complex and diverse as human communities. They resemble collectives, a compulsory assortment of creatures bound together by the law of survival, while human society is a community, a family united by love and loyalty. The human community, furthermore, produces technology and culture. While man is not the only tool-using animal, he has invented the most complicated tools. Working together, men have discovered the means to be victors over, not victims of, the environment. Science and technology are matched by art and literature as expressions of the human spirit.

God has created and preserved humans with unique personality traits. Humans are persons. Alone among the animals man can say, "I am." Animals are conscious, but man is self-conscious. We are, we know that we are, and we know that we know we are. Man can also say, "I think." We are much more than *Homo sapiens*, "thinking man." René Descartes, the French philosopher, perhaps was prone to exaggeration when he said, "Cogito ergo sum" ("I think, therefore I am"). But the point is obvious. Animals form percepts; humans form concepts. Man also can say, "I remember." We transcend the particular moment to recreate the past in our memory and to anticipate the future in imagination. Man also can say, "I admire." We are creators and connoisseurs of beauty. Man can laugh, exhibit loyalty or fraternal love, and say, "I wonder." We seek truth. Cicero, the Roman statesman, said, "The distinguishing property of man is to search for and to follow after truth." Calvin, the French reformer, said we are "by nature captivated by love of truth." Man fears death. We are born believing we will live forever. Leonard Bernstein recently observed, "Every child is born with a belief in his own immortality. One of the painful things about adolesence—about maturing—is coming to terms with one's mortality." God has created in us a desire for immortality.

God has created and preserved humans in His own image, with a capacity to enter into a loving and lasting personal relationship with Him. We alone, of all earthly creatures, have fellowship with God. This is reflected in what the Bible calls "the image of God," which is evident in our capacity for conscience. Man alone can say, "I ought." We alone have moral conscience. Or, as Mark Twain quipped, "Man is the only animal that blushes. Or needs to." Man was made to live by faith, in love, through hope, with God—to enter into a right relationship with the Deity.

The Fall

Lutherans believe, together with other Christians, that God created a good universe, one in harmony with His will. All was in a right relationship with the creator, so that God could say of the physical world, "it was good"; of the biological world, "it was good"; of humankind, "be fruitful, and multiply" (Gen. 1:28) and "have dominion . . . over every living thing" (Gen. 1:28); of the spiritual world—as of all things—"God saw every thing that he had made, and, behold, it was very good" (Gen. 1:31). Lutherans believe that the universe is no longer in a right relationship with God. Evil has entered the world. This introduces an element of absurdity and futility into all dimensions of the cosmos.

There is physical evil. Catastrophies of every category plague the universe. Such happenings puzzle men. For example, during the eighteenth century a vast earthquake destroyed much of the city of Lisbon. Many residents were killed while attending church. To a generation reared on the philosophy that "this is the best of all possible worlds," such an act of apparent "random chance" seemed a discordant note in the symphony of the universe. Nature itself seemed to be in rebellion.

There is biological evil. Disease and death feed on life. The fields bring forth not only corn and wheat but "thorns also and thistles" (Gen. 3:18). From a garden, earth has become a jungle; life is not unalloyed good, but hard work, for "in the sweat of thy face shalt thou eat bread" (Gen. 3:19). Life itself is maintained with difficulty against accidents and illness. Even the process of reproduction is filled with pain, for "I will greatly multiply thy sorrow and thy conception; in sorrow thou shalt bring forth children" (Gen. 3:16). As Erich Fromm, a twentieth-century psychoanalyst, observed, history is a constant struggle of life against death.

There is sociological evil. Not only are nature and life seemingly at cross-purposes, but society itself is filled with frustrations. Accidents and incidents that defy rational explanation cause even the innocent to suffer, as is eloquently illustrated in the ancient story of Job. Add to that the intentional harm humans do to one another—murder and war, exploitation and manipulation, rejection and misunderstanding—and it becomes a frightening world in which we live. From the murder of Abel to the mass executions at Auschwitz, from the tower of Babel to the United Nations building in New York, men of different colors and languages are confused as to their common purposes. The epic of civilization is fraught with both achievement and embarrassment. The problem resides not simply in the failure of right relationships between persons, but within the human heart itself, as Paul wrote,

> For the good that I would I do not: but the evil which I would not, that I do. Now if I do that I would not, it is no more I that do it, but sin that dwelleth in me. . . . O wretched man that I am! who shall deliver me from the body of this death?
>
> [Rom. 7:19–20, 24]

There is spiritual evil. There are forces at work in the world that are contrary to the purposes of God. Invisible but insidious, they work havoc in the mind and in society. Paul talks of these principalities, powers, and angels (Rom. 8:38).

C. S. Lewis confronted these powers in his popular *Screwtape Letters*. A hymn attributed to Andrew of Crete, hymnist of the Eastern church, asks the age-old question,

> Christian, dost thou see them
> On the holy ground,
> How the powers of darkness
> Compass thee around?
>
> Christian, dost thou feel them,
> How they work within,
> Striving, tempting, luring,
> Goading into sin?

Lutherans believe that the world in all its dimensions is engaged in rebellion against God, and is, therefore, not in a right relationship with its source. This occurred in the fall.

Strictly speaking, one ought to speak of two falls.

The first fall occurred in the spiritual world, the metaphysical realm, when certain invisible and spiritual beings—angels and archangels—revolted against God. This rebellion, led by one called Satan (Hebrew, "the Adversary"), Lucifer ("the Morning Star"), or the devil, apparently is the event described in the Apocalypse:

> And there was war in heaven: Michael and his angels fought against the dragon; and the dragon fought and his angels, And prevailed not; neither was their place found any more in heaven. And the great dragon was cast out, that old serpent, called the Devil, and Satan, which deceiveth the whole world: he was cast out into the earth, and his angels were cast out with him.
>
> [Rev. 12:7–9]

The second fall occurred in the world of man—involving his environment, his community, and his relationship to his neighbors, himself, and his God. This is described early in the Bible in the third chapter of Genesis. The Bible makes clear that evil did not originate with man, but with Satan. Humanity, therefore, is savable, for our race was deceived and led into fellowship with the demonic. The story is given in dramatic simplicity, focusing on the three crucial ingredients: doubt, denial, and disobedience.

The primordial pair are first led to doubt the love of God for them; for "God doth know that in the day ye eat thereof, then your eyes shall be opened, and ye shall be as gods, knowing good and evil" (Gen. 3:5).

The second step is to deny the validity of the divine covenant—that a relationship with God depends on faith, or mutual trust and respect—and to desire things other than God. For "the woman saw that the tree was good for food, and that it was pleasant to the eyes, and a tree to be desired to make one wise . . ." (Gen. 3:6). Once faith has shifted—and love has been transferred to any object less than God—idolatry has occurred.

The third step is to disobey—to act contrary to the purposes of God in the universe. "She took of the fruit . . . and did eat, and gave also unto her husband . . . and he did eat" (Gen. 3:6). So sin entered human history and permeated the human spirit, becoming a hereditary condition. Now by nature we fear, not love, God; we distrust Him, placing our faith in lesser things; and we disobey Him, intentionally and accidentally.

If the fall were the end of the Bible, it would be a tragedy in two acts: creation and fall. But another act was yet to be played—that of redemption in Christ, who overcame doubt with love; denial with faith; disobedience with obedience.

> Who on the Tree of the Cross didst give salvation unto mankind; that whence death arose, thence life also might rise again: and that he who by a tree once overcame, might likewise by a Tree be overcome. . . .
>
> [Proper Preface of the Holy Communion for Lent]

CHAPTER

The Lord of Salvation

. . . and in one Lord Jesus Christ, the only-begotten Son of God.

The Question of Christ

"Whom do men say that I the Son of man am?" (Matt. 16:13). The question Christ posed to the disciples in the borderlands of Caesarea Philippi is one that the church has sought to answer through the centuries. The answer given by Simon Peter in ancient Palestine has been called the "first creed of the church." This answer sought to cope with the question of Jesus' identity in a concise theological formula: "Thou art the Christ, the Son of the Living God" (Matt. 16:16). In this statement of faith, we find evidence of Jewish messianic expectations that the disciples held and saw as fulfilled in the person of Jesus of Nazareth. To the disciples, Jesus was the "expected one," the "anointed" (the Messiah, the Christ). This confession built upon a long history of Jewish expectation of a deliverer, the "servant of Yahweh," who would come and save Israel.

Peter's credo involved two separate but integral categories of Jewish messianic expectation. One involved the promise of God to send a divinely appointed and anointed Savior to His people—"Thou art the Christ. . . ." This was the function of Messiah. Another involved the special nature of this selfsame Savior—". . . the Son of the living God." This was the person of Messiah. Both portions of this confession drew upon prophetic themes in the Old Testament literature. For

Philip Melanchthon

(1497–1560)
Confessor of the Faith

the apostles and the Fathers, there was in the Old Testament a bloodline of prophecy that ran from the Pentateuch through the prophets and found its perfection in the work and person of Jesus Christ.

Who was the Messiah of the Hebrew prophets? He was to be the "seed" who would bruise the head of the serpent (Gen. 3:15), the seed of Abraham (Gen. 18:18), the seed of Isaac and Jacob (Gen. 17:19; Num. 24:17), of the tribe of Judah (Gen. 49:10), the heir to the throne of David (Isa. 9:6), the prophet "like unto" Moses (Deut. 18:15), and the "Anointed" (or Christ) of God (Ps. 2; Isa. 11:2). This Christ was seen as a suffering Servant (Isa. 53), rejected by His own people, betrayed by His friends (Ps. 41:9), sold for the price of a slave (Zech. 11:12), and put to an ignominious death (Ps. 22). Christ was seen alternately as a princely ruler (Dan. 9:25) who would enter Jerusalem as a triumphant king (Zech. 9:9), restore true worship as a priest-king (Zech. 6:13) of the order of Melchizedek (Ps. 110:4), and execute "judgment and justice in the earth" (Jer. 23:5). The paradoxical character of these prophecies caused great confusion at the time of Christ. What sort of Messiah could be expected? Some learned rabbis went so far as to speculate that two messiahs were to be looked for! Others despaired of any divine intervention at all. Many, however, still looked for the promised one of God to come and to save. This messianic expectation was in Peter's mind when he identified Jesus of Nazareth as "the Christ."

The second part of Peter's testimony went beyond this initial messianic identification: "Thou art the Son of the living God." This statement drew upon the apocalyptic writings of the Old Testament and Jewish commentaries of the time. Peter's affirmation went beyond merely naming Jesus as the Messiah, for he was speaking of Christ's very nature and His special relationship with the eternal God. Peter comprehended that this Jesus was more than a man. Henry Alford, a New Testament Greek scholar, commenting on this passage, said,

> The excellence of this confession is, that it brings out both the human and divine nature of the Lord: [He] is the Messiah, the Son of David, the anointed King: [He is also] the Eternal

> Son, begotten of the Eternal Father, not 'Son of God' in any inferior figurative sense . . . but the Son of the Living God, having in Him the Sonship and the divine nature *in a sense in which they could be in none else.*[1]

Peter seemed to be echoing many of the Old Testament prophecies that pointed to the eternal or divine nature of the coming Messiah. Micah had spoken of a future ruler "whose goings forth have been from of old, from everlasting" (Mic. 5:2). The prophet Isaiah attributed to the Messiah divine titles and a kingdom that would have "no end" (Isa. 9:6–7). Most prophets promised that Yahweh Himself would save His people. Peter perceived by divine inspiration, not by "flesh and blood," that this Messiah stood before him at Caesarea Philippi.

The question of Christ, "Whom do men say that I am?", has continued to occupy the minds of thinking men through the centuries. Men have sought to answer this question in a variety of ways. These methods have included searches for the life of Christ, studies of the confessions of Christ (creeds), scriptural understanding of the person of Christ (Christology), and exposition of the work of Christ (soteriology).

It is recognized that to grasp Christ is the center and focus of all that has borne the name *Christian.* For, as Henry Drummond, a nineteenth-century Scottish evangelist, said,

> The power to set the heart right, to renew the springs of action, comes from Christ. The sense of the infinite worth of the single soul, and the recoverableness of a man at his worst, are the gifts of Christ.
>
> The freedom from guilt, the forgiveness of sins, come from Christ's cross; the hope of immortality springs from Christ's grave. Personal conversion means for a life a personal religion, a personal trust in God, a personal debt to Christ, a personal dedication to His cause. These, brought about how you will, are supreme things to aim at, supreme losses if they are missed.[2]

1. *Alford's Greek Testament* (Grand Rapids: Guardian, 1976), vol. 1, p. 172. Italics in the original.

2. George Adam Smith, *The Life of Henry Drummond* (London: Hodder & Stoughton, 1900), p. 7.

The Life of Jesus

Secular historians—ancient and modern—have been baffled by the life of Jesus. Christ's contemporaries in both Jewish and classical culture largely ignored Him. Few references to the Master are found in the literature of the time. Except for a passing reference in the writings of Josephus—and a century later some critical comment by Roman historians—His career is lost in anonymity. In a strangely similar fashion, modern secular historians, such as Ernest Renan in France, have been puzzled by the story of Jesus. For more than a century there was a quest for the historical Jesus, an attempt to reconstruct His life without reference to the supernatural elements of that life. Many scholars think these efforts have proven fruitless. At the conclusion of decades of research, one scholar wrote of Christ, "He comes to us as one unknown. . . ."

Our main source for information about the life of Jesus is the New Testament. Most of our material comes from the four Gospels—Matthew, Mark, Luke, and John—though helpful references to the Christ are found in Acts and in the Letters (or Epistles), and certainly the Revelation is a testimony of the presence of the living Christ in the midst of His church. The biblical writers strive to do much more than write a biography of Jesus. They are persuaded that His life cannot be fully explained in terms of time and space or history and geography. Christ was more than merely a product of first-century Palestine; He was the breaking forth of eternity upon history. For that reason the authors of the New Testament describe the main events of the life of Jesus as points of interaction between the natural and the supernatural. They would have found the skeletal outline in most modern history books—which contend that all we can know is that Jesus was born perhaps in 4 B.C., that He was a carpenter and self-appointed rabbi, or teacher, who died around A.D. 29—woefully inadequate, because such an outline denies the unique character of the life of Christ, who is "God in human flesh appearing."

The witness of the New Testament centers around seven

mysteries of the life of Christ. In this context the word *mystery* refers to a secret, hidden from eternity, now manifested in history. Paul wrote to Timothy in a creedal fashion, stating,

> And without controversy great is the mystery of godliness: God was manifest in the flesh, justified in the Spirit, seen of angels, preached unto the Gentiles, believed on in the world, received up into glory.
>
> [I Tim. 3:16]

The Seven Mysteries of Christ

There is the mystery of the incarnation: that in Jesus, the eternal God took on flesh and dwelt among men. We celebrate this mystery in the church at Christmas. Matthew and Luke write of this mystery in their accounts of the virgin birth. John probes the mystery of "the Word [that] was made flesh, and dwelt among us (and we beheld his glory, the glory as of the only begotten of the Father), full of grace and truth" (John 1:14). Paul explains the mystery, writing, "when the fulness of the time was come, God sent forth his Son, made of a woman, made under the law, to redeem them that were under the law" (Gal. 4:4–5). For the earliest Christians, the incarnation taught that God, the high and holy One, was also near and immanent, as close as the man Jesus. The incarnation thus solved a great theological problem: how God can be transcendent and yet immanent, how He can be powerful yet personal. The very name *Jesus Christ* unites the two—Jesus, the man of history, with a human face; yet Christ, the anointed one, who is from all eternity.

There is the mystery of the baptism. We celebrate this mystery in the church on Epiphany. Jesus, believed by Christians to be innocent, without sin, received baptism from John the Baptist in the Jordan, to take upon Himself the iniquity of the fallen world. This is why, some feel, that Mark, whose Gospel possibly is the earliest, begins not with an account of the birth of Jesus, but with the story of His baptism. Certainly accounts of His baptism are present in all the Gospels. The urgency of the gospel is the preaching of "the remission of sins." The dilemma was obvious—since the fall, the human race was in bondage to evil; man must pay the debt; yet only God was capable of paying that debt. In the baptism, Jesus is manifested as the one acceptable to be the sin-bearer. The Son of God came out of the river, "the heavens opened, and the Spirit like a dove descend[ed] upon him: And there came a voice from heaven, saying, Thou art my beloved Son, in whom I am well pleased" (Mark 1:10–11). Christ's baptism thus solved a great ethical dilemma: how can guilty humanity approach a holy God in innocence? Jesus Christ in His person provides a solution through His baptism.

There is the mystery of the transfiguration. We celebrate this mystery in the church on the feast of the transfiguration. At midpoint in His ministry, Jesus went aside to a mountain to pray, taking the apostles Peter, James, and John with Him (Matt. 17:1–8; Mark 9:2–8; Luke 9:28–36). While Christ communed with His Father, He was transformed before the eyes of His followers, and began to converse with Moses and Elijah, who represent the fullness of the Old Testament—both the law and the prophets. The church of all times was potentially present, for the apostles, heralds of the New Testament, watched in wonder. For believers from earliest times the transfiguration reconciled the paradox of time and eternity. As the birth of Jesus harmonizes transcendence and immanence, as His baptism harmonizes innocence and guilt, so His transfiguration demonstrates the reconciliation of time and eternity in an eternal Savior who shows forth His glory and salvation in human history.

There is the mystery of the crucifixion. We remember this mystery in the church on Good Friday. The death of Jesus on the cross around A.D. 29 is for believers not merely an accident or an isolated incident, but a salvific event foreseen from the foundation of the world (see Rev. 13:8). This is why the four Gospels climax in accounts of the crucifixion, and why half of each account is devoted to the passion of Christ. This is why the Epistles are replete with the proclamation of the cross and why Acts and the Apocalypse celebrate the Jesus who died yet lives. For Christians the cross is not a thing of shame, but a sign of glory:

> In the cross of Christ I glory
> Tow'ring o'er the wrecks of time.

For Christians from the first century forward, the cross reconciles holiness and love. God is holy and He cannot tolerate sin. Yet He is loving and compassionate. How can these two traits of the Deity be reconciled? Only in their harmonization is there hope for sinful men. Christians believe that in the sacrifice of Jesus on the cross He offered, out of love, a pure and holy sacrifice, which alone can atone for the sins of men. For this reason Calvary marks the place where justice and grace have met and where a holy God can accept a fallen race.

There is the mystery of the resurrection. We celebrate this mystery in the church on Easter. All the Gospels conclude with accounts about Christ after His resurrection. The Book of Acts begins with an account of the earthly ministry of the risen Savior. This is the foundation of Christians' faith. As Paul wrote,

> And if Christ be not risen, then is our preaching vain, and your faith is also vain. . . . And if Christ be not raised, your faith is vain; ye are yet in your sins. Then they also which are fallen asleep in Christ are perished. If in this life only we have hope in Christ, we are of all men most miserable. But now is Christ risen from the dead, and become the firstfruits of them that slept.
>
> [I Cor. 15:14, 17–20]

In the mystery of Easter, Christians find reconciled two facts: the empirical reality of physical death and the abiding hope for immortal life. From time immemorial women and men have longed for life beyond the grave. That hope could find argumentation in logic and foundation in love, but there was no demonstration in history that it was possible. In Jesus, one dead now lives and is the "firstfruits" of the resurrection of the dead. In His triumph over death, Christ reconciled death and immortality.

There is the mystery of the ascension. We celebrate this mystery in the church on Ascension Day. This event that concludes the Gospels and opens the Book of Acts is the reality that permeates the Epistles and the Apocalypse. Christians make much of the ascension because it explains to them a paradox of the present-day world. On the one hand, evil seems to be strong. Even since the death of Christ believers continue to die. (The implications of this fact plagued even the earliest Christians. Paul's first letter, that to the Thessalonians, deals with this question.) Furthermore, although the resurrection vindicated Christ as the model or paradigm of life, evil continues. Even Christians sin. How can God be in control of a world like this? Yet by faith Christians continue to have fellowship with Jesus, and they know that He is *Christus Rex*, Christ the King, who is seated at the right hand of God the Father, and, as Paul said in comforting the Romans, "all things work together for good to them that love God . . ." (Rom. 8:28). The mystery of the ascension reconciles for Christians the continuation of evil in the world and the affirmation that Christ is in control. Paul, writing to the Ephesians, assured believers of the power of God in Christ:

> Which he wrought in Christ, when he raised him from the dead, and set him at his own right hand in the heavenly places, Far above all principality, and power, and might, and dominion, and every name that is named, not only in this world, but also in that which is to come: And hath put all things under his feet, and gave him to be the head over all things to the church, Which is his body, the fulness of him that filleth all in all.
>
> [Eph. 1:20–23]

There is the mystery of the second advent. Chronologically, this is the one great future mystery of Christ. We anticipate this mystery in the church during Advent. If Christ rules, why do all men not see it? If Christ is righteous, then why does injustice prevail? If Christ is loving, why is there so much deprivation and hardship even yet? This is the paradox of promise and reality. The reconciling answer is that Christ is coming again! For every one prophecy in the Bible about His first coming, there are two about His second advent. This age in which we live is an interim age, a chance for men and nations to repent and receive Him. For soon Christ the King will come again, not in lowly humility, as in the cradle, but in great authority, wearing His crown. He will appear not to suffer but to reign. Then absolute justice will be rendered. Christ will be manifested before the world, reconciling His promises and the reality of fulfillment in His person. Paul, anticipating this last mystery, wrote of a time

> that at the name of Jesus every knee should bow, of things in heaven, and things in earth, and things under the earth; And that every tongue should confess that Jesus Christ is Lord, to the glory of God the Father.
>
> [Phil. 2:10–11]

The Confession of Christ

The Swiss-American church historian, Philip Schaff, said that "creeds will live as long as faith survives, with the duty to confess our faith before men."[3] The church through the centuries has celebrated the mystery of Christ through creedal formulations. Lutherans also have expressed their faith in the creeds of the ancient church. In *The Book of Concord*, the first section contains three ecumenical creeds—the Apostles', the Nicene, and the Athanasian. These are accepted by many main denominations of Western Christendom, such as the Anglican church, the Roman Catholic Church, and certain Reformed churches.

A creed (from the Latin *credo*, "I believe") is a confession, for public or liturgical use, of the faith that one holds. A creed seeks to give a concise formulation of the faith and to express it in an understandable way. Christian creeds have their origin in the New Testament writings themselves. Christ promised eternal rewards for those who would "confess [Him] before men" (Matt. 10:32), and Paul associated confession and salvation: "If thou shalt confess with thy mouth the Lord Jesus [Jesus as Lord] and shalt believe in thine heart . . . thou shalt be saved" (Rom. 10:9). Certainly we may also speak

3. *The Creeds of Christendom*, 3 vols. (1877; reprint ed., Grand Rapids: Baker, 1977), preface to the fourth edition.

of the baptismal formula and the words of institution of the Lord's Supper as protocreeds of the church. In the New Testament, creedal formulas arise out of God's initiative in Christ's own words or in the response of the disciples to the revelation. These confessions of faith could be as simple as "Jesus is Lord" or "I believe that Jesus Christ is the Son of God" (Acts 8:37). Yet even in the pages of the New Testament more complex creeds are alluded to: "But to us there is but one God, the Father, of whom are all things, and we in him; and one Lord Jesus Christ, by whom are all things, and we by him" (I Cor. 8:6; cf. I Tim. 3:16; Heb. 4:1–2).

What is the purpose of a creed? Historically there have been three essential purposes; recently there has been added yet another purpose. The first purpose is demarcation. The initial use of the creeds (in the New Testament) was to identify the church as an entity separate from both Judaism and the pagan world. A second purpose is celebration. The creeds have always had a liturgical function in the church. This is especially true in regard to the Lord's Supper, baptism, and the confirmation of the newly baptized. A third function is preservation. In the age of the church councils (325–787) creeds were employed to distinguish the church from heretical groups, as well as to instruct the laity concerning the decisions of the councils. A fourth purpose is identification. More recently, creeds have been used to point out the particular doctrinal stances of certain denominations within the Christian family. The main purpose of any Christian creed is, of course, to confess Christ. Though each of the creeds that we will examine is trinitarian in structure, the main article and emphasis in each concern the person and work of Jesus Christ. These creeds were given by the church as safeguards to protect the integrity of the believers' faith in Christ.

The Apostles' Creed

I believe in God the Father Almighty, Maker of heaven and earth.

And in Jesus Christ, His only Son, our Lord; who was conceived by the Holy Ghost, born of the Virgin Mary; suffered under Pontius Pilate, was crucified, dead, and buried; He descended into hell;[4] the third day He rose again from the dead; He ascended into heaven; and sitteth on the right hand of God the Father Almighty; from thence He shall come to judge the quick and the dead.

I believe in the Holy Ghost; the holy Christian[5] church; the communion of saints; the forgiveness of sins; the resurrection of the body; and the life everlasting. Amen.

Martin Luther said of this creed, "Christian truth could not possibly be put into a shorter and clearer statement." The Apostles' Creed, insofar as its present form, is not the work of the twelve apostles, as was once popularly believed. It is, however, a summation of apostolic teaching and preaching. The present form is based upon what is called the Old Roman Creed of the fourth century. (It was augmented for use in all the churches and was put into its present form in the sixth or seventh century.) The Old Roman Creed, in turn, had been based on earlier rules of faith that had become popular in the second and third centuries and that are mentioned by a number of church fathers, such as Cyril of Jerusalem, Ambrose, and Augustine. The rules of faith these Fathers refer to were most likely baptismal confessions in which the candidates for baptism would be asked, "Do you believe in God the Father . . . God the Son . . . God the Holy Spirit . . . ," to which they would reply, "I believe." These original rules of faith were regarded in the early church as a portion of the mysteries or the secret discipline of the faith to which only the fully initiated had access.

The Apostles' Creed focuses on the person of Christ as its main subject. It teaches that although the church, like the Jews, worships a transcendent God who is almighty, yet the church believes that God has shown Himself in the man Jesus Christ. Perhaps the most telling phrase in the creed is that this Jesus was "crucified" and "suffered under Pontius Pilate," thus placing the eternal Deity in the realm of history and reconciling the absolute God with the particular person of Jesus of Nazareth. This incarnational emphasis was to

4. The article on the descent into hell (Hades), appears to have been adapted from the local creed of the church of Aquileja.

5. In Latin, *catholica*. It has been customary among Lutherans to translate *catholica* with *christlich*, although this is by no means universal.

place the church on a doctrinal tightrope for the first four centuries of its existence. That God would become man was "a mystery so divine that man scarcely [could] believe it." It was so incomprehensible to the minds of men that many people found it difficult to accept it in all of its glory and majesty. Following a precedent found in the Book of Acts (Acts 15ff.), the church, gathered in council, acted three different times to assure that the fullness of this mystery would be preserved intact for the future.

Although there had been many regional councils before 325, none ever had had the opportunity to act in the sweeping way in which the Council of Nicea did. The council had been called because of a controversy, originating in the church at Alexandria, that had been in the making for more than a century. The problem at hand concerned an Alexandrian parish priest, Arius, who had confronted his bishop, Alexander, and his young deacon, Athanasius. According to Arius, Jesus was indeed a creature of the very highest order, but to say that Jesus and God are substantially the same was unacceptable. From the viewpoint of Alexander and Athanasius this teaching of Arius was heretical because it would lead to idolatry, in that Christians, who worshiped the person of Christ, would be worshiping a mere creature, a practice strictly prohibited. Such a belief would also make the atonement wrought by Christ of no effect, for as a creature His sacrifice would be without eternal significance and value. To settle the issue, the Christian emperor, Constantine, convened a council in the city of Nicea in Asia Minor. The council declared its support for Alexander and affirmed that, in Jesus Christ, God truly appeared on earth as the second person of the holy Trinity—the Son. The council also defined the person of Jesus as "being of one substance with the Father" and as having been "begotten, not made." This allows for generation in and from God but disallows any idea that Christ is a creation. Though this controversy continued in certain regions for a number of years, the church in council had spoken with authority concerning the faith. The formula of faith issued at Nicea had minor changes made in it at the first ecumenical council at Constantinople in 381, and it is substantially in that form that the creed comes to us today.

The Nicene Creed

I believe in one God, the Father Almighty, Maker of heaven and earth, and of all things visible and invisible.

And in one Lord Jesus Christ, the only-begotten Son of God, begotten of His Father before all worlds, God of God, Light of Light, very God of very God, begotten, not made, being of one substance with the Father, by whom all things were made; who, for us men and for our salvation, came down from heaven, and was incarnate by the Holy Ghost of the Virgin Mary, and was made man; and was crucified also for us under Pontius Pilate; He suffered and was buried; and the third day He rose again according to the Scriptures; and ascended into heaven, and sitteth on the right hand of the Father; and He shall come again, with glory, to judge both the quick and the dead; whose kingdom shall have no end.

And I believe in the Holy Ghost, the Lord and Giver of Life, who proceedeth from the Father and the Son, who with the Father and the Son together is worshiped and glorified, who spake by the Prophets. And I believe one holy Christian and Apostolic Church. I acknowledge one Baptism for the remission of sins, and I look for the resurrection of the dead, and the life of the world to come. Amen.

The church had safeguarded the teaching about the deity of Christ and the confession of the holy Trinity at Nicea. For some believers, however, the problem of God as a "wholly other" or absolutely transcendent Being remained. For them, the union of God and man in Jesus compromised God's transcendence. At the beginning of the fifth century, a group arose, led by Bishop Nestorius of Constantinople, who taught that the Son of God in heaven and the man Jesus of Nazareth were actually two distinct persons. Although these two persons were united in Jesus Christ, they remained separate and distinct entities. Thus Mary could be referred to as the mother of the man Jesus, but not the mother of God. To deal with this problem, the Council of Ephesus in 431 declared that in Christ there is a divine and a human nature united in the one person of Christ "without confusion" and "without division." In other words, we can find the fullness of God in the man Jesus. To give full expression to this mystery, the council gave to Mary the designation of *Theotokos*—"the God-bearer." In Western Christendom Mary is still referred to as the mother of God.

The last great christological controversy arose immediately after the decision at Ephesus. Pious people began to put forward the theory that in Christ one may find only divinity, the human nature being nonexistent. Thus, behind the façade of a man there was no true humanity. In this system of thought, Christ feigned human responses for His observers' benefit, but He was not truly a man. Those putting forth this idea were called Monophysites (from the Greek, "one nature"). Another church council was called, this time at Chalcedon in 451. The assembled bishops issued a formula declaring that both a human and a divine nature existed in Christ in their entirety. God had truly appeared in a real man. The decisions and terminology of these two councils, Ephesus and Chalcedon, were included by an anonymous Western theologian in the document that has come down to us as the Athanasian Creed. Though not written by the great defender of orthodoxy, it was so called because it included many of the fourth-century conciliar concepts. It is without doubt one of that age's most precise documents concerning the person of Christ. It has been used for various festivals and celebrations of the church throughout Western Christendom. Due to its length and polemical quality, it is used less often than the Apostles' or Nicene creeds.

The Athanasian Creed

Whosoever will be saved, before all things it is necessary that he hold the catholic faith.

Which faith except everyone do keep whole and undefiled, without doubt he shall perish everlastingly.

And the catholic faith is this, that we worship one God in Trinity and Trinity in Unity,

Neither confounding the Persons nor dividing the Substance.

For there is one Person of the Father, another of the Son, and another of the Holy Ghost.

But the Godhead of the Father, of the Son, and of the Holy Ghost is all one: the glory equal, the majesty coeternal.

Such as the Father is, such is the Son, and such is the Holy Ghost.

The Father uncreate, the Son uncreate, and the Holy Ghost uncreate.

The Father incomprehensible, the Son incomprehensible, and the Holy Ghost incomprehensible.

The Father eternal, the Son eternal, and the Holy Ghost eternal.

And yet they are not three eternals, but one eternal.

As also there are not three uncreated nor three incomprehensibles, but one uncreated and one incomprehensible.

So likewise the Father is almighty, the Son almighty, and the Holy Ghost almighty.

And yet they are not three Almighties, but one Almighty.

So the Father is God, the Son is God, and the Holy Ghost is God.

And yet they are not three Gods, but one God.

So likewise the Father is Lord, the Son Lord, and the Holy Ghost Lord.

And yet not three Lords, but one Lord.

For like as we are compelled by the Christian verity to acknowledge every Person by Himself to be God and Lord,

So are we forbidden by the catholic religion to say, There be three Gods or three Lords.

The Father is made of none, neither created nor begotten.

The Son is of the Father alone, not made nor created, but begotten.

The Holy Ghost is of the Father and of the Son, neither made nor created nor begotten, but proceeding.

So there is one Father, not three Fathers; one Son, not three Sons; one Holy Ghost, not three Holy Ghosts.

And in this Trinity none is before or after another; none is greater or less than another;

But the whole three Persons are coeternal together and coequal, so that in all things, as is aforesaid, the Unity in Trinity and the Trinity in Unity is to be worshiped.

He, therefore, that will be saved must thus think of the Trinity.

Furthermore, it is necessary to everlasting salvation that he also believe faithfully the incarnation of our Lord Jesus Christ.

For the right faith is that we believe and confess that our Lord Jesus Christ, the Son of God, is God and Man;

> God of the Substance of the Father, begotten before the worlds; and Man of the substance of His mother, born in the world;
>
> Perfect God and perfect Man, of a reasonable soul and human flesh subsisting.
>
> Equal to the Father as touching His Godhead and inferior to the Father as touching His manhood;
>
> Who, although He be God and Man, yet He is not two, but one Christ:
>
> One, not by conversion of the Godhead into flesh, but by taking the manhood into God;
>
> One altogether; not by confusion of Substance, but by unity of Person.
>
> For as the reasonable soul and flesh is one man, so God and Man is one Christ;
>
> Who suffered for our salvation; descended into hell; rose again the third day from the dead;
>
> He ascended into heaven; He sitteth on the right hand of the Father, God Almighty; from whence He shall come to judge the quick and the dead.
>
> At whose coming all men shall rise again with their bodies and shall give an account of their own works.
>
> And they that have done good shall go into life everlasting; and they that have done evil, into everlasting fire.
>
> This is the catholic faith; which except a man believe faithfully and firmly, he cannot be saved.

The councils of the church sought to defend and define key articles of faith in regard to the person of Christ. The Council of Nicea, in 325, was concerned with His divinity; that of Ephesus, in 431, was concerned with His unity; and that of Chalcedon, in 451, spoke concerning His humanity. It is noteworthy that these councils expressed themselves in what have become liturgical documents—meant for use, not just in the study of theology, but for worship. The earliest known hymn we possess outside of the New Testament, "The Hymn to the Evening," says it best in its praise to Christ, the joyous light of holy glory:

> It is right to praise Thee
> At all times with Holy Songs
> Son of God, who has given life;
> Therefore the world glorifies Thee.

The Person of Christ

It would be wrong to assume that the teaching about the identity of Christ was established by councils, bishops, and decrees. The creedal formulas of the conciliar age only confirmed and conserved that which was already believed by the majority of Christians. Luther felt that the councils "established nothing new . . . but defended the old faith." Lutherans, as a whole, agree with this. If not established, then, by bishops and councils, how was the doctrine of the identity and nature of Christ arrived at? For this answer we have to turn back to the source and norm of all Christian teaching—the sacred Scriptures.

The New Testament employs many images to describe the person of Christ. Many of these descriptions denote Christ's relationship with mankind in general and the church in particular. Of the many images, we have chosen five—Christ as our brother, our God, our mediator, our servant, and our master. The last two images stand in a dialectical relationship, as do the first two. The image of Christ our mediator is the central and unifying factor.

Christ Our Brother: The Humanity of Our Lord

The Gospels portray Jesus as our brother. To this the remainder of the New Testament gives assent. The Gospels begin with the very human genealogy of our Lord (that of His mother's family in Luke 3:23–38, and that of His adopted father's family in Matthew 1:1–17); they end with His suffering, death, and resurrection. In the accounts of Christ's suffering, Pilate exclaims before the scoffing crowd, "Behold the man!" (John 19:5).

Jesus always claimed to be a man and was called a man by others. In response to those who sought to kill Him, Christ said, "But now ye seek to kill me, *a man* that hath told you the truth" (John 8:40; italics added). From the accounts of the evangelists, we know that He possessed the essential elements of a man, namely, a physical body and a rational soul. Christ could speak of "my body" and "my blood" (Matt. 26:26, 28). He could say His "soul [was] exceeding sorrowful" (Matt. 26:38), and could assure the disciples after the resurrection that He still consisted of "flesh and bones" (Luke 24:39). Jesus, in His life here, was subject to all that is common to man. He experienced hunger (Matt. 4:2), thirst (John 19:28), and weariness (John 4:6). He expressed compassion (Matt. 9:36), love (Mark 10:21), and even anger (Mark 3:5).

Although the birth of Jesus involved supernatural factors, we know that His growth as a child and adolescent was, for the most part, very normal. We are told by Luke that "Jesus increased in wisdom and stature, and in favour with God and man" (Luke 2:52). This indicates that Christ followed the usual pattern of physical, intellectual, spiritual, and social development. Yet Jesus, the babe and the boy, became a man and partook of real suffering and death on the cross (John 19:30).

There was, however, a factor that separated Jesus from other men. He was a perfect man, untainted by sin. He was free from inherited sin (original sin) due to His supernatural conception by "the power of the Most High." He was free from actual sin due to the purity and divinity of His character (John 8:46). He possessed a personality that was in complete union with the second person of the holy Trinity and expressed itself in perfection. He was to be the perfect sacrifice "without blemish and without spot" (I Peter 1:19), sent for our salvation. As Luther wrote,

> The Son obeyed His Father's will,
> Was born of virgin mother,
> And God's good pleasure to fulfill,
> He came to be my brother.
> No garb of pomp or power He wore,
> A servant's form, like mine, He bore,
> To lead the devil captive.

Christ Our God: The Divinity of Our Lord

The Gospels portray Jesus as our God. To this the rest of the New Testament gives assent. Both Matthew and Luke open their narratives with the account of the miraculous conception and birth of Christ. In Matthew He is announced as "Emmanuel"—"God with us" (Matt. 1:23). Luke reports that He is to be called "the Son of God" (Luke 1:35). Mark, in the early portion of his record, states that Christ forgives sins, something only God Himself can do (Mark 2:5–11). John, in the first sentence of his account, declares that "in the beginning was the Word, and the Word was with God, and the *Word was God*" (italics added). He afterward affirms that this "Word was made flesh, and dwelt among us" (John 1:14). John had no doubts concerning the divinity of our Lord. At the end of the Johannine account, another of the disciples comes to this realization and falls at the feet of Jesus, saying, "My Lord and my God" (John 20:28).

It was the conviction of all the New Testament writers that Jesus possessed divine attributes. They could speak of Him having "*life* in himself" (John 5:26; italics added), being without change (immutable; Heb. 13:8), and retaining absolute love (I John 3:16), truth (John 14:6), and holiness (John 6:69). Christ is recognized as being eternal (John 1:1), omnipresent (Eph. 1:23), omniscient (John 16:30), and omnipotent (Matt. 28:18). These same writers acknowledge Jesus as the creator and sustainer of this world (John 1:3; Heb. 1:3) and therefore worthy of adoration and worship (Phil. 2:10; Heb. 1:6). Paul, speaking of the incarnation, tells us that "Christ came, who is over all, God blessed forever" (Rom. 9:5). To this Luther agreed when he wrote,

> This is the Christ, our God and Lord,
> Who in all need shall aid afford;
> He will Himself your Saviour be
> From all your sins to set you free.

Christ Our Mediator: The Unity of Our Lord

The Gospels portray Jesus as our mediator. To this the rest of the New Testament gives assent. At His birth, Jesus was a mediator between the rich and the poor, the wise and the simple. Both shepherds and magi came to worship. He was born between the epochs of time and in the meeting place of continents. At His death, Jesus was stretched upon a cross between heaven and earth. He was placed between an innocent Mary and guilty thieves, set before believing disciples and scoffing scribes. All of this pointed to the role of Christ as mediator.

For Jesus to be a true mediator between the creator God and His creation, man, it was necessary to Him to be both true God and true man in a perfect union of natures, in a single person (hypostatic union). In this union, each nature communicates its attributes to the other, without confusion or deletion. Thus we may, with the Council of Ephesus, speak of Mary as the "mother of God," and with Paul we may speak of God purchasing the church "with His own Blood" (Acts 20:28). It has been the conviction of Lutheran theologians through the centuries that in Christ's humanity, God has "really and actually suffered" on our behalf.

It is also due to this communication of attributes that we may describe divine qualities as being "given" to Jesus during His earthly ministry. For although eternal and omnipotent, according to His divine nature, Christ says that "all power is *given* unto me in heaven and in earth" (Matt. 28:18; italics added). This is an example of a divine attribute, communicated to the person of Christ, *in time.* Because of this unique union we may say that the God-man is eternal, but was born in the reign of Caesar Augustus; that Jesus was weary, hungry, suffered, and died, yet is "the same yesterday, and to day, and for ever" (Heb. 13:8).

All this was accomplished so that Jesus Christ might be a true mediator between God and man. As an ancient father of the church declared, "what God has not assumed, he has not redeemed." To this Luther agreed when he wrote,

> Oh, then rejoice that thro' His Son
> God is with sinners now at one;
> Made like yourselves of flesh and blood,
> Your brother is th' eternal God.

Christ Our Servant: The Humiliation of Our Lord

The Gospels portray Jesus as a servant. To this the rest of the New Testament gives assent. The gospel accounts begin with Jesus being born in a stable—servants' quarters. His mother, Mary, bears for all generations the title of "the handmaid of the Lord" (Luke 1:38). Jesus is reared not as a king but as a carpenter. In the first act of public ministry He comes to John the Baptist, not as a king seeking pomp and glory, but as a servant asking to be baptized. At His death, Christ carries His own cross, is mocked by those He made, and serves by bringing comfort to a penitent thief who is dying beside Him. At His burial, a tomb must be borrowed, for this servant of men "has not a place to lay his head," even in death.

Christ's humiliation did not consist in becoming man, but in the kind of man He became. Though He was the eternal Son of God, He voluntarily laid aside the independent exercise of divine power and veiled from human eyes the greatness of His glory. At times, such as at the transfiguration, this glory and power shone through. But these occasions were the exceptions, not the rule. The final humiliation of His servant's life was a shameful suffering and death upon a Roman cross. This is the point of Paul's exhortation to the Philippians, when he writes,

> Let this mind be in you, which was also in Christ Jesus: Who, being in the form of God, thought it not robbery to be equal with God: But made himself of no reputation, and took upon him the form of a servant, and was made in the likeness of men: And being found in fashion as a man, he humbled himself, and became obedient unto death, even the death of the cross.
>
> [Phil. 2:5–8]

Luther, commenting on this passage in a sermon, said,

> Above and beyond being found in fashion as a man and comporting Himself as a man, He became lower than all men . . . by submitting to a death which was the most ignominious, namely, the death on the cross; He died as an archknave, above all knaves. . . . So, then, He was made entirely nothing.[6]

Christ Our Master: The Exaltation of Our Lord

The Gospels portray Jesus as our master. To this the rest of the New Testament gives assent. He was born of a royal line, worshiped by kings, feared by Herod, and beheld by

6. Franz Pieper, *Christian Dogmatics* (Saint Louis: Concordia, 1951), vol. 2, p. 291.

angels. In His earthly ministry Jesus showed mastery over nature, men, death, and disease. At His death He was called "King of the Jews," and so He was. Yet all of the aforementioned events were only precursors to the exaltation of Jesus that was to take place after His death on the cross.

Following Christ's death and burial was His exaltation. Paul, writing to the Philippians, moves beyond the humiliation of Jesus to state that after His death, God "highly exalted him, and [gave] him a name which is above every name" (Phil. 2:9).

Lutherans traditionally have believed that there were six stages in this process of exaltation. The first stage was revivification. This refers to the quickening of the entire Christ in the tomb, by which He was made alive in body and soul. The second was proclamation. Jesus, having been quickened by the Holy Ghost, went and "preached unto the spirits in prison" (I Peter 3:19). We confess this in the Apostles' Creed, saying "he descended into hell." Classical Lutheranism taught that Christ by a "supernatural motion" made a "triumphal proclamation" of His victory over death to those certain spirits in bondage. The third stage was resurrection. Christ arose from the tomb by the power of the holy Trinity, in the very body borne by the Virgin Mary. This was the first day of the week, Sunday, the day of the new creation. The stone was rolled away from the tomb—not to let Christ out, but that the disciples might look in and know that Christ was risen indeed. The fourth was manifestation. Following His resurrection, Christ appeared to His disciples over a period of forty days, "speaking of the things pertaining to the Kingdom of God" (Acts 1:3). It was during this time that He taught the disciples again and "opened . . . their understanding, that they might understand the scriptures" (Luke 24:45). The fifth was ascension and coronation. "While they beheld, He was taken up; and a cloud received Him out of their sight" (Acts 1:9). Traditionally this event has been likened to and celebrated as a coronation. Jesus is crowned as king and given dominion, glory, and authority by God the Father. The sixth stage was session and intercession. After Christ's ascension into heaven, Lutherans believe that Christ is seated "at [the] right hand [of God]" (Eph. 1:20). This indicates not the place of Christ's session, but the extent of His glory and dominion. He is in this place of dominion on our behalf and exercises both intercession and power for us (Heb. 7:25).

Christ's exaltation is the seal and the assurance that His work for us has been accepted by God. It is also our hope and life. As Luther wrote in his Easter hymn,

> Christ Jesus lay in death's strong bands,
> For our offenses given;
> But now at God's right hand he stands
> And brings us life from heaven;
> Therefore let us joyful be
> And sing to God right thankfully
> Loud songs of hallelujah. Hallelujah!

The Work of Christ

It is often difficult to separate the person of Christ from the work of Christ. This is because all we know of Jesus is in His revelation to man; and in His revelation to man, He is seen doing work on our behalf. This work that Christ has done and is doing for man's salvation may be placed under three titles that have been ascribed to Him—prophet, priest, and king. The Bible tells us that Christ was acknowledged to be a "prophet mighty in deed and word" (Luke 24:19), was set apart as a "faithful high priest" (Heb. 2:17), and is expected at His return to bear the inscription "King of kings, and Lord of lords" (Rev. 19:16). These three offices had been the types and symbols of authority in the Old Testament and were applied to Christ by the New Testament writers and the church fathers. The early church historian, Eusebius of Caesarea (260?–?340), wrote of this tripartite designation being fulfilled in

> . . . the true Christ, the divinely inspired and heavenly Word, who is the high *priest* of all, and the only *King* of every creature and the Father's only supreme *prophet* of prophets.[7]

7. *Nicene and Post-Nicene Fathers of the Christian Church*, second series, ed. Philip Schaff and Henry Wace (Grand Rapids: Eerdmans, 1976), vol. 1, p. 86.

Luther was the first of the reformers to use these designations to categorize the ministries of our Lord. This system of categorization was then expanded upon by John Calvin in *The Institutes of the Christian Religion.* Since the time of the Reformation, most Protestant theologians have found these headings helpful in describing the work of Christ.

An American Presbyterian, James M. Boice, has pointed out that the concept of Christ's threefold office corresponds to the threefold need of fallen man.[8] Man has a need for the knowledge of God. Jesus comes to us as the prophet par excellence to reveal the Father. Man has a need for salvation. Jesus comes to us as the reconciling priest, to offer Himself as a sacrifice for sin and to intercede at the right hand of God for us. Man has a need for loving direction and rule. Jesus comes to us as the shepherd-king, bearing both the rod of discipline and the staff of guidance. This correlation of office and need is helpful in understanding the application of Christ's work to our lives. Let us now examine these offices of Christ in greater detail.

Christ the Prophet

Most people think of a prophet as one who foretells future events. The Bible includes accounts of many men who did receive this particular gift from God, such as Moses, Samuel, Isaiah, and Ezekiel. There is, however, another designation for a prophet as one who "forthtells," or proclaims, the message of God to a people. The Bible also includes accounts of this type of person, such as David, Abraham, Nathan, and John the Baptist. A prophet is anyone who is a medium of divine communication or revelation. Many prophets of the Old Testament are also credited with working miracles and signs, which validated their ministry. In all of these respects, Jesus Christ showed Himself to be a true prophet.

Jesus, the eternal Word of God (John 1:1), was the source of prophecy and all prophetic work previous to His incarnation. He was "the true Light, which lighteth every man that cometh into the world" (John 1:9). All that was revealed concerning God was mediated through the Son, the second person of the Trinity.

8. *Ibid.,* p. 162.

In His incarnation, Jesus was *the* "Prophet" promised by Moses (Deut. 18:15) and expected by Israel. In His earthly ministry, Christ did the work of a prophet (Acts 3:22), taught the people (Matt. 5–7), made predictions (Matt. 24–25), performed miracles (Matt. 8–9), and consistently revealed the Father (John 8:26). Jesus called Himself a prophet (Matt. 13:57) and was given that title by others (John 6:14).

Since His ascension, Christ's prophetic office has continued in the preaching and teaching of His church. This activity originated with the apostles and has, by the enlightening influence of the Holy Spirit, continued in the successive varied ministries of the church (John 16:12–14). It is noteworthy that when Luke wrote his account of the early church he reminded his reader of "the former treatise have I made, O Theophilus, of all that Jesus *began* both to do and to teach" (Acts 1:1; italics added). This statement indicates that the work of Jesus as prophet had just begun and was going to be continued in His body—the church.

Christ the Priest

In the Old Testament a priest fulfilled a divinely appointed office. The duty of the priest was to appear before God on man's behalf and, in a certain way, to appear before man on God's behalf. Under the old covenant the priest fulfilled this office in two ways. First was the offering to God of a sacrifice; second was the making of intercession. In both ways Christ fulfilled the office of a priest. This was the theme dwelt upon by the author of the Book of Hebrews. In comparing the priesthood of the Old Testament to the present and eternal priesthood of Jesus, the apostolic writer observed,

> But this man, because he continueth ever, hath an unchangeable priesthood. Wherefore he is able also to save them to the uttermost that come unto God by him, seeing he ever liveth to make intercession for them. For such an high priest became us, who is holy, harmless, undefiled, separate from sinners, and made higher than the heavens; Who needeth not daily, as those high priests, to offer up sacrifice, first for his own sins, and then for the people's: for this he did once, when he offered up himself. For the law maketh men high priests which

> have infirmity; but the word of the oath, which was since the law, maketh the Son, who is consecrated for evermore.
>
> [Heb. 7:24–28]

While all of Christ's ministry has a priestly character, two events especially reveal His sacerdotal role—His crucifixion and His ascension. The first indicates His priestly function as the one who offers sacrifice for sin; the second indicates His priestly function as the one who offers intercessory prayer for sinners. Let us consider each of these priestly actions.

The first priestly action was the crucifixion. On Calvary, Christ the priest offered Himself as a sacrifice for the sins of humankind. As Paul exclaimed, "Christ died for our sins" (I Cor. 15:3).

Through the centuries the church has contemplated the mystery of the cross in liturgical expression. The Lutheran service often opens and closes with participants making the sign of the cross. Luther wrote, "In the morning, when you get up, make the sign of the holy Cross. . . ." Babies at baptism are often "signed" with the cross. Sometimes communicants at the altar "cross themselves" after receiving Christ's body and blood. The last act of a believer's life is sometimes the sign of the cross and anointing. When the body is returned to the earth, the officiating minister often makes the sign of the cross as he commits the body to rest. Lutherans from birth to death can say with integrity and certainty, "In the cross of Christ I glory," because

> When the woes of life o'ertake me,
> Hopes deceive, and fears annoy,
> Never shall the cross forsake me;
> Lo! it glows with peace and joy.

The church has also contemplated the mystery of the cross in theological expression. Four fundamental and compatible interpretations of the crucifixion have existed in the church from earliest times, though each is often associated with a particular era and individual. Each theology of the cross reveals a different dimension of the cross's influence. Figure 4 illustrates these varying interpretations.

Figure 4 **Views of Christ's Atonement**

Luther and Gerhard

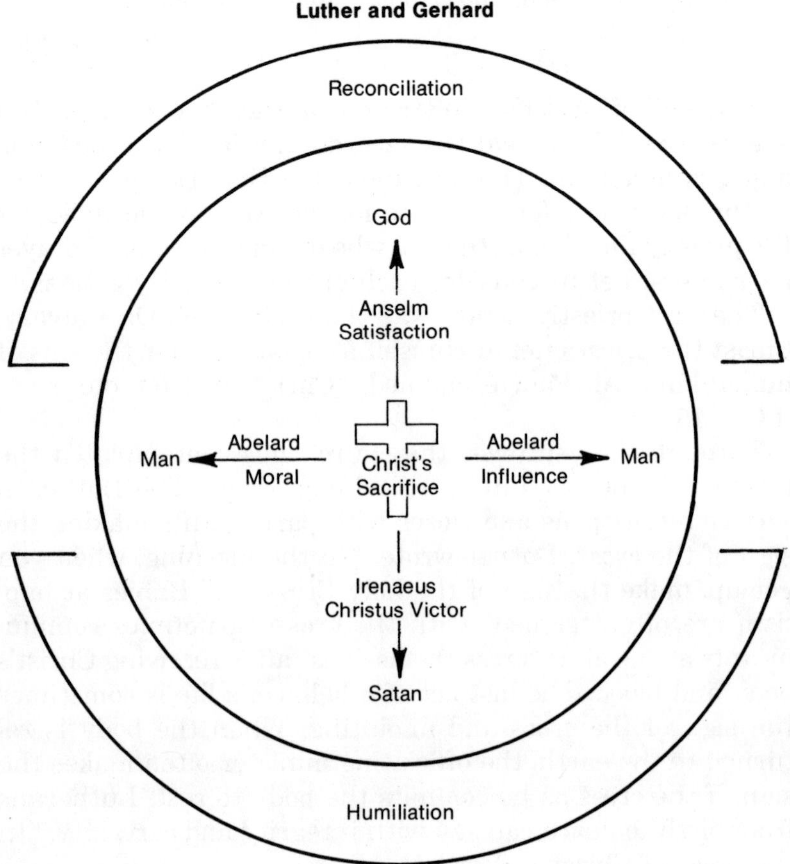

In the ancient world a popular and powerful interpreter of the theology of the cross was Irenaeus (A.D. 130–200), teacher of both the Eastern and Western churches, theologian in Anatolia and bishop in Gaul. According to tradition, Irenaeus was taught the faith by Polycarp, a disciple of Saint John the Divine. Irenaeus perceived the cross in terms of its impact on Satan, who has held man in bondage since the fall. Christ is the conqueror of hell and evil. Jesus is *Christus Victor*, who "bound the strong man, and set free the weak, and endowed His own handiwork with salvation by destroying sin." The theology of Irenaeus is reflected in the classical Lutheran understanding of Christ's descent into hell as a "harrowing of the inferno that the Evil One might have no more dominion over man." It is also evident in Luther's confession in the Large Catechism:

> There was no counsel, no help, no comfort for us until this only and eternal Son of God, in his unfathomable goodness, had mercy on our misery and wretchedness and came from heaven to help us. Those tyrants and jailers now have been routed, and their place has been taken by Jesus Christ, the Lord of life and righteousness and every good and blessing. He has snatched us, poor lost creatures, from the jaws of hell, won us, made us free, and restored us to the Father's favor and grace.[9]

Both Irenaeus and Luther reflect and echo the doctrine of Paul, who celebrated our Lord Jesus Christ, "who gave himself for our sins, that he might deliver us from this present evil world, according to the will of God and our Father . . ." (Gal. 1:4).

In the medieval world a popular and powerful interpreter of the theology of the cross was Anselm (1033–1109), author of *Cur Deus Homo? (Why the God-man?)*, a native of Italy who became Archbishop of Canterbury, and a teacher of both the Northern and Southern churches. Schaff esteemed Anselm as "a man of spotless integrity, and simple devotion to truth and righteousness. . . ." Many regard him as the most original thinker in the church since the time of Augustine. Anselm perceived the cross in terms of its impact on God. For Anselm, the crucifixion reveals that "satisfaction must be made for man's sins" to the holy Father. He remarked, "Sinful man owes God a debt for sin which he cannot repay and at the same time that he cannot be saved without repaying it. . . ." This Christ, as true God and true man, has done.

To Luther this understanding of the atonement was eminently satisfying. Commenting on the Book of Galatians, Luther wrote,

9. *The Book of Concord*, trans. and ed. Theodore G. Tappert (Philadelphia: Fortress, 1959), p. 414.

> He verily is innocent, because he is the unspotted and undefiled Lamb of God. But because he beareth the sins of the world, his innocence is burdened with the sins and guilt of the whole world. Whatsoever sins, I, thou, and we all have done, or shall do hereafter, they are Christ's own sins as verily as if he himself had done them. To be brief: our sins must needs become Christ's own sin, or else we shall perish for ever.[10]

Anselm and Luther both reflect and echo the prophecy of Isaiah:

> Surely he hath borne our griefs, and carried our sorrows: yet we did esteem him stricken, smitten of God, and afflicted. But he was wounded for our transgressions, he was bruised for our iniquities: the chastisement of our peace was upon him; and with his stripes we are healed. All we like sheep have gone astray; we have turned every one to his own way; and the Lord hath laid on him the iniquity of us all.
>
> [Isa. 53:4–6]

They also mirror the theology of the Isaiah of the New Testament, Paul, who affirmed, "And not only so, but we also joy in God through our Lord Jesus Christ, by whom we have now received the atonement" (Rom. 5:11)

Also in the medieval world, another popular and powerful interpreter of the theology of the cross was Peter Abelard (1079–1142), a younger contemporary of Anselm. Abelard was a French philosopher and theologian, a professor at the University of Paris, who ended his career as a contemplative at the monastery of Cluny. Regarded as "a great scholar and keen theologian," Abelard has been a teacher of both the medieval and the modern churches. The man whose mind spans both scholasticism and humanism, Abelard perceived the cross in terms of its impact on man. For Abelard, the crucifixion reveals the eternal love of God for man expressed in Christ. As Paul wrote, "But God commendeth his love toward us, in that, while we were yet sinners, Christ died for us" (Rom. 5:8). Sinful persons, beholding the crucified Jesus,

10. Robert H. Culpepper, *Interpreting the Atonement* (Grand Rapids: Eerdmans, 1966), p. 94.

are compelled by His sacrifice to repent and to return to the waiting Father. This is the moral influence of the cross on humankind. Abelard wrote, in his *Commentary on Romans*,

> Now it seems to us that we have been justified by the blood of Christ and reconciled to God in this way: through this unique act of grace manifested to us—in that his Son has taken upon himself our nature and persevered therein in teaching us by word and example even unto death—he has the more fully bound us to himself by love; with the result that our hearts should be enkindled by such a gift of divine grace, and true charity should not now shrink from enduring anything for him.
>
> Wherefore, our redemption through Christ's suffering is that deeper affection in us which not only frees us from slavery to sin, but also wins for us the true liberty of sons of God, so that we do all things out of love rather than fear. . . .[11]

To Luther this understanding of the atonement was helpful. It is reflected in the reformer's conception of God—not as a tyrant, but as a loving father, head of a great extended family on earth and in heaven. The moral influence of the cross is taught by Luther, as when he writes,

> If you have a true faith that Christ is your Saviour, then at once you have a gracious God, for faith leads you in and opens up God's heart and will, that you should see pure grace and overflowing love. This it is to behold God in faith that you should look upon his fatherly, friendly heart, in which there is no anger nor ungraciousness. He who sees God as angry does not see him rightly but looks only on a curtain, as if a dark cloud had been drawn across his face.[12]

Both Abelard and Luther reflect and echo the doctrine of Saint John the Theologian: "In this was manifested the love of God toward us, because that God sent his only begotten

11. *Ibid.*, pp. 89–90.

12. Quoted by Roland H. Bainton, *Here I Stand: A Life of Martin Luther* (New York: Abingdon-Cokesbury, 1950), p. 65.

Son into the world, that we might live through him." (I John 4:9).

In early modern times a popular and powerful interpreter of the theology of the cross was Johann Gerhard (1582–1637), the expositor of Lutheran high orthodoxy, a professor at Jena, in spite of twenty-four calls to other universities. Though intensely confessional, Gerhard influenced Roman Catholic, Anglican, and Reformed thought, as he in turn was influenced by Greek, Latin, and German theology. Regarded as the greatest theologian of Lutheranism since Luther, Gerhard synthesized Catholic and evangelical thought and gave the Lutheran churches a holistic perspective on the cross. Gerhard, interpreting the many themes found in Luther's theology, perceived the cross in terms of its impact on God and man as reconciliation and its impact on Satan as humiliation.

For Gerhard, one manifestation of this will become evident at Christ's return, especially in his treatment of the redeemed:

> He will not, therefore, come as a severe Judge, producing the sins of the godly to the public gaze of all, and calling them to a rigid examination. For it is the part of an advocate not to publish, but to cover; not to accuse, but excuse; not to convict, but to favor. . . . For as the only Mediator between God and man, He took our sins upon Himself, and afforded a perfect satisfaction for them, which believers apply to themselves by true faith. . . . But if He were to reveal the sins of the godly in judgement, He would act contrary to His own office, since He would reveal the sins which He suffered to be placed upon Him, in order that He might afford a most sufficient ransom whereby they might be abolished and removed. . . . He has not reproached those for their sins, who in this life have been converted to God by true repentance, but, according to his promise, has not remembered their sins, and has treated such persons as a most indulgent and mild father, who receives into his open arms a wayward son who returns, without upbraiding him for his former life. . . . For they are described as those who are not to be judged . . . who will not come into judgement, for whom there is no condemnation as washed, sanctified, jus-

> tified, whom none can accuse or condemn, as without spot of wrinkle or any such thing. . . .[13]

This is the eschatological implication of the gospel as summarized by John, evangelist and seer: "For God so loved the world, that he gave his only begotten Son, that whosoever believeth in him should not perish, but have everlasting life" (John 3:16).

For Luther, as he wrote in the Small Catechism, this was a source of enormous comfort, renewed each time we pray, "Our Father, who art in heaven," because, for Christ's sake,

> God would by these words tenderly invite us to believe that He is our true Father, and that we are His true children, so that we may with all boldness and confidence ask Him as dear children ask their dear father.

Christ's other priestly action, besides the crucifixion, is his intercessory prayer for sinners. This transpires not at the right hand of thieves but at the right hand of the giver of all good gifts, the Father. As one eminent theologian wrote, "The priesthood of Christ does not cease with his work of atonement but continues forever. In the presence of God he fulfills the second office of the priest, namely that of intercession." John confessed, "If any man sin, we have an advocate with the Father, Jesus Christ the righteous" (I John 2:1). Paul affirmed, "It is Jesus Christ that died, yea rather, that is risen again, who is even at the right hand of God, who also maketh intercession for us" (Rom. 8:34).

Christ the King

Christ the prophet and priest also reigns as the "King of kings" (Rev. 19:16). Traditionally, Lutheran theologians have spoken of three kingdoms over which Jesus rules. His kingly authority in these spheres is not the sovereignty that He possesses as a result of His divine nature. His kingship is that of the eternal Redeemer: His by birth in the stable at

13. Quoted by Henry Eyster Jacobs, *A Summary of the Christian Faith* (Philadelphia: The United Lutheran Publication House, 1905), p. 525.

Bethlehem, His by decree on the cross, His by victory in the resurrection, and His by right at the ascension.

The first of the three kingdoms of Jesus is the kingdom of power. This kingdom extends over the entire universe, and includes every created order, both physical and spiritual. In this kingdom all things are upheld by "the word of his power" (Heb. 1:3), and Jesus is the absolute authority (Matt. 28:18). Christ reigns over the kingdom of power as an omnipotent ruler. The rule of Jesus over the universe will be manifested to all men at His coming again in glory when He will "rule them with a rod of iron" (Rev. 19:15). The second is the kingdom of grace. This kingdom extends over the people of God on earth—the church militant. In this kingdom, Jesus reigns in love over a "redeemed and blood bought band." His instruments of rule are the Holy Spirit and the revealed Word of God. Jesus is "the head over all things to the church" (Eph. 1:22), whose throne reaches from this world to the next (Heb. 1:8). The third is the kingdom of glory. This kingdom extends over the people of God in heaven—the church triumphant. In this kingdom Jesus reigns, in the full revelation of Himself, over "the city of the living God, the heavenly Jerusalem and . . . an innumerable company of angels" (Heb. 12:22). It is here that Jesus shares with the redeemed the vision of His glory, concerning which He prayed, in the garden of Gethsemane, "that they also, whom thou hast given me, be with me where I am; that they may behold my glory" (John 17:24).

Christ the King, *Christus Rex*, is the present reality and the future hope for all who believe. He is the ruler and judge for the believer and the unbeliever alike. We confess this in the Nicene Creed when we declare that "He shall come again, with glory, to judge both the quick and the dead; whose kingdom shall have no end."

We are left at the end of this chapter with the question of Christ, "Whom do men say that I the Son of man am?" We may find answers in the Christ of history, the Christ of the creeds, the Christ of the theologians, or in the Christ of the cross; but He still comes to each of us as a person, unknown and often hidden in His work. Jesus comes to us to be known of us, and to apply His saving work to our lives. This is the message of reconciliation. As the Episcopal bishop Phillips Brooks wrote,

> ... Christianity is knowing Christ, and personal knowledge can come only by experience: and experience takes time. A truth you may embrace, and embrace completely, as soon as you understand the terms of its statement and have learned its evidence. But you cannot bring a person, as you can a proposition, up to a man, and say, 'Here, know him!' and you say 'Know this,' and be at once obeyed. 'I cannot,' he replies, 'However thoroughly you vouch for him, I cannot know him till he shows himself to me. I thank you for bringing him to me. I thank you more than if I could know him all at once, for if he is really all you say, then there lies before me a long career of gradual knowledge that shall be all delight to me till I shall know him perfectly.' This seems to me one difference of Christians. Make Christianity a doctrinal system, and when your new disciple has learned his catechism, he is all done; and pretty soon you will find him sitting with his hands in his lap, complaining that there is nothing more to learn, and either finding his well-learned faith dull and uninteresting, or supplementing it with dogmatic speculation of his own. Make Christianity a personal knowledge of Christ, and then, with ever new enticements, each little that he knows opens to him something more to know of the infinite personal life, obedience feeding love, and love stimulating obedience, he presses on in the never stale, never weary ambition of 'knowing Christ.'[14]

14. *The Candle of the Lord and Other Sermons* (London: Macmillan, 1905), pp. 52–53.

CHAPTER

3

The Spirit of Conviction

> And I believe in the Holy Ghost, the Lord and Giver of Life, who proceedeth from the Father and the Son, who with the Father and the Son together is worshiped and glorified, who spake by the Prophets. . . .

Twenty years ago the Holy Spirit was the forgotten person of the Trinity. During a seminary class on pneumatology, the science of the Holy Spirit, Edward C. Fendt exclaimed, "Pitney Van Deusen is right. The Holy Spirit is the anonymous member of the Trinity." Or, to put it another way, to most seminarians of the fifties, the Spirit, at best, was a vague, oblong blur.

Today the Holy Spirit has become the controversial person of the Trinity. During a seminary class in the 1980s on the Lutheran confessions, Robert Preus discussed the claims of charismatic renewal. Then Preus referred to one of his books:

> If one were to read only what Lutheran theology says about the Holy Spirit in its locus on God, one could only conclude that Lutheranism teaches a quite truncated Pneumatology.[1]

During the discussion he spoke of "the innate Lutheran fear of all enthusiasm." Preus continued, "Certainly the Spirit is more prominent in our thinking today than when I was a student in the seminary." Students then shared their reactions—either positive or negative—to the charismatic movement, which is so widespread within the Lutheran church

1. *The Theology of Post-Reformation Lutheranism* (Saint Louis: Concordia, 1972), vol. 2, p. 157.

Kramer Chapel

Concordia Theological Seminary
Fort Wayne, Indiana
Eero Saarinen, architect

Contemporary Lutheran sanctuary situated on the first campus to receive a first-honor award from the American Institute of Architects.

today. The Holy Spirit is "a present reality to many people." One-fifth of all Lutherans claim to have received the Paraclete in a special way. More than a fourth of all Americans testify to rebirth through His power. The Spirit is a "force at work in the hearts and minds of millions."

In this chapter we will look at the Holy Spirit (Holy Ghost, Comforter, or Paraclete) to examine His divinity, activity, ministry, and position in the holy Trinity.

The Divinity of the Holy Spirit

The Holy Spirit is God. That is the confession of the church. Together with the Father and the Son, the Spirit "is worshiped and glorified. . . ." How did the Christian community arrive at this conviction? On the basis of the sacred Scriptures, the source and norm of all teaching in the church, believers have arrived at four affirmations concerning the divinity of the Holy Spirit.

The Holy Spirit is identified as God in the Bible. At the beginning of the gospel the Spirit appears, together with the Father, to proclaim Jesus, in His baptism, as the beloved Son. Luke reports,

> Now when all the people were baptized, it came to pass, that Jesus also being baptized, and praying, the heaven was opened, And the Holy Ghost descended in a bodily shape like a dove upon him, and a voice came from heaven, which said, Thou art my beloved Son; in thee I am well pleased.
>
> [Luke 3:21–22]

At the conclusion of the gospel the Spirit is mentioned in the Great Commission, for Jesus said, "Go ye therefore, and teach all nations, baptizing them in the name of the Father, and of the Son, and of the Holy Ghost" (Matt. 28:19).

Throughout the New Testament the Spirit is given names or titles that can legitimately be applied only to the Deity. He is known as the Comforter (John 14:26) and the Spirit of God (I Cor. 2:10–11). To lie to him, Peter told Ananias, is to deceive God, for "why hath Satan filled thine heart to lie to the Holy Ghost? . . . Thou hast not lied unto men, but unto God" (Acts 5:3, 4). Or Paul could inform the Corinthians that they were "the temple of God" because "the Spirit of God dwelleth in you" (I Cor. 3:16). Or again, writing to the same congregation, Paul could associate the Spirit with the Lord (Christ) and with God (the Father), saying, "Now there are diversities of gifts, but the same Spirit. And there are differences of administrations, but the same Lord. And there are diversities of operations, but it is the same God which worketh all in all" (I Cor. 12:4–6). To the apostolic church, the Spirit is God.

The Bible ascribes the attributes of God to the Holy Spirit. The Spirit is omnipresent, for "whither shall I go from thy Spirit? or whither shall I flee from thy presence?" (Ps. 139:7). He is omniscient, "for the Spirit searcheth all things, yea, the deep things of God" (I Cor. 2:10). He is omnipotent, "for God hath not given us the spirit of fear; but of power . . ." (II Tim. 1:7). He is "the *eternal* Spirit" (Heb. 9:14; italics added), holy and without imperfection (Matt. 28:19). He is the "Spirit of *life*" (Rom. 8:2; italics added), the "Spirit of *truth*" (John 16:13; italics added), and the "*holy* Spirit of God" (Eph. 4:30; italics added). Christians dwell in the "*love* of the Spirit" (Rom. 15:30; italics added). To the apostolic church, the Spirit is God.

The Holy Spirit is credited with the works of God in the Bible. With the Father and the Son, He is the God of creation, for "by the word of the LORD were the heavens made; and all the host of them by the *breath* [Spirit] of his mouth" (Ps. 33:6; italics added). With the Son and the Father He is the God of salvation, for "he saved us, by the washing of regeneration, and renewing of the Holy Ghost" (Titus 3:5). Jesus told Nicodemus that regeneration is the work of the Spirit, for "the wind bloweth where it listeth, and thou hearest the sound thereof, but canst not tell whence it cometh . . . so is every one that is born of the Spirit" (John 3:8). Furthermore, resurrection occurs by the power of the Holy Spirit (Rom. 8:11). Sanctification is His task also, for He is the *Holy* Spirit. To the apostolic church, the Spirit is God.

The Holy Spirit is worshiped as God in the Bible. The baptismal formula itself, reported in the closing verses of Matthew's Gospel (Matt. 28:19) is liturgy, an act of worship by the church. Paul, writing to the Galatians, employs an ancient triune blessing, “that the blessing of Abraham might come on the Gentiles through Jesus Christ; that we might receive the promise of the Spirit through faith” (Gal. 3:14). The God of Abraham together with Jesus Christ and the Spirit are all invoked and adored as one deity. In closing his letter to the Corinthians Paul employs the apostolic benediction, which can be understood not simply as a blessing of the people, but as a prayer to the Spirit: “The grace of the Lord Jesus Christ, and the love of God, and the communion of the Holy Ghost, be with you all” (II Cor. 13:14). To the apostolic church, the Spirit is God.

The Holy Spirit is God. This is what Martin Luther confessed, praying,

> Come, Holy Ghost, God and Lord;
> Be all thy gifts in plenty poured
> To save, to strengthen and make whole
> Each ready mind, each waiting soul.
> O, by the brightness of thy light
> In holy faith all men unite,
> And to Thy praise, by every tongue,
> In every land, our hymn be sung.

The Activity of the Holy Spirit

Classic Lutheran theology, on the basis of the sacred Scriptures, has taught a threefold activity of the Holy Spirit. Together with the Father and the Son, He is the God of creation, the God of redemption, and the God of sanctification.

Let us consider this threefold activity of the Holy Spirit.

The Holy Spirit is the God of creation. The Bible opens with the story of creation as “the Spirit of God moved upon the face of the waters” (Gen. 1:2). The psalmist could state, “Thou sendest forth thy spirit, they are created: and thou renewest the face of the earth” (Ps. 104:30). Man, the apex of creation, is made in “the image of God” (Gen. 1:27) and is said to be “a temple of God, and that the Spirit of God dwelleth in you” (I Cor. 3:16). In the Spirit, Saint John the Divine was able to foresee the "new heaven and the new earth," the great creation following the consummation of history. No wonder the words of a ninth-century hymn (translated by John Dryden) connected the Spirit with creation and re-creation:

> Creator Spirit, by whose aid
> The world's foundations first were laid,
> Come, visit every pious mind,
> Come, pour thy joys on humankind;
> From sin and sorrow set us free,
> And make thy temples worthy thee.

The Holy Spirit is the God of redemption. As the creed confesses, Jesus "was conceived by the Holy Ghost, born of the Virgin Mary. . . ." The Spirit was crucial to the incarnation. Gabriel told the Virgin Mary, "The Holy Ghost shall come upon thee, and the power of the Highest shall overshadow thee: therefore also that holy thing which shall be born of thee shall be called the Son of God" (Luke 1:35). When Christ was presented in the temple, Simeon, "just and devout, waiting for the consolation of Israel" (Luke 2:25) "came by the Spirit into the temple" (Luke 2:27) to see and proclaim baby Jesus as the Messiah. John the Baptist said of Jesus, "He shall baptize you with the Holy Ghost" (Luke 3:16). At Christ's baptism "the Holy Ghost descended . . . upon him" (Luke 3:22). Jesus, "being full of the Holy Ghost" (Luke 4:1), was "led by the Spirit into the wilderness" for the temptation (Luke 4:1). By the power of the Spirit Jesus conducted His ministry—preaching and teaching, helping and healing—for He said, "I cast out devils by the Spirit of God" (Matt. 12:28). The resurrection of Christ also involved the Spirit, for Paul spoke of "the Spirit of him that raised up Jesus from the dead" (Rom. 8:11). Christ promised his followers the Spirit, for "it is expedient for you that I go away: for if I go not away, the Comforter will not come unto you; but if I depart, I will send him unto you" (John 16:7). Christ, after his ascension, sent the Spirit on the apostles, "and they were all filled with the Holy Ghost . . ." (Acts 2:4). No wonder Simon Browne, a seventeenth-century poet, could connect the Spirit and Christ, praying,

Lead us to Christ, the living way,
Nor let us from his pastures stray;
Lead us to holiness, the road
That we must take to dwell with God.

The Holy Spirit is the God of sanctification. That is the activity of the Paraclete that is best known in the church. *A Short Explanation of Dr. Martin Luther's Small Catechism* taught, "The Holy Ghost sanctifies me, that is, He *makes me holy*, by bringing me to faith in Christ and by imparting to me the blessings of redemption. (Sanctification in the wider sense includes everything that the Holy Ghost does in me.)"[2]

Paul stated the matter this way: "But ye are washed, but ye are sanctified, but ye are justified in the name of the Lord Jesus, and by the Spirit of our God" (I Cor. 6:11).

Luther testified, in the Small Catechism,

> I believe that I cannot by my own reason or strength believe in Jesus Christ, my Lord, or come to Him; but the Holy Ghost has called me by the Gospel, enlightened me with His gifts, sanctified and kept me in the true faith; even as He calls, gathers, enlightens, and sanctifies the whole Christian Church on earth, and keeps it with Jesus Christ in the one true faith; in which Christian Church He daily and richly forgives all sins to me and all believers, and will at the Last Day raise up me and all the dead, and give unto me and all believers in Christ eternal life. This is most certainly true.

Johann Gerhard, the prince of Lutheran theologians in the age of orthodoxy, felt that the climax of sanctification was found in the mystical union of the believer and God. This union is made possible by the power of the Holy Spirit—so that the Father and the Son could dwell in the heart of the believer. Gerhard read these words of Jesus: "If a man love me, he will keep my words: and my Father will love him, and we will come unto him, and make our abode with him" (John 14:23). Then Gerhard commented,

> Think of the majesty of these guests (the Father and the Son, John 14:23), and you will better understand the kindness of this coming ('We will come unto him'). Since in this life, we

2. (Saint Louis: Concordia, 1943), pp. 125–126. Italics in the original.

> cannot ascend to God, so as to be present with him (2 Cor. 5:8), but as long as life lasts, 'We are absent from the Lord' (v. 6), God, of His immense kindness, descends to us, and comes to us, i.e., the highest majesty comes to the most abject vileness, heaven to earth, the Creator to the creature, the Lord to the servant. What love for man! 'Lord, what is man that thou art mindful of him, or the son of man that thou visitest him?' (Ps. 8:4). How men are pleased when earthly kings and princes turn aside to visit them! But what is this, compared with the coming of God! Earthly kings become a burden to those whom they visit, because of the expense attending their entertainment; but these heavenly guests come, not with empty hands, but with a store of priceless gifts.[3]

The Spirit unites us with the Father and the Son. No wonder Edwin Hatch, the celebrated nineteenth-century Anglican scholar, could pray,

> Breathe on me, Breath of God,
> Until my heart is pure,
> Until with thee I will one will,
> To do and to endure.
>
> Breathe on me, Breath of God,
> Unite my soul with thine,
> Until this earthly part of me
> Glows with thy fire divine.

The Ministry of the Holy Spirit

While Lutherans do not recognize an order of salvation as such, nor do these events follow in any set order, usually classical Lutheran theology has spoken of a fivefold ministry of the Holy Spirit: invitation, or vocation; illumination; regeneration and conversion; incorporation, or the mystical union; and renovation.

Let us consider these five ministries of the Holy Spirit.

First is the ministry of invitation, or vocation. This is

3. Quoted by Henry Eyster Jacobs, *A Summary of the Christian Faith* (Philadelphia: The United Lutheran Publication House, 1905), p. 246.

commonly known as the call. David Hollaz, a theologian in the era of orthodoxy, said,

> The Call is the act of grace by which the Holy Spirit manifests by means of the Word of God His will in regard to the salvation of sinners to those persons who are out of the Church, and offers them benefits from Christ the Redeemer, that they may be led to the Church, converted, and obtain eternal salvation.[4]

The witness of the New Testament is that God the Holy Spirit calls persons to faith. Peter, writing to the diaspora church, remembered how God "called you out of darkness into his marvellous light" (I Peter 2:9). Paul said to the Thessalonians, "He called you by our gospel" (II Thess. 2:14). To Timothy Paul wrote that God "hath saved us, and called us with an holy calling" (II Tim. 1:9), just as John reported that "the Spirit and the bride say, Come" (Rev. 22:17). Invitation is the initial ministry of the Spirit, as Luther noted, for "the Holy Ghost has called me by the Gospel. . . ."

This teaching of the New Testament has continued to be a living reality in the lives of millions across the centuries. Illustrative of the invitation of the Spirit to discipleship is the story of Augustine of Hippo.

Born in 354 in the North African town of Tagaste and reared by a Christian mother, Monica, Augustine had avoided both baptism and a public profession of Christ. A creative mind, a restless spirit, and aimless energy characterized Augustine in his youth. As a young man of twenty he began his feverish quest for truth, which led him to embrace several of the popular philosophical systems of his time, including both Manichaeism and Neoplatonism. Concurrently he had acquired a mistress, by whom he fathered a son. Indulgence in both philosophy and the flesh did not bring Augustine the certainty he sought. The question haunted him: "How is it that so many humble persons find peace so speedily in reli-

4. Quoted by Heinrich Schmid, *The Doctrinal Theology of the Evangelical Lutheran Church*, trans. Charles A. Hay and Henry E. Jacobs, third rev. ed. (Minneapolis: Augsburg, 1961), p. 442.

gion, while I, with all my philosophy and anxious reasonings, remain year after year in darkness and doubt?"[5]

What followed has been eloquently described by John S. C. Abbott:

> Conscious that the difficulty was to be found in his own stubborn will, he retired in great agitation to a secluded spot in the garden, and, as he writes, 'with vehement indignation I rebuked my sinful spirit because it would not give itself up to God.' His anguish was great, and he wept bitterly. Falling upon his knees beneath a fig-tree, with tears and trembling utterance he exclaimed,—
>
> 'O Lord! how long shall I say to-morrow? Why should not this hour put an end to my slavery?'
>
> Just then, he fancied that he heard a voice saying to him, 'Take up and read.' He had with him Paul's epistles. Opening the book, the first passage which met his eye was this, found in the thirteenth chapter of Romans, thirteenth and fourteenth verses:—
>
> 'Let us walk honestly, as in the day; not in rioting and drunkenness, not in chambering and wantonness, not in strife and envying. But put ye on the Lord Jesus Christ, and make not provision for the flesh to fulfill the lusts thereof.'[6]

The invitation of Christ, coming through the written Word, was directed precisely at the evil that held Augustine in bondage, his sensuality. In his case, the calling of Jesus was effective. Augustine committed his life to the Savior and was baptized on Easter, 387. His subsequent career altered the course of Western Christianity. It is significant to recall that Luther was an Augustinian monk and that the twice-born saint of Hippo was his mentor in theology.

Second is the ministry of illumination. Hollaz wrote of this activity of the Holy Spirit that

> illumination is the act of applying grace, by which the Holy Spirit, through the ministry of the Word, teaches a man who is a sinner and called to the Church, and continues to instruct

5. Quoted by John S. C. Abbott, *The History of Christianity* (Portland, ME: George Stinson, 1889), p. 380.

6. *Ibid.*, pp. 380–381.

> him in an ever-increasing measure, with the earnest purpose to remove the darkness of ignorance and error, and imbue him with the knowledge of the Word of God, by instilling from the Law the conviction of sin, and from the Gospel the apprehension of divine mercy, founded upon the merit of Christ.[7]

The witness of the New Testament is that God the Holy Spirit enlightens men and women with His gifts, grants them saving knowledge of Christ, and causes them to trust and rejoice in Him. Paul spoke of this when he wrote to the Corinthian church: "God, who commanded the light to shine out of darkness, hath shined in our hearts, to give the light of the knowledge of the glory of God in the face of Jesus Christ" (II Cor. 4:6). Illumination is a vital ministry of the Spirit, as Luther noted, for "the Holy Ghost has . . . enlightened me with His gifts, sanctified and kept me in the true faith. . . ."

Luther knew this truth not only deductively from the Scriptures but also experientially from his own life. Born in 1483 in the German town of Eisleben, reared by a traditional Roman Catholic father and mother, Luther possessed an agile mind, a sensitive conscience, and a questing spirit. Peace of soul evaded him. Young Luther did not believe himself to be in favor with God. Luther's struggles led him into the Augustinian monastery in Erfurt, to advanced theological study resulting in an earned doctorate, to much activity in church, community, and university, and to an amazing discovery of the gospel that changed Christian history. In terms of emotional anguish, intellectual struggle, and anxiety of soul, Luther's illumination ranks alongside the equally dramatic episode of the calling of Augustine. Recall how one historian described Luther's experience:

> . . . [Luther] turned to the famous chapter in Romans 1:16–17, in which the Gospel is characterized as the saving power of God for all who believe, because in it the righteousness of God is revealed from faith to faith. But at first the study of this passage only made his heart grow heavier and the darkness deeper. 'Thus the Gospel, too,' he said to himself, 'is only a

7. Quoted by Schmid, *Doctrinal Theology*, p. 45.

> revelation of the punitive righteousness of God, only a means of further torturing men who are already fearfully burdened with original sin and the Ten Commandments.' And just as often before, as he pondered this, there now rose up in him a feeling of passionate hatred for this cruel God who always requires love, love, and yet actually makes it impossible for His creatures to love Him. 'So he raged in his little room in the tower of the Black Cloister' with a wounded and confused spirit, and beat importunately on that passage in St. Paul, thirsting with a most ardent desire to know what the Apostle really meant, until finally, after days and nights of thinking, he hit upon the idea of examining the context more carefully. 'The righteousness of God is revealed in the Gospel.' 'The just shall live by faith.' Therefore, he concluded, what is meant here is not the punitive righteousness of God, but rather the forgiving righteousness of God by which in His mercy He makes us just, as it is written, *justus ex fide vivit*. 'Thus it seemed to me as if I were born anew and that I had entered into the open gates of Paradise. . . . As much as I had heretofore hated the word 'righteousness of God,' so much the more dear and sweet it was to me now. And so that passage of St. Paul became for me in very truth the gate to Paradise.[8]

The illumination of Christ, coming through the written Word, was directed precisely at the ignorance that held Luther in bondage, his confusion of law and gospel, of works and grace. In this case the calling of Jesus was effective. Luther became the illuminator of the Western church (many of his contemporaries saw a striking symbolism in the similarity of the German word *Luther* and the Greek term for "light") and the father of the Protestant Reformation when he posted his Ninety-five Theses in October, 1517.

Third is the ministry of regeneration and conversion. These two actions of the Holy Spirit belong together. Of regeneration, one classical Lutheran theologian wrote, "Regeneration is the act of grace by which the Holy Spirit gives the sinner saving faith, that, his sins being pardoned, he may become a son of God and an heir of eternal life."[9] Conversion has

8. Heinrich Boehmer, *Martin Luther: Road to Reformation*, trans. John W. Doberstein and Theodore G. Tappert (New York: Meridian, 1957), pp. 110–111.
9. Quoted by Schmid, *Doctrinal Theology*, p. 459.

been defined by John Theodore Mueller as "the bestowal of faith in the divine promise of salvation for Christ's sake upon a sinner who from the divine Law has learned to know and lament his sins."[10] Henry Eyster Jacobs, longtime professor of historical theology at the Lutheran seminary in Philadelphia, wrote concerning conversion,

> In the wide sense of the term, it includes Regeneration, being the activity of God through which the entire change with respect to man, both inwardly and outwardly, is accomplished. Illumination, Regeneration, and Sanctification . . . are thus comprised in one term. In a more restricted sense, it is used to describe the process whereby Repentance is effected. A man partially illumined, and not regenerated, could not be said to be converted. Regeneration, therefore, when regarded as the culmination of the call and Illumination, is Conversion in the most ordinary sense of the term.[11]

The witness of the New Testament is that through regeneration and conversion the Holy Spirit works saving faith in people. This saving faith, which is entirely the gift of God, has been described by Luther in his introduction to the Book of Romans:

> Faith is a divine work in us, which transforms us, and begets us anew of God. It makes us entirely different men in heart, mind, sense and all powers, and brings with it the Holy Spirit. . . . Faith is a living, wide-awake confidence in God's grace, that is so certain that one who has it is ready to die a thousand times for it. . . . Pray God to work faith in thee; otherwise thou shalt remain eternally without faith, though thou thinkest and doest whatever thou wilt or canst.[12]

That is the faith that can say, with Peter, "Being born again, not of corruptible seed, but of incorruptible, by the word of God" (I Peter 1:23). Paul, like Peter and Luther, knew that "the righteousness of God . . . is by faith of Jesus Christ" (Rom. 3:22) and that God is "the justifier of him which believeth in Jesus" (Rom. 3:26).

10. *Christian Dogmatics* (Saint Louis: Concordia, 1955), pp. 336–337.
11. *A Summary of the Christian Faith*, p. 241.
12. Quoted, *ibid.*, p. 189.

The further witness of the New Testament is that saving faith trusts in God for the justification of the sinner. Man's fundamental problem since the fall has been his inability to fulfill the law of God. Christ on the cross did this. The righteousness of Jesus is now imputed or accounted to those who believe in him. Paul developed this teaching at great length in his letter to the Romans, an epistle that, we have seen, so profoundly influenced Augustine and Luther. In the fourth chapter of that book alone, Paul used the term *impute* or *reckon* eleven times. By doing so, Paul informed us, God has put to the account of Christ our sin, and to our account His righteousness. In the next chapter of the epistle Paul exclaimed, "For as by one man's disobedience many were made sinners, so by the obedience of one shall many be made righteous" (Rom. 5:19). This is grace. The acrostic *grace*—God's righteousness at Christ's expense—explains this concept.

The still further witness of the New Testament is that saving faith consists of three parts. First is knowledge, an acquaintance with the gospel that has come as a result of the invitation and illumination of the Spirit through the Word, for, as Paul asks, "How shall they believe in whom they have not heard?" (Rom. 10:14). Second is assent, or a judgment of the intellect, so that what is taught in the Scriptures is received as true and as true for me. Both the general and special forms of assent are referred to in Paul's famous credo: "This is a faithful saying, and worthy of all acceptation, that Christ Jesus came into the world to save sinners [general assent]; of whom I am chief [special assent]" (I Tim. 1:15). Third is confidence, the reliance of the entire heart and will upon the merit of Christ, or, as Peter preached, "Through his name whosoever believeth in him shall receive remission of sins" (Acts 10:43).

Conversion occurs differently in the case of children than in that of adults. The offspring of Christian parents, baptized as infants, are regenerated at the font, belong to Christ, grow up in the faith, and "know not when they were not" the disciples of Jesus. This is the way of Christian nurture, made so famous in the United States in the ministry of Horace Bushnell. Representative of this approach is the life of America's most famous preacher of the last century, Henry Ward

Beecher. Born into the home of a prominent clergyman, reared a believer, Beecher was always a Christian. In those days congregations in the Puritan tradition were often reluctant to admit that such was possible, indeed, quite normal, and even very desirable: Lyman Abbott, Beecher's successor at Plymouth Church, wrote,

> He had not yet joined the church, for he had not been converted [dramatically in a revival]; but in a letter to his sister he quite unconsciously illustrates the kind of religious life which has grown up in him. . . . 'I do not like,' he says, 'to read the Bible as well as to pray, but I suppose it is the same as it is with a lover, who loves to talk with his mistress in person better than to write when she is afar off.' A little later than this there was a revival at Mt. Pleasant, and a wave of feeling passed over him which he thought might be conversion. His father was quite satisfied on the subject, and partly from a kind of shamefacedness which kept the boy from saying he did not think he was a Christian, he 'let them take me into the Church.' Like a ship built on the land that on some moment must be launched into the sea are some souls; like a fish born in the sea and growing up there are others. Henry Ward Beecher belong to the latter class; he never was launched and needed no launching.[13]

Those brought to the font as infants, baptized and reared in belief, know the church as their natural habitat.

The case of adults reared outside the church is different. Representative is the history of August Wilhelm Neander (1789–1850), an eminent Lutheran church historian. Born to Jewish parents, reared as David Mendel, he was not converted until he had read the sermons of Friedrich Schleiermacher. At the age of seventeen he was baptized, taking the name *Neander*, meaning literally, a "new man." "Warmly and deeply religious, with a childlike Christian trust," Neander won "the affection of hundreds of students and sought to lead them into an earnest and joyous Christian experience."[14]

13. *Henry Ward Beecher*, ed. William B. McLoughlin, American Men and Women of Letters series (New York: Chelsea House, 1980), p. 36.

14. Kenneth Scott Latourette, *A History of Christianity*, first edition (New York: Harper, 1953), p. 1133.

Beecher and Neander are but two illustrations of the power of the Spirit to convert, for as Jesus answered Nicodemus, "Verily, verily, I say unto thee, Except a man be born of water and of the Spirit, he cannot enter into the kingdom of God" (John 3:5).

Fourth is the ministry of incorporation. This is commonly known as the mystical union. It has been defined by Hollaz as

> . . . the spiritual conjunction of the triune God with justified man, by which He dwells in him as in a consecrated temple by His special presence, and that, too, substantial, and operates in the same by His gracious influence.[15]

The witness of the New Testament is that God the Holy Spirit causes Christ to dwell in us. Paul could write the Galatians, "Yet not I, but Christ liveth in me" (Gal. 2:20); to the Ephesians, "that Christ may dwell in your hearts by faith" (Eph. 3:17); and to the Corinthians, "he that is joined unto the Lord is one spirit" (I Cor. 6:17). This is what Jesus meant when He said, "My Father will love him, and we will come unto him, and make our abode with him" (John 14:23). Summarizing this mystery of incorporation, Luther said, "Christ thus inhering and bound up with me . . . and abiding in me, lives in me the life which I am living; yea, the life by which I thus live, is Christ Himself. . . ."

This teaching of the New Testament has continued to be a living reality in the lives of millions across the centuries. Illustrative of this ministry of the Holy Spirit is an incident in the life of C. F. W. Walther, spiritual father of the Lutheran Church-Missouri Synod, one of the four or five great Lutheran theologians who labored in North America. Born in 1811 in a pastor's home in Germany, trained for the ministry at the University of Leipzig, Walther knew that the biblical training received in his youth "accompanied me through my life like an angel of God." In spite of this he could write that "I was in deep spiritual affliction . . . doubting my salvation, wrestling with despair." Walther found that "no praying, seeking, fasting, or struggling seemed able to help. The peace of God had departed from my soul." At that point he heard

15. Quoted by Schmid, *Doctrinal Theology*, p. 482.

of the ministry of the Reverend Martin Stephan, pastor of Saint John's Church in Dresden. Walther wrote Stephan for counsel.

> When he received Stephan's reply, he did not open the letter until he had knelt in prayer and asked God to prevent his receiving false comfort should such be contained in Stephan's missive. But after reading it, he felt himself elevated from the depths of hell to the bliss of heaven. His tears of penitent grief changed to tears of joyful faith, for Stephan demonstrated to him that he had long experienced the contrition he sought in the Law and that he lacked nothing but faith. Walther says that he could not resist, he had to come to Jesus. And so the peace of God entered his heart.[16]

The close walk of Walther with Christ continued through much of the century, enabling this remarkable theologian, author, editor, preacher, and synod president to reach thousands for Jesus, not simply in Saint Louis, but across the United States.

Fifth is the ministry of renovation. As one theologian of the era of orthodoxy wrote, "Renovation is an act of grace, whereby the Holy Spirit, expelling the faults of a justified man, endows him with inherent sanctity."

The witness of the New Testament is that God the Holy Spirit works renovation or sanctification in us. In a passage by Paul, which was a favorite of Paul Tillich, we read that "if any man be in Christ, he is a new creature: old things are passed away; behold, all things are become new" (II Cor. 5:17). Or again Paul could write to the Ephesians:

> That ye put off concerning the former conversation the old man, which is corrupt . . . And be renewed in the spirit of your mind; And that ye put on the new man, which after God is created in righteousness and true holiness.
>
> [Eph. 4:22–24]

God pours upon us the Spirit. We receive His gifts and are enabled to function as a member of His body, ministering in the world.

16. Walter A. Baepler, *A Century of Grace: A History of the Missouri Synod, 1847–1947* (Saint Louis: Concordia, 1947), p. 44.

This teaching of the New Testament has continued to be a living reality for millions across the centuries. Illustrative of this ministry of the Holy Spirit is the career of Francis of Assisi (1182–1226). Born in the late twelfth century to a prosperous cloth merchant, Francis aspired to many things in his youth. Especially he desired to become a knight, as did Ignatius Loyola. His military ambition reminds us that Luther, while in exile at the Wartburg, was known as Squire George. It is also reminiscent of Ulrich Zwingli, who was not only a pastor and preacher in Zurich, but also a chaplain in the Swiss army. But it was made clear to Francis that soldiering was not his calling. Francis beheld poverty, in the form of beggars; he saw sickness, in the form of a leper; he reckoned with the decay of the church, symbolized by the ruins of a small chapel by the way. Then during a service on the feast of Saint Matthias, Francis heard a reading from the holy Gospel that spoke directly to him:

> And as ye go, preach, saying, The kingdom of heaven is at hand. Heal the sick, cleanse the lepers, raise the dead, cast out devils: freely ye have received, freely give. Provide neither gold, nor silver, nor brass in your purses. Nor scrip for your journey, neither two coats, neither shoes, nor yet staves: for the workman is worthy of his meat.
>
> [Matt. 10:7–10]

Francis took that summons literally, taking up a life of service that not only gave him fulfillment, but also brought renewal to the entire Western church. The Spirit, through the renovation of the individual, brought renovation to the institution, the Latin Catholic community.

The ministry of the Holy Spirit is a mystery—God comes to us as a servant! Comprehension fails, logic gives way to poetry, as we sing, Creator Spirit,

> Plenteous of grace, descend from high
> . . . .
> Make us eternal truths receive,
> And practice all that we believe;
> Give us thyself, that we may see
> The Father and the Son by thee.

The Holy Trinity

Christians pray to the Holy Spirit, "Give us thyself, that we may see/The Father and the Son by thee." This act of piety, present in the church from earliest times, was expressed theologically by Augustine of Hippo, bishop and doctor of the faith, when he wrote,

> Now we are to speak about the Holy Spirit, insofar as God the Giver shall permit. According to the Sacred Scriptures, this Holy Spirit is neither the Spirit of the Father alone, nor of the Son alone, but the Spirit of both, and, therefore, He insinuates to us the common love by which the Father and the Son mutually love each other.[17]

This echoes the Athanasian Creed, which confesses, "The catholic faith is this: that we worship one God in Trinity and Trinity in Unity." The Christian God is the holy Trinity, "Father, Son, and Holy Ghost, three distinct Persons in one divine Being."

One can reflect on the mystery of the holy Trinity biblically, historically, practically, and liturgically.

The teaching of the holy Trinity is a biblical reality. As Jacobs wrote of this doctrine, "It is neither taught by Natural Revelation, nor can it be demonstrated from that source. . . ." This is the "Knowledge of God that is peculiar to Christianity." Alleged trinities in other world religions simply are not comparable to the Divinity worshiped by the church. The God of the Bible is the holy Trinity. While in the Old Testament the unity of God is emphasized, there are suggestions of the divine Trinity. Stress placed on the oneness of God was a necessary measure for the Hebrews, who lived with the external threat of polytheism and the internal menace of idolatry. Thus, the credo of the Jewish church, the *Shema*, stated, "Hear, O Israel: The LORD our God is one LORD . . ." (Deut. 6:4).

There are, however, subtle and veiled references to the Trinity throughout the Old Testament as a preparatory min-

17. *The Fathers of the Church*, trans. Stephen McKenna (Washington, DC: The Catholic University of America Press, 1963), vol. 45, Saint Augustine, *The Trinity*, p. 491.

istry to the full revelation of God in Jesus. The triune character of God is suggested in the Aaronic benediction:

> The LORD bless thee, and keep thee: The LORD make his face shine upon thee, and be gracious unto thee: The LORD lift up his countenance upon thee, and give thee peace.
>
> [Num. 6:24–26]

This liturgical action is continued and evidenced in the vision of Isaiah the prophet: “And one cried unto another, and said, Holy, holy, holy, is the LORD of hosts: the whole earth is full of his glory” (Isa. 6:3). The Psalter is also replete with trinitarian praise, as in David’s intercession: “God be merciful unto us, and bless us; and cause his face to shine upon us” (Ps. 67:1).

It is in the New Testament, with the advent of Christ, sent of the Father and empowered by the Spirit, that the Trinity is clearly revealed. The holy Trinity is made known in many places, of which we cite three examples. The first is at the baptism of Christ.

> And Jesus, when he was baptized, went up straightway out of the water: and, lo, the heavens were opened unto him, and he saw the Spirit of God descending like a dove, and lighting upon him: And lo a voice from heaven, saying, This is my beloved Son, in whom I am well pleased.
>
> [Matt. 3:16–17]

The second is in the upper room, where Jesus promised, “And I will pray the Father, and he shall give you another Comforter, that he may abide with you for ever” (John 14:16). Jesus also promised, “But when the Comforter is come, whom I will send unto you from the Father, even the Spirit of truth, which proceedeth from the Father, he shall testify of me” (John 15:26).

The third example is at the ascension of the Savior, where we hear His imperative: “Go ye therefore, and teach all nations, baptizing them in the name of the Father, and of the Son, and of the Holy Ghost” (Matt. 28:19). Christ and His Father are incomprehensible apart from the Spirit, who remains anonymous apart from His association with the Savior and the One who sent Him.

The teaching of the holy Trinity is a historical reality. Though the term *trinity* was first employed by Tertullian (160?–230), a Latin theologian of the second century, the doctrine was evident in the church, starting with Pentecost. Paul, apostle to the Gentiles, wrote to the Corinthians,

> Now there are diversities of gifts, but the same Spirit. And there are differences of administration, but the same Lord. And there are diversities of operations, but it is the same God which worketh all in all.
>
> [I Cor. 12:4–6]

He also informed the Ephesians,

> There is one body, and one Spirit, even as ye are called in one hope of your calling; One Lord, one faith, one baptism, One God and Father of all, who is above all, and through all, and in you all.
>
> [Eph. 4:4–6]

John's Gospel is rich in trinitarian theology (see John 1:29–36; 14:16, 26; 16:15). The confession of the apostles is accurately preserved in the confessions of the Fathers, such as Irenaeus, who also believed

> in one God Almighty,
> from whom are all things;
> and in the Son of God, Jesus Christ,
> our Lord,
> by whom are all things,
> and in his dispensations,
> through which the Son of God became man;
> the firm persuasion also in the Spirit of God,
> who furnishes us with a knowledge
> of the truth, and has set forth the
> dispensations of the Father and
> the Son, in virtue of which he
> dwells in every generation of
> men, according to the will of
> the Father.[18]

18. Quoted by Philip Schaff, *The Creeds of Christendom*, 3 vols. (1877; reprint ed., Grand Rapids: Baker, 1977), vol. 2, p. 16.

No wonder the Apostles' Creed, employed widely at the close of the ancient era and mandated as the baptismal confession, reiterates the Great Commission of Jesus, given centuries before, to baptize "in the name of the Father, and of the Son, and of the Holy Ghost."

The teaching of the holy Trinity is a practical reality. The pastoral work of the church is inconceivable apart from it. Christ, in the Great Commission (Matt. 28:19), connects the doctrine of the Trinity with proclamation (preaching), education (teaching), incorporation into the church (reaching), personal regeneration (baptizing), evangelization (sharing), and world missions (going). Earlier, in the upper room (John 14, 15), the Master associated the Spirit and the Father with all forms of pastoral ministration—comforting, assuring, exhorting, confessing, praying, and believing. The Fathers and the doctors of the church felt that the unity, purity, vitality, integrity, and apostolicity of the Christian community would be impaired beyond recognition if this teaching were deliberately and consistently ignored.

The teaching of the holy Trinity is a liturgical reality. The earliest references to the Trinity in the New Testament are within the context of worship. Paul blesses the Corinthians in the name of the Trinity, saying, "The grace of the Lord Jesus Christ, and the love of God, and the communion of the Holy Ghost, be with you all. Amen" (II Cor. 13:14). Jesus instructs the apostles to baptize in the name of the Trinity, saying, "Go ye therefore, and teach all nations, baptizing them in the name of the Father, and of the Son, and of the Holy Ghost" (Matt. 28:19). Peter, in his first catholic epistle, greets the faithful with an apostolic invocation, saying, "Elect according to the foreknowledge of God the Father, through sanctification of the Spirit, unto obedience and sprinkling of the blood of Jesus Christ: Grace unto you, and peace, be multiplied" (I Peter 1:2). The creeds of the early church, which were trinitarian in structure and substance, were intended for use in the Mass, for theology was also doxology.

The holy Trinity is both reality and mystery. It is the solution of the age-old problem of the one and the many, the universal and the particular, the reconciliation of community and unity. As such, it transcends human comprehension. To unbelievers, it is absurdity. George Bernard Shaw once quipped that he would be a Christian if it were not for the doctrine of the Trinity. To us, as to our peers and forebears in the faith, this teaching, while a mystery, is not absurdity but ultimate reality. In it our faith transcends human reason and perceives eternal wisdom. As Cecil Frances Alexander (1818?–1895), Anglican hymnist, confessed,

> . . . 'The faith of the Trinity lies,
> Shrined for ever and ever, in those grand old words and wise;
> A gem in a beautiful setting; still, at matin-time,
> The service of Holy Communion rings the ancient chime;
> Wherever in marvelous minster, or village churches small,
> Men to the Man that is God out of their misery call,
> Swelled by the rapture of choirs, or borne on the poor man's word,
> Still the glorious Nicene confession unaltered is heard;
> Most like the song that the angels are singing around the throne,
> With their "Holy! holy! holy!" to the great Three in One.'[19]

19. Quoted, *ibid.*, vol. 1, p. 27.

PART TWO

A Way of Belonging

Thou art the Way:
To Thee alone from sin and death we flee;
And he who would the Father seek,
  Must seek Him, Lord, by Thee.

George W. Doane

CHAPTER

4

The Means of Grace

. . . who for us men and for our salvation came down from heaven.

"Where Christ is, there is the Church." This is an ancient confession of faith. Its antecedents are as old as the New Testament. To be a Christian was to respond positively to the invitation of Jesus to be a disciple. In the Gospel of Mark we read that one day Jesus was walking by the seashore, and beholding Simon and Andrew, He said, "Come ye after me" and "straightway they forsook their nets, and followed him" (Mark 1:16–18). In such a fashion the apostolic band was formed and the nucleus of the church was created, with Christ in its midst.

How can Jesus Christ come to us today? In the days of His incarnation Jesus was present immediately to His followers. His body was visible, His voice was audible, His companionship was physical and local. When strangers desired to learn more of the Lord, they came, as did the searching Greeks to Philip, saying, "Sir, we would see Jesus" (John 12:21). Like Nicodemus, they came privately to inquire of Christ, "How can a man be born [again] when he is old?" (John 3:4). In such instances Jesus could teach an inquirer directly. But our situation in the twentieth century is somewhat different from that of believers in the first. Since His ascension Christ is in a certain sense absent from us, because we do not have His bodily companionship as did the apostles. Christ prepared His followers for this separation. In the upper room He said to them, "Yet a little while I am with you" (John 13:33) and "whither I go, thou canst not follow me now" (John

Kramer Chapel (Chancel)

Concordia Theological Seminary
Fort Wayne, Indiana

13:36). After His death and resurrection, Jesus ascended to heaven, for “he was taken up; and a cloud received him out of their sight” (Acts 1:9). Two angels appeared to the apostles, assuring them of Christ’s return in glory in the parousia, when “this same Jesus, which is taken up from you into heaven, shall so come in like manner as ye have seen him go into heaven” (Acts 1:11).

In the interim between the two advents—the one in His birth, the other in His return—believers have not felt themselves bereft of Christ’s presence. He is spiritually present among His people. Jesus promised this, saying before He ascended to heaven, “Lo, I am with you alway, even unto the end of the world” (Matt. 28:20). The Master had said earlier, “Where two or three are gathered together in my name, there am I in the midst of them” (Matt. 18:20). That was spoken in the context of Christ’s teaching about the church. His ascension proved to be a prelude to the reality of the mystery of the church. It is important to note that though the Gospels conclude with Christ’s ascension into heaven, they are immediately followed by the Book of Acts, the story of the birth and growth of the Christian church. The New Testament reports that “the Lord added to the church daily such as should be saved” (Acts 2:47).

How is this possible that Christ, though ascended and seemingly absent, is able to be present among His people?

Lutherans believe an explanation can be found in the concluding section of the Gospel of Matthew. This book, often regarded as a catechism of the early church, contains formal instruction concerning the Christian life. It is significant that the Gospel closes by connecting Christ’s ascension with the Great Commission.[1] The apostolic band had gathered as the church, for

> when they saw him, they worshipped him: but some doubted. And Jesus came and spake unto them, saying, All power is given unto me in heaven and in earth. Go ye therefore, and teach all nations, baptizing them in the name of the Father, and of the Son, and of the Holy Ghost: Teaching them to ob-

1. See C. George Fry, “A Day to Remember,” *Christianity Today*, vol. 13, May 9, 1969, pp. 3–5.

> serve all things whatsoever I have commanded you: and lo, I am with you alway, even unto the end of the world.
>
> [Matt. 28:17–20]

In this context Christ makes it clear that His ascension will make it possible for Him to actively reign throughout time and space, permitting an extension of His ministry throughout all history and geography. The creed confesses this when it states that He sits at "the right hand of God the Father." Lutherans teach that the right hand of God is everywhere. Christ is omnipresent. That is why Jesus "is able also to save them to the uttermost that come unto God by him. . ." (Heb. 7:25).

Lutherans believe that the Great Commission is also the charter of the church. Jesus indicates the means whereby He saves. Lutherans call these the means of grace. They constitute the means by which Christ's people are gathered to the church. The means are indicated in the three activities made incumbent upon the apostles: communicating the Word, for they are to "teach all nations"; initiating by water, for they are to go "baptizing them in the name of the Father, and of the Son, and of the Holy Ghost"; and facilitating believers to keep "all things whatsoever I have commanded you." The greatest of these commands concerns the Lord's Supper. In the night in which He was betrayed, Jesus

> took bread, and blessed it, and brake it, and gave it to the disciples, and said, Take, eat; this is my body. And he took the cup, and gave thanks, and gave it them, saying, Drink ye all of it; For this is my blood of the new testament, which is shed for many for the remission of sins.
>
> [Matt. 26:26–28]

This meal, almost universally observed among Christians, is commemorated during Holy Week on Maundy Thursday, probably named from the commandment (Latin, *mandatum*) that Christ's followers "love one another" (John 13:34) and keep this feast.

Lutherans believe that these means—Word, baptism, and the Lord's Supper—are ways by which Jesus comes to minister to us. Often, as a sort of theological shorthand, Lutherans speak of the two means of grace, Word and sacrament (both baptism and the Lord's Supper are called sacraments by Lutherans). The Holy Spirit, who was poured out on Pentecost, works through these means, so that Christ comes to us now—not immediately (or directly) as in the days of His flesh, but mediately (or indirectly) in these times of the Spirit. It is the Spirit who unites women and men to Christ through Word and sacrament.

The Word of God

The term *Word of God* has come to have at least three related meanings in Christian usage. It can refer to Jesus Christ, the personal or incarnated Word, as John does in his Gospel when he writes, "In the beginning was the Word, and the Word was with God, and the Word was God. . . . And the Word was made flesh, and dwelt among us" (John 1:1, 14). It can refer to the proclaimed or inculcated word of preaching and teaching, as Paul does, writing of "the word of faith, which we preach" (Rom. 10:8). It can refer to the written or inscripturated Word, the sacred Scriptures, as Peter does, exhorting believers, "We have also a more sure word of prophecy; whereunto ye do well that ye take heed. . . ." (II Peter 1:19).[2] The three operate in conjunction, as is illustrated in Paul's experience at Berea, where "the word of God was preached of Paul" and "they received the word with all readiness of mind, and searched the scriptures daily, whether those things were so" (Acts 17:13, 11). On the basis of Scripture (the inscripturated Word) Jesus (the incarnated Word) is preached as Lord and Savior (the inculcated word) and is personally received by faith. Through these means Christ saves.

The Bible is the written Word of God. Our word *Bible* is derived from the Greek word *biblia*, meaning "the books." The Bible is literally a library of sacred literature. It is also

2. See C. George Fry, "The Doctrine of the Word in Orthodox Lutheranism," *Concordia Theological Quarterly*, 43, January 1979, pp. 26–44.

called the sacred Scriptures, the Writings, and the oracles of God.

Lutherans believe that God guided the composition of the Bible. As special revelation of God's saving purpose, the Bible was given by inspiration. This is taught by Peter, who wrote, "For the prophecy came not in old time by the will of man: but holy men of God spake as they were moved by the Holy Ghost" (II Peter 1:21). The Lutheran confessions, however, have never taught any one mode of divine inspiration. Individual Lutheran theologians have propounded many theories of inspiration, including the belief that every detail of the Scriptures, even to the Hebrew vowel points, was divinely dictated. Most Lutheran scholars recognize that God employed a wide variety of means, such as direct discourse (as on Mount Sinai, when "God spake all these words, saying . . . ," Exod. 20:1), dreams and visions (Isa. 6:1; Matt. 2:19–20), historical investigation (Luke 1:1–4), and human recollection (John 14:25–26). Most Lutherans, furthermore, have been able to live with the paradox that the Bible is both the Word of God and word of man. This is in keeping with the New Testament itself. Paul, for example, is confident that his message is "the word of God" and "the things that I write unto you are the commandments of the Lord" (I Cor. 14:36, 37). That does not rule out purely personal statements within the Pauline corpus, such as Paul's advice to Timothy concerning his health (I Tim. 5:23) or his request that his disciple bring his cloak from Troas (II Tim. 4:13). With the apostle, Lutherans recognize that "we have this treasure in earthen vessels" (II Cor. 4:7) but nevertheless "all scripture is given by inspiration of God, and is profitable for doctrine, for reproof, for correction, for instruction in righteousness" (II Tim. 3:16).

Lutherans believe that God guided the compilation of the Bible. His providence prevailed through the centuries as authors, as far removed as Moses and Paul, David and Peter, wrote in several languages, in many locations, in different styles, expressing themselves in literary forms as varied as poetry and history, prophecy and liturgy, parable and hymnody. Of course writings have been lost—such as "the book of Jasher" (Josh. 10:13) or Paul's initial letter to the church at Corinth (I Cor. 5:9)—but the Spirit gathered and preserved and transmitted those materials necessary for our edification. Today sixty-six books form what is called the canon (from the Greek word for "standard" or "measuring rod"). Thirty-nine of these books were recognized by the Jews of Jesus' day as forming the Old Testament. By the fourth century, the church accepted twenty-seven of these books as constituting the New Testament. The criteria for the inclusion of a book within the canon (especially of the New Testament) were content, authorship, and acceptance by the believing community. Lutherans recognize that other Christians, such as those of the Roman Catholic Church, accept additional books, which are called the Apocrypha (writings from the era between Malachi and Matthew; for example, I and II Maccabees). Lutherans have always regarded these texts as useful, though not canonical, and the Wittenberg reformer included them in his German Bible. Unlike some Protestants, Lutherans do not regard the canon as "closed." We believe, however, that the consensus of the centuries and the Christian community stand behind the Bible as we now know it.

Lutherans believe that God has guided the preservation of the Bible. Composed through the centuries, gathered together in many different countries, transmitted by often unknown and forgotten scribes, the Bible maintains its integrity. It possesses unity and continuity of theme. Its many and sundry parts all unite to make us "wise unto salvation" (II Tim. 3:15). It reflects a catholicity of spirit and a universality of scope that prevent it from becoming narrow, partisan, or sectarian. All the while it radiates beauty and power that cause the Bible to be considered a masterpiece of world literature. That literary quality survives even in translation. It has been said that three of the vernacular versions of the Bible—Jerome's Vulgate, Luther's German Bible, and the King James Version of the English Bible—are classics in their own right. Central to the sacred anthology is the person of Christ. Jesus said, "Search the scriptures; . . . they . . . testify of me" (John 5:39). Charles Porterfield Krauth, a great American Lutheran theologian of the nineteenth century, compared the Bible with a musical score:

> Why take many lutes and pipes, unless revelation were designed to be a symphony as well as melody, whose unity should not be that of the simple strain, but that by which the Great Composer pours His own divine spirit of music into many parts, whilst wind and touch on instruments faithful to their own nature, unite in 'Creation' or 'Messiah,' to form what is once truly theirs, and, because such, truly His?[3]

Lutherans believe that God has endowed the Bible with certain attributes. Four are usually cited.

There is the sufficiency of Scripture. The Bible teaches everything that is necessary for salvation and it does so accurately and truthfully. As the psalmist wrote, "The law of the LORD is perfect, converting the soul: the testimony of the LORD is sure, making wise the simple" (Ps. 19:7). To speak of Christ, Bernard of Clairvaux asked, "What language shall I borrow?" To describe the canon, Lutheran theologians have struggled to find the right vocabulary. Attempting to do justice to the sufficiency of the Bible, conservative Lutherans often speak of its accuracy, infallibility, and inerrancy.

There is the efficacy of Scripture. The Bible is able to accomplish the purpose for which God gave it—the salvation of humankind. As Isaiah wrote, "So shall my word be that goeth forth out of my mouth: it shall not return unto me void, but it shall accomplish that which I please, and it shall prosper in the thing whereto I sent it" (Isa. 55:11).

There is the perspicuity of Scripture. The Bible is clear and understandable in all matters that pertain to our salvation. As the Scriptures remind us, God's Word "is a lamp; and the law is light" (Prov. 6:23) and "ye do well that ye take heed, as unto a light that shineth in a dark place" (II Peter 1:19).

There is the authority of Scripture. The Bible is the source and norm of faith and practice for the Christian. Other authorities—conscience, reason, experience, and tradition—are not to be despised, but are to be evaluated by Scripture. As Paul counseled Timothy, "All Scripture is given by inspiration of God, and is profitable for doctrine, for reproof, for

3. Quoted by Henry Eyster Jacobs, *A Summary of the Christian Faith* (Philadelphia: The United Lutheran Publication House, 1905), p. 269.

correction, for instruction in righteousness" (II Tim. 3:16), so he would instruct us. Lutherans confess in the Formula of Concord, ". . . the Word of God is, and should remain the sole rule and norm of all doctrine, and that no human being's writings dare be put on a par with it, but that everything must be subjected to it."[4] Lutherans believe that God guides the church into the proper interpretation and application of the Bible. It is beyond the scope of this volume to discuss the principles of hermeneutics. However, crucial to any Lutheran reading of the Bible is the careful distinction between law and gospel. God's Word can be divided into the law, which tells us what we ought to do for God, and the gospel, which informs us what God has done for us. Martin Luther wrote,

> By the Law, nothing else is meant than God's Word and command, wherein He enjoins what we should do and leave undone, and demands our obedience. But the Gospel is that doctrine or Word of God that neither requires works of us, nor enjoins the doing of anything, but announces only the offered grace of the forgiveness of sins and eternal life. The Gospel offers God's gifts and bids us only open the sack to receive them, while the Law gives nothing, but only takes and demands of us.[5]

The law, summarized in the Ten Commandments and the Sermon on the Mount, has a threefold function: it convicts of sin, for it reveals our iniquity, as Paul confessed that "by the law is the knowledge of sin" (Rom. 3:20); it leads to Christ, for it becomes, in Paul's words, "our schoolmaster to bring us unto Christ, that we might be justified by faith" (Gal. 3:24); and it instructs the redeemed in godliness, for it serves as a standard for the regenerate person, for, as Paul wrote to the Ephesians, "we are his workmanship, created in Christ Jesus unto good works, which God hath before ordained that we should walk in them" (Eph. 2:10).

The gospel is summarized in many places in the Scriptures. Jesus said, "For God so loved the world, that he gave

4. *The Book of Concord*, Theodore G. Tappert, trans. and ed. (Philadelphia: Fortress, 1959), p. 505.
5. Quoted by Jacobs, *A Summary of the Christian Faith*, p. 299.

his only begotten Son, that whosoever believeth in him should not perish, but have everlasting life" (John 3:16). Paul testified, in the text that transformed Luther's life,

> I am not ashamed of the gospel of Christ: for it is the power of God unto salvation to everyone that believeth; to the Jew first, and also to the Greek. For therein is the righteousness of God revealed from faith to faith: as it is written, The just shall live by faith.
>
> [Rom. 1:16–17]

In such passages we find the primary purpose of the Scriptures. The major intention of the Bible is not to inform us concerning secular matters or to give us a divine blueprint for a perfectly organized society. We have the Bible so that we might come to know Jesus Christ, experience the power of His presence, the joy of His pardon, and the wonder of His fellowship.

J. H. C. Helmuth, one of the most learned Lutheran ministers of the early American republic, was for many years pastor of Zion's and Saint Michael's churches in Philadelphia (1779–1822). Concurrently he was a professor at the University of Pennsylvania. Well-versed in Hebrew, he was celebrated for his scholarly attainments. He had amassed much information about the Bible, but the real role of the Word became clear to him in 1793. That year an epidemic of yellow fever struck Philadelphia and within a short time more than six hundred of his parishioners died. Thus, in the words of Henry Eyster Jacobs, "he learned more of the reality and efficacy of God's Word, than a hundred life-times of scholarly research could have ever afforded." Helmuth came to know the power of God, as Isaiah had written:

> When thou passest through the waters, I will be with thee; and through the rivers, they shall not overflow thee; when thou walkest through the fire, thou shalt not be burned; neither shall the flame kindle upon thee. For I am the LORD thy God, the Holy One of Israel, thy Saviour.
>
> [Isa. 43:2–3]

Baptism

Christ comes to us in ways other than the Word written or spoken. Events also communicate His presence, pardon, and power. Lutherans believe there are two such repeatable actions that manifest Christ to us—baptism and the Lord's Supper. Collectively these two means of grace are called sacraments.

While the word *sacrament* is not used in the Bible, the concept is implicit. Biblical Greek speaks of the "mysteries" of the church. Paul, writing to the Corinthians about the ministry, said, "Let a man so account of us, as of the ministers of Christ, and stewards of the *mysteries* of God" (I Cor. 4:1; italics added). The clergy of the early church did more than preach or teach. They also presided at events called mysteries. Very soon the gospel spread to Latin-speaking areas. The Western fathers, such as Tertullian, struggled to find a Latin term that would do justice to the Greek word *mysterion* ("mystery"). They used the Latin expression *sacramentum*, which had rich meaning for the Romans. The word means "an oath" or "a promise." Among soldiers it conveyed a sense of allegiance. In the courtroom it referred to a deposit of money by the parties in a suit. Command, promise, action, gift—all were connoted by the Latin expression. Jerome followed Tertullian's lead, using the word *sacrament* in his Latin Bible, the Vulgate, to render the Greek word *mysterion*. Augustine, greatest of the Latin theologians, defined a sacrament as an action that gives "a visible form of invisible grace." Since then the word has been part of the theological vocabulary of the Western church. The Eastern church retains the Greek term.

From the pages of the New Testament we learn that Jesus did and commanded many things. Why do Lutherans, along with most other historic Protestant denominations, identify only two of these deeds as being formative and normative for the church, as actions to be repeated at stated intervals by the community? For Lutherans, as for Presbyterians and Anglicans, a sacrament is identifiable in terms of three realities: it must have been instituted by Christ, rest on His command, and derive from His Word. In the upper room Jesus instructed His disciples, "Take, eat. . . . And he took the cup . . . saying, Drink ye all of it" (Matt. 26:26, 27); "this do in remembrance of me" (I Cor. 11:24). On the Mount of Ascension Christ stated, "Go ye . . . and teach all nations, baptizing them. . ." (Matt. 28:19). A sacrament must employ a physical means instituted by Christ, such as water, bread, and wine. It must also embody a promise of Christ, as when Peter said, "Repent, and be baptized . . . for the remission of sins" (Acts 2:38) or as when we participate in Holy Communion, we realize the New Testament witness that this is "given for you" (Luke 22:19), "shed for you" (Luke 22:20), "poured out for many unto remission of sins" (Matt. 26:28). While the Lutheran churches, like the Eastern Orthodox and the Roman Catholic, have marriage, confirmation, confession, ordination, and the burial of the dead, they do not normally regard these as sacraments but as rites, for these fail to meet the threefold criteria that identify a sacrament. While the Lutheran churches—like the Free churches—recall all actions of Jesus, such as washing the feet of the disciples, they do not normally regard this as a repetitive action filled with promise to be performed in the church. For Lutherans a sacrament is a means of grace, facilitating the presence of the ascended Savior in our midst.

Baptism is the first sacrament in both history and liturgy. Forerunners of Christian baptism are found in late Judaism. The most famous example is John the Baptist, preacher of repentance, and many who "were all baptized of him . . . , confessing their sins" (Mark 1:5). Jesus accepted baptism of John, transforming the significance of this experience (see Mark 1:9–11). It became the Lord's participation in our sin, a foretype of His death, burial, and resurrection—that we, through baptism, might have "the remission of sins" (Mark 1:4). Christ commanded baptism in the Great Commission (Matt. 28:19) and the church was born on Pentecost with the outpouring of the Spirit and the mass baptism of more than three thousand persons (Acts 2:41). As the church was born of water and the Spirit, so are individual Christians. Baptism, the application of water in the name of the holy Trinity, with the confession of faith and Christ's promise of forgiveness, is the sacrament of initiation into the Christian life. Normally baptism is performed by an ordained minister before the congregation. In case of emergency, any Christian may baptize. The essentials are water and the Word. Lutherans do not insist on any one mode of baptism. Pouring, sprinkling, and immersion are all accepted among Lutherans as biblical means of baptism. The amount of water is incidental. Paul, for instance, preached repentance to the Philippian jailer. The jailer took Paul and Silas "the same hour of the night, and washed their stripes; and was baptized ..." (Acts 16:33). Immediate baptism at midnight in a prison precluded the possibility of much water. The washing of wounds (with the water undoubtedly contained in a basin), mentioned in the same context as the baptism of the jailer and his family, suggests strongly that the method of baptism was by pouring. Luther once compared baptism to an engagement ring, saying it is the sign by which Christ marries His church. As we know, it is the quality of love, not the cost of the ring, that determines the character of a relationship.

Baptism is for believers and the children of believers, as Peter said on Pentecost: "Be baptized every one of you.... For the promise is unto you, and your children" (Acts 2:38, 39). For adults who have not known Christ, the sequence is often one of hearing the Word, repenting of sin, receiving Christ as Lord, confessing Him before the church, and accepting the waters of baptism. Baptism is also for the children of believers. The sequence, however, is different. Believing parents and sponsors present the infant for baptism. This normally transpires in the setting of the service. Christ's words are recalled: "Suffer little children to come unto me, and forbid them not: for of such is the kindgom of God" (Luke 18:16). Parents and sponsors confess their faith in Christ and promise to rear the child in the covenant. Then the sacrament is administered. In Lutheran practice both routes are known—that of a sudden new nature through adult conversion, and that of a gradual growth in faith through childhood nurture.

Only in modern times has infant baptism been seriously challenged. The argument of history indicates that infant baptism has been the custom from time immemorial. The consensus of the Christian community is overwhelmingly in favor of the initiation of infants into the church. This is now and has been the predominant practice—among the Catholic, Orthodox, Oriental, and historic Reformation churches. The rational for this custom is theological and historical.

The theological rational is stated by Paul, writing to the Romans: "By one man sin entered into the world, and death by sin; and so death passed upon all men, for that all have sinned" (Rom. 5:12). Babies die. Death is the price of sin. Children of fallen parents inherit original sin and its guilt. Baptism is the means whereby Christ comes to forgive sin and to bestow eternal life. Baptism is the only means we have to communicate Christ to those who are unreachable through the spoken or written Word.

The historical rationale rests on the practice of the apostolic and patristic church. Family baptisms are reported in the New Testament—those of Cornelius and his family (Acts 10), Lydia and her household (Acts 16:15), the Philippian jailer "and all his" (Acts 16:33), and "the household of Stephanas" (I Cor. 1:16). Behind this understanding of baptism was the history of circumcision, the Old Testament rite of initiation, administered on the eighth day. The concepts of nation, family, and people so common to the Scriptures and the early church indicate that the rugged individualism of modern times was not part of the biblical attitude. A strong sense of social solidarity pervaded both Judaism and ancient Christianity, so that the deliberate exclusion of children from the promise would have seemed incomprehensible.

Baptism is, under normal circumstances, a necessity. While the absence of baptism does not damn, contempt for the sacrament does, for it is a rejection of Christ. Reception of baptism confers upon us nothing less than Jesus and His life, as Paul wrote:

> . . . according to his mercy he saved us, by the washing of regeneration, and renewing of the Holy Ghost; Which he shed on us abundantly through Jesus Christ our Saviour; that being justified by his grace, we should be made heirs according to the hope of eternal life.
>
> [Titus 3:5–7]

Luther, in the Small Catechism, wrote of baptism, "It works forgiveness of sins, delivers from death and the devil, and gives everlasting salvation to all who believe, as the word and promise of God declare."

The Lord's Supper

Jesus recognized that persons are dynamic entities, composed of physical and spiritual components. To be human is to be a creature with both body and soul. For that reason Christ has provided several means for communicating Himself to us. There is a Word—invisible, intangible, appealing to our conscious faculties of mind and memory, conscience and will. Cognitive response is elicited. There are also the sacraments—visible, tangible, appealing to our senses of sight and taste, smell and touch. Baptism, a kind of bath or washing, is the unrepeatable act of initiation into Christ. The Lord's Supper, the sacrament of preservation in faith, is a repeated action. In many respects, it is the "earthy" sacrament, for we take the grain of the field and the fruit of the vine, one baked into the loaf, the other pressed into wine, each the product of labor at hearth or press, and as we "eat this bread, and drink this cup, [we] do shew the Lord's death till he come" (I Cor. 11:26).

This action is repeated frequently in the church, sometimes daily, often weekly, usually monthly, under many names: the Lord's Supper, the Table of the Lord, the Holy Communion, the Mass, the Sacrament of the Altar, the Eucharist.

Lutherans believe that the Lord's Supper was instituted by Christ Himself. This occurred on Thursday of Holy Week, when Jesus met with His friends in the upper room. It was the night of His betrayal. Jesus apparently was keeping the passover meal with His disciples. Taking bread, Christ "gave thanks, and brake it, and gave unto them, saying, This is my body . . ." (Luke 22:19). Taking wine, Christ said, "This cup is the new testament in my blood . . ." (Luke 22:20). Together with most Christians, Lutherans regard this supper as a repeatable feast. There is every indication that the Jerusalem Christians kept the Eucharist: "And they continued stedfastly in the apostles' doctrine and fellowship, and in *breaking of bread*, and in prayers" (Acts 2:42; italics added). Many exegetes regard the term *breaking of bread* as a technical one for the Lord's Supper. The Supper was known in Gentile churches, for Paul instructs the Corinthians concerning it (see I Cor. 11). It is the consensus of the Christian community that this meal is to be observed "until the kingdom of God shall come" (Luke 22:18).

Lutherans believe that the Lord's Supper has a fivefold significance.

The Lord's Supper is an act of recollection, by which we remember the things Christ did "for us men and for our salvation." As Christ commanded, "This do in remembrance of me" (Luke 22:19). Especially we recall His death and resurrection. This aspect of the Supper is stressed in the hymn of James Montgomery, "According to Thy Gracious Word," in which we sing,

> Thy body, broken for my sake
> My bread from heav'n shall be;
> Thy testamental cup I take,
> And thus remember thee.

The Lord's Supper is an act of anticipation, by which we await Christ's return "with glory to judge both the quick and the dead: Whose kingdom shall have no end." As Christ indicated, "I will not drink of the fruit of the vine, until the kingdom of God shall come" (Luke 22:18). The Supper, therefore, pertains not only to history, but also to our eternal destiny. There is a strong eschatological overtone, as suggested by Thomas Aquinas in his eucharistic hymn, "Thee We Adore, O Hidden Saviour," where we sing,

> O Christ, whom now beneath a veil we see
> May what we thirst for soon our portion be,
> To gaze on thee unveiled, and see thy face,
> The vision of thy glory and thy grace.

The Lord's Supper is an act of participation, by which we experience Christ's presence among us "for the remission of sins." As Paul instructed the Corinthians, "The cup of blessing which we bless, is it not the communion of the blood of Christ? The bread which we break, is it not the communion of the body of Christ?" (I Cor. 10:16). The Supper is a means by which Christ is sacramentally present among His people. It is more than history or destiny; it is a current reality. Luther explained this in the Small Catechism, saying "In the Sacrament forgiveness of sins, life and salvation are given us through these words. For where there is forgiveness of sins, there is also life and salvation." The real presence of the Savior is proclaimed in such hymns as "Let All Mortal Flesh Keep Silence," where, in the words of the Liturgy of Saint James, we sing;

King of kings, yet born of Mary
As of old on earth he stood,
Lord of lords in human vesture,
In the Body and the Blood
He will give to all the faithful
His own self for heavenly food.

The Lord's Supper is an act of association by which we realize "the communion of saints." As Paul informed the Corinthians, "We being many are one bread, and one body: for we are all partakers of that one bread" (I Cor. 10:17). The supper is incorporation into the death and resurrection of Christ, an actualization of His presence now among His people, and an expression of our fellowship with one another. At the altar we join in a common confession of faith, in a common act of adoration and dedication, in a common consecration of ourselves to each other—in mutual ministration, in shared life and labor. This blessed fellowship of the faithful is reflected in many Lutheran hymns, as in one by Jacobs, "Lord Jesus Christ, We Humbly Pray," where we sing,

One bread, one cup, one body, we
United by our life in thee,
Thy love proclaim till thou shalt come,
To bring thy scattered loved ones home.

The Lord's Supper is an act of celebration, by which we express our gratitude to one triune God who "is worshipped and glorified." With Paul we cry out, "Thanks be unto God for his unspeakable gift" (II Cor. 9:15). From earliest times the Supper has been called the Eucharist, or Thanksgiving, a name retained in many Lutheran liturgies. In one order the minister faces the people at the beginning of the Holy Communion, saying, "Let us give thanks unto the Lord our God." To which the faithful reply, "It is meet and right so to do." Then the pastor continues, "It is truly meet, right and salutary, that we should at all times, and in all places, give thanks unto thee, O Lord, Holy Father, Almighty, Everlasting God. . . ." As people of the new covenant we show our appreciation to God for our salvation. This sentiment is shared in the hymn by Thomas Hansen Kingo, "O Jesus, Blessed Lord," in which we sing,

> Break forth, my soul, for joy and say,
> 'What wealth is come to me this day,
> My Saviour dwells within me now,
> How blest am I, how good art thou!'

Lutherans have always felt uncomfortable with the various theories offered in the church to explain how Christ is present in the Supper. Lutherans certainly regard the meal as more than a memorial, for Christ is not totally absent from His people; He is sacramentally present. Lutherans, furthermore, view the Supper as more than a moment of aspiration when the senses receive physical elements while the soul devoutly meditates on Christ. Lutherans also are reluctant to name it a miracle, and for that reason they usually have avoided the term *transubstantiation*. (This doctrine maintains that in the Mass, when the priest speaks the words of institution, the bread and wine are miraculously changed into the body and blood of Christ. While retaining the outward appearance of natural elements they are in fact inwardly the supernatural reality of Christ). Lutherans believe that the communicant receives both bread and body, wine and blood. These are not mixed together (described by the term *consubstantiation*, a teaching wrongly ascribed to Lutherans). Nor is the corpus of Christ radically localized as in the notion of impanation, a doctrine rejected by the Lutheran reformers. Lutherans affirm that the Supper is a mystery; their confessions refuse to define the mode of Christ's presence; their liturgies steadfastly celebrate the reality that the entire Christ—body and spirit—is there to bless.

In the words of the creed, all that Christ has done for "us men and our salvation" has involved His coming to us. This has not changed in the age of the church, for Jesus Christ is "the same, yesterday, today, and forever." The means of grace are the mode of Christ's coming to us in a way that satisfies the needs of our humanity. He remains with us to preserve, pardon, and empower us. His promise remains: "Lo, I am with you alway, even unto the end of the world" (Matt. 28:20).

CHAPTER

5

The Congregation of Christ

And I believe one holy Catholic and Apostolic Church.

The English language has its dangers. Words don't always mean what we think they mean. This is especially true when we use theological terms. Surely one of the most confusing words in our vocabulary today is "church." Let us begin this chapter about the Lutheran understanding of the church by considering some definitions.

The Church: A Definition

The word *church* in the English language has many different meanings. Among them are the following six usages.

The word *church* can refer to a building used for worship. One of the authors, for instance, was confirmed in Saint Paul's Lutheran Church, Stewart and Bruck, Columbus, Ohio. In that connection, the word *church* refers to a large red brick edifice, with stone trim, set at the corner of the intersection of two streets on the south side of Ohio's capital.

The word *church* can mean a denomination, an organized group of religious congregations. The word is employed in that sense when we speak of the American Lutheran Church, the Lutheran Church in America, the United Methodist Church, the Church of England, the Christian Reformed Church, or the United Presbyterian Church. It indicates a collection of Christian congregations sharing a common heritage and a conviction of mutual identity and ministry.

The word *church* can mean a religious service. The term

Saint Paul's Lutheran Church

Fort Wayne, Indiana

Dedicated on September 15, 1889, and considered one of the finest examples of nineteenth-century Gothic-revival architecture in the American Midwest.

is used in such a manner when a mother calls to her children on Sunday morning, “Hurry up, Mary; hurry up, Billy, or we will be late for church.” That is what we mean when we say, “Church is at eleven o’clock.” We are thinking of an act of worship when a congregation gathers under the leadership of its ministers to offer prayer and praise to God, to be instructed by a sermon, or to participate in communion.

The word *church* can mean an ecclesiastical or social power, sometimes in opposition to the secular establishment, as suggested in the phrase *the separation of church and state*. The word in this context indicates a complex of individuals, institutions, ideas, and influences—a kind of spiritual corporation composed of congregations set over against other natural orders such as the state, the family, work, or school. The term *church* in this sense indicates an entity in society that exercises political influence.

The word *church* can mean a congregation, that is, a local assembly of Christians within a given community. Several denominations have placed strong emphasis on this meaning of the word *church*, as is reflected in names such as Congregational Christian churches. Baptists, Disciples, Congregationalists, and many Lutherans use the term *church* in this sense when they speak of “gathering a new church in Indianapolis.” They are referring to the calling together of a local society of believers in Jesus Christ, which is then “the church in Louisville” or “the church in Upper Arlington.”

The word *church* can mean all Christians, both living (the church militant) and dead (the church triumphant), of all generations and locations, who constitute the body of Christ. The word was used in this way when Samuel J. Stone spoke of “The Church’s One Foundation” and confessed that

> . . . she on earth hath union
> With God the Three in One,
> And mystic sweet communion
> With those whose rest is won.

This is the great church, the catholic church, the church universal, from which no one who truly believes in Christ is excluded.

There are probably other usages of the word *church* in English, but these are six of the most common. Of these six definitions, all, save the last two, are postbiblical. The term *church* in the Scriptures does not indicate a building, a denomination, a service, or an establishment.

In the Scriptures, the word *church* has but two meanings, both of which are synonymous with the term *congregation* (the preferred Puritan translation for both the English Bible and *The Book of Common Prayer*, a translation suppressed by High-Church Anglicans).

In a primary sense the word *church* means the great congregation, the universal church, the Christians of all areas and eras, the "saints and believers," "the congregation of the elect," or, in the words of the Apology of the Augsburg Confession, those "who truly believe in the Gospel of Christ and have the Holy Ghost" (*Ap. Conf.*, 4.28).

In a secondary sense the word *church* means the local congregation, the gathered assembly, the Christians of a specific vicinity. The New Testament word for "church" (*ekklesia*) indicates an "assembly" of those "called out" from the world. This Koine Greek term corresponds to the Hebrew *qāhāl*, or "gathered congregation." The word *church* is similar in meaning to the name applied to a Jewish fellowship, the synagogue, which literally means "a come-together" or "an assembly." The term *synagogue* was a Hellenistic Greek word used by Hebrew believers to translate *'ēdāh*, a term in their mother tongue that signified "society" or "association." In New Testament usage, the word *church* often refers to such Christian assemblies in various localities. At least thirty-five different churches are named in the New Testament, being societies of believers in Philippi, Berea, Troas, Colosse, Smyrna, and elsewhere. Early Lutherans were quick to recover this apostolic usage. Johann Gerhard, called the greatest of all Lutheran theologians, wrote,

> The word Church generically signifies an assembly or congregation, whence it is applied to political and secular assemblies. In order, therefore, that the holy assembly of the Church may

> be distinguished from secular assemblies, it is called the Church of God. . . .[1]

According to the New Testament, these entities are not two different realities. There is but one church. Both the smaller and greater congregation are one. Particular churches are manifestations of the universal church. John Theodore Mueller, a twentieth-century American Lutheran theologian, noted,

> With respect to the relation between the Church Universal and the local churches, Scripture teaches clearly that these are not two different churches or two different kinds of churches, but the Church Universal consists of all true believers who are found in the local churches.[2]

The Church: A Description

The church can be described in many ways. One approach is to indicate its appellations. Many names are given to church members in the New Testament. Jesus spoke of them as his family (Mark 3:33) and "little flock" (Luke 12:32) who were to be "salt" and "light" (Matt. 5:13, 14). Those who accepted Christ were known as brothers (Acts 1:16), believers (Acts 2:44), "disciples" (Acts 6:1), those who "call on the name of the Lord" (Acts 2:21), those "called" (Rom. 1:6), "the saints" (Acts 9:13), those of the way or of "that way" (Acts 19:9), and "Christians" (Acts 11:26). The term by which we most often refer to disciples, "Christian," is used only three times in the New Testament (Acts 11:26; 26:28; I Peter 4:16) and was possibly a name invented by enemies of the church. Christians collectively are called "the body" or "the bride" of Christ (I Cor. 10:17; Rev. 22:17). Paul, when he wished to employ the plural, spoke of "the churches of God" (I Thess. 2:14). Later

1. As cited in Heinrich Schmid, *The Doctrinal Theology of the Evangelical Lutheran Church*, trans. Charles A. Hay and Henry E. Jacobs, third revised edition (Minneapolis: Augsburg, 1961), p. 585.
2. *Christian Dogmatics: A Handbook of Doctrinal Theology* (Saint Louis: Concordia, 1955), p. 554.

Christian leaders began to talk of the catholic or orthodox church.

Following the Reformation, Lutherans continued to refer to the great congregation as the catholic church. However, they were quickly required to find a designation for their own movement of renewal within the Western church. Enemies called them Lutherans. This name has endured. Luther's own preference was that his followers should simply call themselves evangelicals. "Evangelical" is a word from Greek that means "gospel" or "good news." Luther hoped that the adherents of the Reformation churches in Europe would be known as evangelical Catholics. In subsequent centuries the word *evangelical* has come to have meanings other than "Lutheran," including all Protestants who embraced the Reformation, Low-Church Anglicans, and conservative American Protestants. Often in the United States one speaks of the evangelical Lutheran churches in order to differentiate this branch of evangelicalism from the other churches of the Reformation. Most Lutherans in America today employ the name *Lutheran*, not only to honor the reformer, but also to indicate a confessional position: they are Protestants who follow Luther's articulation of the evangelical faith.

Local Lutheran congregations are named in a variety of ways. While today most Lutheran parishes use the name *Lutheran*, that has not always been the case. In colonial America, Lutheran churches employed a variety of appellations. The first organization of Lutherans in New Netherlands was known as "the Christian Community Adhering to the Unaltered Augsburg Confession of Faith." Justus Falckner, a pioneer German preacher in Pennsylvania, spoke of "the Christian Apostolic Protestant Lutheran Congregation." Often Lutheran societies were known as "Congregations Adhering to the Augsburg Confession." Eventually the label *Lutheran* became almost universal in America. As Lutheran congregations were gathered, they named themselves by geographical location (North Community Lutheran Church), historical preeminence (First Lutheran Church), ethnic or linguistic origin (the German Lutheran Church, First English Lutheran Church), or in honor of a biblical saint (Saint Mark's Lutheran Church), a medieval Christian hero (Saint Olaf's Lutheran Church), a reformer (Martin Luther Lutheran Church, Melanchthon Lutheran Church), a church father (Walther Memorial Lutheran Church), a cherished doctrine (Trinity Lutheran Church), a desired virtue (Faith Lutheran Church), an honored credo (Augsburg Lutheran Church), a biblical place name (Bethlehem Lutheran Church), or a title of Christ (Redeemer Lutheran Church). Imagination has seldom faltered among founders of Lutheran churches! There are Epiphanies, Wittenbergs, Centennials, Gloria Deis, Immanuels, and many more.

In America, local Lutheran congregations have been gathered by pious folk using the means of grace. Sometimes a pastor, seminarians, or others will be sent to canvass a community, seeking persons who wish to confess Christ and nurture one another in His fellowship. Other times a district or a synod will establish a "mission," complete with pastor, parsonage, and "church plant" in a suburb that is being developed. Often Lutheran congregations will establish satellite or daughter churches. Occasionally a large congregation will voluntarily divide. There is, in fact, a host of ways in which new churches may be planted. No single method may be viewed as normative or better than another.

The Church: Its Attributes

The church also can be described in terms of its attributes. Churches—the local and the universal—derive their character from Christ. The church, whether by Lake Michigan or the crystal sea, is the body of Christ. We are attached to Him, by faith, in baptism, through the Word, and at the Supper. Because of this there is an interesting communication of attributes between Christ and His church. With great audacity the New Testament writers use the same terms to describe both Jesus and the church. The noted Presbyterian theologian, James D. Smart, wrote,

> If it were not for the plain words of Jesus and his apostles ... it would seem to us almost blasphemy to set the divine Lord and a human ministry in such close relation: It is star-

> tling that Jesus, who, whether he said it of himself or had it said of him by John, is uniquely 'the light of the world' (John 8:12), is reported by Matthew to have said of his disciples what they would never have dared to say of themselves; 'Ye are the light of the world' (Matthew 5:14). Surely it is this same continuity of ministry which is reflected in the words, 'As the Father has sent me, even so send I you.' (John 20:21; cf. Luke 10:16). He who was himself the great Fisher of Men, casting the net of his word into the sea of humanity to catch men and women for the life of his Kingdom, called his disciples to take up this same occupation and 'become fishers of men.' (Mark 1:17)[3]

In this communication of attributes between Jesus and His saints there is a dialectical tension. Through God's grace we are what Christ has shared with us. By faith we seek to become what we already are. Perhaps a German phrase will help explain our relationship to these attributes. They are both *Gabe und Aufgabe*, both "gift and task," or both potentiality and responsibility. For that reason the life of the church on earth consists in becoming what it already is in heaven.

While the older dogmaticians could never quite agree on how many attributes there are, many theologians identify four, all of which are drawn from the third article of the Nicene Creed, "I believe one holy Catholic and Apostolic Church." Let us consider each of these.

The church is one. It possesses the attribute of unity. For that reason Paul can express this as already given, for "there is one body, and one Spirit, even as ye are called in one hope of your calling; One Lord, one faith, one baptism, One God and Father of all, who is above all, and through all, and in you all" (Eph. 4:4–6). Yet Jesus recognized that the manifestation of this unity will be a task, for why else did He pray "that they all may be one; as thou, Father, art in me, and I in thee, that they also may be in us: that the world may believe that thou hast sent me" (John 17:21)? In Christ all genuine Christians, on earth and in heaven, are one family. Within the context of history, taking into account man's fallen state, this unity is a responsibility—on both the congrega-

3. *The Rebirth of Ministry* (Philadelphia: Westminster, 1960), p. 30.

tional and the global level. Perhaps that is why some Lutheran dogmaticians talked of invisibility as an attribute of the church. By using this term they did not mean to imply that the church is a Platonic dream or an abstract ideal. The word indicated the spiritual unity of all believers in Christ, no matter how much they might be divided by the pluralisms of history.

The church is holy. It possesses the attribute of sanctity. Because of that, Paul praised this "glorious church, not having spot, or wrinkle, or any such thing; but that it should be holy and without blemish" (Eph. 5:27). Peter, in inspired prose, defined the church as "a chosen generation, a royal priesthood, an holy nation, a peculiar people . . ." (I Peter 2:9). Because of its participation in Christ, the church is declared perfect in God's eyes. But this is to be made real in our humanity. If this were not the case, why then are the Scriptures filled with injunctions such as that of the Lord in Leviticus, "ye shall be holy" so "therefore sanctify yourselves" (Lev. 11:44)? The holiness of the church is both a quality and a quest.

Lutherans insist that congregations do include both true and false believers, for as Jesus taught us, the tares cannot be destroyed without harming the wheat in the field. Separation must await the harvest. Among the apostolic twelve there was a Judas, and Ananias and Sapphira were members of the earliest church. Even within devout Christian people there are what John Wesley called "unconverted areas." For this reason Lutherans contend that sanctity is realized in the churches through reformation. Reformation comes by preaching the Word and administering the sacraments. This calls sinners to faith, and faithful Christians to greater obedience.

The church is catholic or universal. It has the attribute of catholicity. The word *catholic* was first used by Ignatius of Antioch in the second century when he wrote, "Wherever Jesus Christ is, there is the Catholic Church." He wrote this to designate that the church that operated in fullness or with catholicity operated with the fullness of Christ. It has all that Christ is, and all the truth that He imparts. He fills all that the church is, as Paul confessed:

> For by him were all things created: . . . all things were created by him, and for him: And he is before all things, and by him all things consist. And he is the head of the body, the church: who is the beginning, the firstborn from the dead; that in all things he might have the preeminence. For it pleased the Father that in him should all fulness dwell.
>
> [Col. 1:16–19]

This fullness or catholicity relates to the universality of Christ's atonement and the extension of His kingdom in both history and geography. Thus, the church catholic, the body of Christ, is cosmopolitan. Saint John the Divine testified:

> After this I beheld, and, lo, a great multitude, which no man could number, of all nations, and kindreds, and people, and tongues, stood before the throne, and before the Lamb, . . . And cried with a loud voice, saying, Salvation to our God which sitteth upon the throne, and unto the Lamb.
>
> [Rev. 7:9–10]

As the church makes its pilgrimage through the centuries it can be assured of its catholicity in time. Jesus said, "I will build my church; and the gates of hell shall not prevail against it" (Matt. 16:18). This applies not only to the immortality of the individual believer, but also to what some of the older dogmaticians described as the perpetuity of the church. There will always be a church on earth. One should not understand this attribute to imply that the church will prevail forever in all parts of the world. It is easy to pinpoint parts of our planet, such as North Africa or the Middle East, where the church was once extensive and where it is now virtually extinct.

C. F. W. Walther, the patriarch of Missouri Synod Lutheranism, liked to quote Martin Luther's statement that the gospel is like a refreshing summer shower, moving across the land with its graces, dispensing life in its path. After its departure, the ground is once more parched. God's Word comes to a people, a church flourishes; but if the people abuse, misuse, or disuse the ordinances of the Lord, the Spirit will move with the message to more promising regions. We work and pray that there may always be a church among us. Surely one of the reassuring prophecies of the latter day is that the gospel will be proclaimed throughout the world.

Within geography, the realm of space, the church seeks to realize its catholicity. This transpires in both home and foreign missions. Extension is a natural process of the church as a living organism. In this process people of all kinds are added to the congregation of Christ. While one normally regards the Lutheran church as a predominately Germanic and Scandinavian faith, today one can find blacks, American Indians, Asians, Anglo-Saxons, and Hispanics within its membership. This was dramatically illustrated for one of the authors more than a decade ago when he still lived in Columbus, Ohio. Asked to minister at First English Lutheran Church, he arrived early to become acquainted with the parish. First English was once a mighty "platform parish." But by 1970 the neighborhood had changed. "White flight" was common and the community was predominantly black. Muhammad's mosque was but a few blocks away. As the author parked in front of the church and stepped onto the sidewalk, his clerical collar and vest became evident. A young black boy, perhaps about eleven years old, was sitting on the steps and rose to ask, "Father, can I help you?" "Why, yes," the author replied. "Could you show me to the church office?" "Why sure," the boy said, a broad smile on his face. Off they went on a tour of old First Church. Edward, the author's newfound friend, pointed out the exceptional characteristics of the very lovely church—nodding to the steps leading to the great pulpit, explaining the meaning of the golden sanctuary lamp, genuflecting to the resplendent altar—and then, guiding the author around the communion rail, led him to the sacristy. Edward's familiarity with the church and its furnishings was so impressive that the author asked, "Son, are you a custodian?" "Oh, no, Father," he replied, "I'm a Lutheran." In that moment of humor came recognition of the catholicity of the church. Here a seventh-generation American of English descent and a seventh-generation American of African ancestry found a brotherhood in Christ that transcended race and that will endure into eternity.

The church is apostolic. It has the attribute of apostolicity.

This indicates its identity and continuity with the fellowship founded by Jesus twenty centuries ago. Christ Himself is the apostle, the one sent by God. This Jesus then commissioned the Twelve, saying, "As my Father hath sent me, even so send I you" (John 20:21). Because of that, Paul described the church as "built upon the foundation of the apostles and prophets, Jesus Christ himself being the chief corner stone" (Eph. 2:20). That is a gift. But it is also a task, for it is the responsibility of each generation of Christians to compare their principles and practices with those of the primitive church.

Much confusion has occurred as to the criteria of this comparison. Through the centuries some extremists have insisted on total conformity to all the customs prevalent in first-century Palestine. Churches have at times condemned pipe organs, robes, creeds, or any other additions made to the Christian tradition since the days of Peter and Paul. Lutherans regard such an attitude to be harmful, not helpful, in our approximation of apostolicity. Apostolicity does not mean identity in all areas—else we could not have pews, electric lights, air conditioning and central heating, or microphones (or even church buildings).

Lutherans traditionally have been committed to innovation in the church in all areas that will not compromise its apostolicity. For Lutherans apostolicity consists in continuity in the apostles' message and mission. Since the faith of the apostles is recorded in the New Testament, Lutherans contend that apostolicity consists in fidelity to the Word. Scripture, the written testimony of the apostolic community, becomes the norm of church life today. All that is not forbidden by the Word is allowed. Like the noble Bereans, commended by the apostles, Lutherans "received the word with all readiness of mind, and searched the scriptures daily, whether those things were so" (Acts 17:11). This principle, *sola Scriptura*, was the test of the Reformation in restoring authentic New Testament Christianity in the sixteenth century. The principle remains the means for preserving Christianity today.

The Church: Its Institutions

In response to the Master who comes in Word and sacrament, the church—at Christ's command and by His behest—creates certain institutions. These are necessary for the church to fulfill its task within history. Invented in a variety of situations, designed to meet the necessities of different conditions, these institutions are to be understood as human creations that have originated in a faithful and obedient response to divine revelation. They have been compared with machinery, devised by an engineer, to be driven by the power provided by God in nature, to meet the needs of people. As circumstances change, they may be altered. Another analogy is that of travel. Christ invites us to be pilgrims and He provides for us along the way. How we make the journey depends on the culture of our times.

During its pilgrimage through time the church has created certain institutions. Let us consider two of these: polity and ministry.

Polity concerns the ordering of the church. Order in the church is not optional. God is not the author of confusion. Government is necessary. Just as individual believers are to belong to a Christian community, so the members of that fellowship are to order their affairs in a God-pleasing manner. Lutheran theologians found no one polity prescribed in the New Testament. This set them apart from the leading divines of other Protestant traditions, who, by the name they used for their followers—Episcopalian or Presbyterian—indicated their contention that there was a divinely instituted form of church government.

Lutherans contend that the only abiding structure surviving from New Testament times is the congregation. Anything above and beyond that is of human derivation, not divine origin. Furthermore, Lutherans insist that the local congregation is complete, full, lacking nothing, having the fullness of Christ in all matters. Lutherans have also pointed out that the congregation is the only universal Christian form of order. All of us have seen churches without diocesan bishops or presbyteries, but none of us has ever observed a church that lacked a congregation. The congregation has the right and the responsibility to decide all matters—faith, life, and order—not clearly settled in the sacred Scriptures. Congregations create an instrument of government, the constitution, that provides for government on the local level. Congregations meet in deliberative bodies to discuss, debate, and settle issues pertaining to the parish, hear reports, and transact other business. Congregations determine the criteria for membership, establish a ruling body (often called the church council or the vestry), elect officers (elders or trustees), and call pastors and commit to their care the public administration of the means of grace. Congregations create committees and task forces, generate agencies and institutions (such as a parish school), employ persons needed (such as a parish secretary, director of Christian education, youth worker, teachers, organist, or sexton), and do whatever else may be useful or necessary for the work of Christ in that specific community. Under the lordship of Christ, there is, quite literally, no end to the work that a congregation may do.

Congregations for a variety of reasons join together in voluntary associations. These associations of congregations are functional and fraternal, intended to conduct those tasks that normally are beyond the ability of a single local church. This could include the publication of Christian literature, the education of church leaders (pastors, teachers, and layworkers), world evangelization, church extension, provision for philanthropic works, care for the aged and disabled, provision of pension funds for retired church workers, and utilization of the mass media. Such a consortium of congregations may be named a synod, a presbytery, a convention, or a diocese. (Lutherans in the Missouri Synod hold to a congregational-connectional polity. The American Lutheran Church has congregational polity but employs episcopal nomenclature for its district and national officers. The Lutheran Church in America is the only major Lutheran body in North America to employ a strictly presbyterian form of order). Historically Lutherans have been free to join congregations into any kind of association they desire and find helpful. Recently there has been renewed interest and study concerning both episcopal polity and nomenclature in American Lutheranism.

Yet another institution is the ministry. The ministry of Word and sacrament (the particular priesthood; the public ministry) is of divine origin. While all Christians (the universal priesthood) may baptize, counsel (confess and absolve), teach and preach, for the sake of order and evangelical continuity the congregation elects pastors. If on a Sunday morning each believer within the universal priesthood insisted on the public exercise of his rights, there would be anarchy. For that reason the congregation meets in solemn assembly, with prayer and deliberation, and sets one or more aside for the office of the ministry. Many things are desirable in a minister. It is a good thing for one to desire this office (I Tim. 3:1–7). There ought to be a sense of vocation, an inner longing to be a pastor. One ought to have a good general education as well as a thorough course of theological study. Lutherans have traditionally valued an educated clergy. Peer group recognition is not to be despised. Fellow clergy, through certification, ordination, and installation, should support the newly called minister. Historically the essential requirement for the office is the election of a congregation. After this election, the public ministry of Word and sacrament is committed to the person elected. As Gerhard wrote,

> The ministry of the Church is a sacred and public office divinely appointed, and entrusted, through a legitimate call, to certain men, in order that being instructed they may teach the Word of God with peculiar power, may administer the Sacraments, and preserve church discipline, for the purpose of effecting the conversion and salvation of men, and truly advancing the glory of God.[4]

Within Lutheranism, one may find many understandings of the public ministry. It often depends upon the polity of the church body involved. The ministry may be seen as an order, as in Swedish Lutheranism; as a profession or "occupation by call," as in certain portions of American Lutheranism; or

4. Quoted by Schmid, *Doctrinal Theology*, pp. 606–607.

in rarer situations as a personal inclination, as in certain independent Lutheran churches. Whatever the understanding of the church may be, all agree on the special distinction of the ministerial office.

The Church: Its Faith and Work

Preeminently Lutherans like to evaluate a church in terms of its faith and work. Theology is the major identifying institution of a church. It reveals what a body of people believes. Work is the constant manifestation of that faith. The two exist in a causal relationship. Lutheran dogmaticians speak in terms of "faith active in works" or *credenda est agenda*, "that which is believed is that which is done." Dogma determines duty. For a Lutheran to separate the two is inconceivable. The manifestation of the church as the body of Christ in the world depends on the church's clear comprehension of its message and mission as articulated in a creed or a confession. Theology reflects the self-understanding of a Christian community and is prerequisite to its effective ministration.

In the broadest sense of the word every Christian is a theologian. A theologian is essentially one who talks about God. Some individual Christians are professionally trained theologians, having spent years studying the Scriptures, church history, systematics, and pastoral care. Some of these persons have produced theological texts that are widely read. Examples are Franz Pieper and Mueller within the Missouri Synod, Matthias Loy of the old Ohio Synod, Michael Reu of the former Iowa Synod, Franklin R. Weidner, Charles Porterfield Krauth, and Henry Eyster Jacobs in the General Council, Edward C. Fendt of the previous American Lutheran Church, or J. A. Singmaster of the old United Lutheran Church in America. These men's systematic theologies, however eminent and esteemed, were not the official creeds or confessions of the Lutheran churches. A confession is a publicly accepted statement of faith for a Christian community. Such testimonies are not normally the work of an individual. Usually they are the products of much deliberation, often by a number of committees and councils. Even if a confession is penned by a single person (as was the case of Philip Melanchthon and the Augsburg Confession), it becomes the common witness of the churches when it is subscribed to by the ministers and members of those communities.

There is, of course, another sense in which a systematic theology differs from a creed or a confession. A creed does not pretend to cover all points of doctrine. No confession could possibly do that. One searches the Apostles' Creed in vain for any information on the earthly ministry of Jesus Christ. Certainly the venerable Lutheran confessions of the sixteenth century do not speak directly to many issues confronting Christians today, such as the charismatic movement, the authority of the Bible, or the proper role of women within the church. While a systematic theology attempts, in logical and rational form, to cover all the points of doctrine (or teaching), a confession is a situational statement of the faith by a community of believers to speak to certain problems. Creeds and confessions come into being when the churches concur in a judgment concerning a contended issue. The so-called ecumenical creeds arose out of the christological controversies that rocked the ancient church. The Lutheran confessions are a product of the sixteenth-century soteriological debates surrounding justification. They represent the consensus of the evangelical church as to the proper doctrines. In that sense they are received as a faithful response to the sacred Scriptures in the matters that had previously been disputed.

Both authors are acquainted with pious Christians who contend that it is not necessary to have a creed. Their motto is "no book but the Bible, no creed but Christ." Of course that sentence denouncing creeds is itself a creed! When we ask such persons about their beliefs—about the authority of the Bible, or the deity of Christ, or the way of salvation—they quite often have evangelical and orthodox answers. If we then show them the Apostles' Creed or the Augsburg Confession, which repeats in official language what they have just said, they often blush and own that they have a creed, but out of stubbornness refuse to subscribe to that same faith as it has been articulated by others.

Certainly those in American church history who have opposed creeds have had a point—and that is the evil of credalism. We are all familiar with bishops, presbyteries, synods, and church boards that abuse and misuse statements of faith to tyrannize the sensitive consciences of fellow Christians. In the hands of the unscrupulous elder or the dogmatic dean, a creed can become an instrument of intellectual torture rather than the shared testimony of joyous hearts. But to abandon creeds because they are misused is as absurd as to prohibit automobiles because thieves use them in the process of robbing banks. Normality—not abnormality—shall be the test of any institution.

In this century an eminent Lutheran minister, Robert Emory Golladay, preached a series of sermons about the Apostles' Creed. He began with a homily on "The Need of a Creed." Golladay defined a creed as "a free, joyous, fearless, declaration of the faith" by a community of Christians. Certainly all creeds and confessions are human institutions, created in response to God's revelation in His Word. No creed, however ancient or universal, can ever claim to have the same authority as Scripture. All creedal authority is derivatory, as that of the Bible is primary. As Golladay noted,

> . . . the creeds, as to their form, are not inspired; but the truth expressed, being a faithful epitome of Biblical doctrine, is just as much of God when embodied in the creed as the same statements are when scattered through a dozen or twenty books of the Bible.[5]

As there can be no body without a skeleton, no church without polity, no worship without pattern, so there can be no consistent public teaching within a denomination without a creed.

The creed or the confession indicates the public teaching of a church. Lutherans contend that there is an evangelical succession, that is, a Christian succession that is "our one-

5. *The Apostles' Creed* (Columbus, OH: Lutheran Book Concern, 1917), p. 10.

ness in the faith of the apostles and saints of every age." The confessions normally received within the Lutheran churches are bound together in *The Book of Concord*. Within that book are creeds of three kinds.

First are the ecumenical, catholic, or universal creeds. These are the Apostles', the Nicene, and the Athanasian creeds. They come to us from the ancient church. While Lutherans realize that there never has been (and probably never will be) a truly ecumenical creed, accepted by all Christians, these statements of faith have been widely used within the Christian churches. By endorsing them, the Lutherans manifest their unity with the church of the Greek and Latin fathers.

Next are the evangelical confessions. These include the Augsburg Confession and its Apology, as well as Luther's Small and Large catechisms. While these were written by Lutherans to articulate their stand on justification over against the position of the Roman Catholic Church, the truths of these documents commended themselves to other evangelicals. Reformers in Switzerland and England employed these confessions in part in the construction of their own statements of faith. Both authors know of churches that are not formally members of a Lutheran denomination but use the Small Catechism and adhere to the Augsburg Confession.

Last are the distinctively Lutheran confessions. These include the Formula of Concord, which states the consensus of Lutherans concerning controversies that divided them from one another and from other Protestants during the late sixteenth century. To our knowledge, while the ecumenical creeds are received by most Catholic Christians and the evangelical confessions are acknowledged by many Protestant believers, no group outside the Lutheran family has given assent to these documents.

Normally a Lutheran congregation contains in its constitution some reference to *The Book of Concord*, or, at the very least, to the ecumenical creeds and the Augsburg Confession. Theoretically a church could be impeccably Lutheran without any mention of these creeds. It would be quite possible for a gathering of believers to compose a new statement of faith, *ex corde*, *ex tempore*, *ex nihilo*, and still be recognized as Lutheran. If the affirmations made in that congregational testimony were harmonious with biblical truth and, therefore, compatible with the existing Lutheran confessions, such a community could be acknowledged as Lutheran, no matter what its name or creed.

Such a situation arose when the Batak churches, indigenous evangelical communities in Indonesia, sought membership in the Lutheran World Federation. After examination of their statement of faith, they were accepted, even though the creed of the Batak churches makes no reference to the historic creeds of Lutheranism. Both authors contend, however, that while the absence of such references does not necessarily preclude the possibility of a church being Lutheran, we think that once such a fellowship has become aware of the traditional Lutheran confessions it will want to make some kind of formal identification with those confessions. Solidarity in the truth has been a hallmark of Lutheranism. When one can, in good conscience, hold an identical creed and confess it in the same way, it is helpful to do so.

Lutherans evaluate churches on the basis of their formal or public profession of faith. While no one can determine the sincerity of the faith of a person or a community (only God can read the heart), it is possible to evaluate theology in terms of its fidelity to the Word. Lutherans generally have considered this to be an important task. This becomes the basis for altar and pulpit fellowship between church bodies.

Theology and the confessions are human responses to the Word of God. They establish the agenda for the community. Confessing is followed by working.

Traditionally Lutherans have spoken of the proper work of the church as the preaching and teaching of the Word and the administration of the sacraments. By these actions God calls the community into existence. The general work of the church then follows. It includes at least seven tasks: *kerygma*, or preaching, which is the exposition of the Word of God; *didache*, or teaching, which is the instruction of the people of God; *koinonia*, or fellowship, first in the sacraments, then in love and mutual service, that exhibits the charity so characteristic of the Christian church; *propheteia*, or reforming, the witness of the church in the world for righteousness and justice; *diakonia*, or serving those in distress (Christ, at the last judgment, will indicate that when we fed the hungry, gave drink to the thirsty, visited the prisoner, welcomed the stranger, or clothed the shivering, we were ministering to the Master); *leitourgia*, or worship, the loving response to God by the people of God; and *martyria*, or evangelization, the obtaining and retaining of members of the body of Christ by witnessing in the world.

"I believe in the . . . church." For Lutherans that statement is forever connected with their confirmation day. One recalls a class of boys and girls, dressed in white robes, proceeding to the front of the sanctuary to be seated in the front pew. Following the lessons, they would all be catechized by the pastor. Many questions would be asked, affording the opportunity to give testimony to their faith, to demonstrate their biblical knowledge, and to indicate their readiness for reception as communicant members of the church. A sermon would follow to emphasize the commitment these young people were making. They then would be invited forward to kneel at the altar, receive the laying on of hands, and then with the right hand of fellowship to be received as communicant members of their particular church. In this rite of confirmation, the Lutheran has pledged loyalty, faithfulness, and lifelong commitment to his church. By this rite Lutherans confess anew the truth of "the communion of saints," the "congregation of Christ."

CHAPTER

The Worship of God

And I believe in the Holy Ghost, . . . who with the Father and Son together is worshiped and glorified.

The Importance of Worship

Worship is a perennial human activity. According to the Scriptures, worship is the most enduring of all human endeavors. Worship began before the fall, for as soon as man was created, God instituted the Sabbath (Gen. 2:2). The garden was the initial temple. Worship will also continue after the parousia. God's people in paradise will praise Him directly, for John reports of New Jerusalem, "I saw no temple therein: for the Lord God Almighty and the Lamb are the temple of it" (Rev. 21:22). Worship is the work of believers in this interim era between the advents. Saints on earth, in the church militant, worship, even as Paul commanded, "I will therefore that men pray every where, lifting up holy hands . . ." (I Tim. 2:8). Saints in heaven, in the church triumphant, worship, for John "heard a great voice of much people in heaven, saying, Alleluia; Salvation, and glory, and honour, and power, unto the Lord our God" (Rev. 19:1). The world, begun with an invocation, will conclude with a benediction and continues with a doxology.

Worship is an essential human activity. In part, man is man because he worships. Humans are made in the image of God (Gen. 1:26). This means they have a capacity to enter into a meaningful relationship with the Eternal. Worship, therefore, reveals a portion of that which is distinctive about man. It becomes the supreme expression of our humanity.

Saint Paul's Lutheran Church (Chancel)

Fort Wayne, Indiana

Worship is a beneficial human activity. Men worship because they must. As Augustine confessed, "Our hearts are restless until they rest in Thee." In the absence of the true God, people turn to idolatry. Prayer to someone or something is necessary. Man, made in the image of the immortal Spirit, hungers and thirsts for God. As the psalmist put it, "As the hart panteth after the water brooks, so panteth my soul after thee, O God" (Ps. 42:1).

In the worship of God, man satisfies seven of his spiritual needs.

Man has a need to express adoration, for he is a spirit filled with reverence for the beauty and bounty of nature, and he praises the majesty and mercy of the Creator. The expression of wonder and awe is the origin of worship.

Man has a need for reconciliation, for he is an estranged spirit, alienated from God, his neighbor, and himself. He longs to be restored to full fellowship with his heavenly Father, to transcend his fallen state. Confession and absolution are integral ingredients of worship. In Isaiah 6, the seer first beheld God "sitting upon a throne, high and lifted up" and then sensed the human tragedy, for "woe is me! for I am undone; because I am a man of unclean lips, and I dwell in the midst of a people of unclean lips . . ." (Isa. 6:1, 5). Pardon, as much as wonder, is involved in worship.

Man has a need for edification, for he is a searching spirit, filled with curiosity and rationality. If we are spiritually alive, we are mentally active. Learning is as essential to worship as praising and confessing, for truth is added to glory and grace in the hour of prayer.

Man has a need for association, for he is a communal spirit, longing for communion with others. Even paradise lacked fulfillment for Adam as long as he was by himself, and God admitted, "It is not good that the man should be alone . . ." (Gen. 2:18). Begotten of the love of God, man is made to give love to others. The great commandment is that "thou shalt love the Lord thy God with all thy heart, and with all thy soul, and with all thy strength, and with all thy mind; and thy neighbour as thyself" (Luke 10:27). To know God truly is to love Him. In worship, affection joins instruction and there is food for heart and mind.

Man has a need for affirmation, for he is a believing spirit, eager to confess his faith. Worship provides adequate opportunity for people to give expression to their values and ideals. Worship at its best becomes the articulation of the fundamental principles and practices by which we order our lives. "I believe" is as much a part of prayer as "I belong."

Man has a need for intercession, for he is a caring spirit, concerned about the welfare of others. In worship man enters into a conversation with God. This communication includes, as Paul noted, "supplications, prayers, intercessions, and giving of thanks . . ." (I Tim. 2:1). There is the expression of appreciation, and then intercession, to bring before our heavenly Father the needs of all people. "I beseech Thee" is as central to worship as "I believe in Thee."

Man has a need for resolution, for he is a working spirit, a sharing creature, filled with compassion for others. Man has a determination to sacrifice, to give. He is able to do that which is beneficial for himself and others. *Ora et labora*, "Pray and work," said Martin Luther. Worship includes an offering—a commissioning for service. In work, worship finds its fulfillment (the word *liturgy* is derived from Greek words meaning "work of the people"; in English the word *service* has the happy double connotation of "worship" and "work"). The prophet Micah stated it well, confessing, "He hath shewed thee, O man, what is good; and what doth the LORD require of thee, but to do justly, and to love mercy, and to walk humbly with thy God?" (Mic. 6:8).

Worship is an obligatory human activity. It is mandatory, not voluntary. God commands worship, not because He is arbitrary but because He knows that it is necessary to the full development of our humanity. This is evident from a study of the sacred Scriptures.

A Biblical Imperative

Worship is a biblical imperative. This is made clear in the covenant made by God with Moses at Sinai. Three of the Ten

Commandments deal with worship.[1] The first commandment proscribes idolatry and prescribes piety, stating, "Thou shalt have no other gods before Me." Luther explained this injunction in the Small Catechism: "We should fear, love, and trust in God above all things." God alone is deserving of our total loyalty. The word *worship*, derived from the Anglo-Saxon word *weorthscipe*, means "the ascription of worth to any object, person, or group." God is the ultimate value. The second commandment prohibits blasphemy and promotes sanctity, stating, "Thou shalt not take the name of the Lord thy God in vain." Luther taught that "we should fear and love God so that we do not curse, swear, conjure, lie, or deceive by His name, but call upon Him in every time of need, and worship Him with prayer, praise, and thanksgiving." The third commandment, "Remember the Sabbath day, to keep it holy," commends worship and condemns spiritual indifference. Luther commented, "We should fear and love God so that we do not despise his Word and the preaching of the same, but deem it holy, and gladly hear and learn it." Luther believed that the first three commandments of the Decalogue inform us of our duty to God, or the service of God (*Gottesdienst*, which is a German name for the Lutheran service), just as the latter seven (the second table of the law) instruct us in our duty to our neighbor. The Mosaic code thus begins in worship and continues in work.

Worship is a biblical imperative. This is made clear in the covenant made by Christ in His ministry. A survey of the works and words of Jesus indicates that Christ commanded worship.

The works of Jesus reveal His high regard for worship. Christ fulfilled all the law perfectly, including the injunction to worship. As a child of twelve Jesus was in the temple (Luke 2:46). As an adult Jesus attended the synagogue regularly "as his custom was" (Luke 4:16). During His career Christ kept the holy days of Judaism (see John 2; 5; 7; 10; 12).

1. Lutherans and Roman Catholics number the Ten Commandments differently from Anglican and Reformed Christians. The prohibition against idolatry, counted as a second commandment by others, is included by Lutherans in the first commandment. The tenth commandment, proscribing coveting, is divided by Lutherans into two laws.

To those outside the Jewish covenant Jesus issued an invitation to "worship the Father in spirit and in truth: for the Father seeketh such to worship him" (John 4:23). Christ was born to the sound of angel songs and He died with the words of Psalm 22 upon his lips.

The words of Jesus reveal His high regard for worship. In the master prayer, or the model prayer, or the Lord's Prayer (also correctly called the disciples' prayer), Jesus taught as the initial petition, "Our Father . . . Hallowed be thy name" (Matt. 6:9; Luke 11:2). Jesus repeatedly urged His followers to pray, promising them, "Ask, and ye shall receive, that your joy may be full" (John 16:24).

Christ also instituted actions, which are called sacraments, that He commanded His followers to observe. During Passion Week, Jesus took bread and wine, blessed it, and distributed it to His disciples, saying, "This do in remembrance of me" (I Cor. 11:24). On the day of ascension, Christ added preaching and baptizing to communing as one of the three means of grace, for He said, "Go ye therefore, and teach all nations, baptizing them in the name of the Father, and of the Son, and of the Holy Ghost; Teaching them to observe all things whatsoever I have commanded you . . ." (Matt. 28:19–20). From the Master's mouth came the injunction to do those three things that now constitute the core of Christian worship—baptizing, preaching, and communing.

Worship is a biblical imperative. This is made clear by the conduct of the first Christians. The disciples obeyed the ordinances of Christ and received strengthening through them. From the pages of the New Testament it is clear that Christ established a ministry of Word and sacrament.

The earliest Christians had a ministry of the Word. It is obvious that the earliest believers assembled for worship. To neglect this community activity was condemned. The author of Hebrews noted, "Let us consider one another to provoke unto love and to good works: Not forsaking the assembling of ourselves together, as the manner of some is; but exhorting one another . . ." (Heb. 10:24–25). Such worship included intercession. When Peter was in prison, "prayer was made without ceasing of the church unto God for him" (Acts 12:5). Worship included adoration, for Paul urged the Colossians to keep "teaching and admonishing one another in psalms and hymns and spiritual songs, singing with grace in your hearts to the Lord" (Col. 3:16). Worship involved the reading and preaching of the Word, for the apostles went about "confirming the souls of the disciples, and exhorting them to continue in the faith" (Acts 14:22). Services were often held "upon the first day of the week" (Acts 20:7), and they contained announcements and reports, for the apostles "gathered the church together [and] rehearsed all that God had done with them" (Acts 14:27). Such meetings occasionally included the election and ordination of church officers (see Acts 14:23). Praying, singing, reading, teaching, preaching, reporting, sharing, and commissioning of leaders were some of the events that transpired during the service of the Word.

The earliest Christians had a ministry of the sacraments. According to the Book of Acts, the church was born with a mighty baptismal service, for "they that gladly received His Word were baptized: and the same day there were added unto them about three thousand souls" (Acts 2:41). Sometimes baptisms were individual, such as those of the Ethiopian eunuch by Philip (Acts 8:38) and of Paul by Ananias (Acts 9:18). Sometimes entire families were baptized, as were those of Cornelius (Acts 10:48), Lydia (Acts 16:15), and the Philippian jailer (Acts 16:33). Baptism could occur in private, but it seems normally to have happened in public, for it was not only a "washing of regeneration" (Titus 3:5) but also an open profession of faith and the rite of initiation into the congregation. The Lord's Supper, the rite of preservation, was also regularly observed by the first believers. Exegetes disagree if the term *breaking of bread* always refers to the Lord's Supper when it is used in the New Testament. Surely in many contexts the phrase is a synonym for the Eucharist. One such instance transpired in Troas when the church "came together to break bread" upon "the first day of the week" and "Paul preached unto them" (Acts 20:7). From the Pauline correspondence we learn that the Lord's Supper was universally observed in the churches. If the Corinthian congregation is representative, then the problem in earliest Christianity was not the neglect of the Eucharist but its abuse (see I Cor. 11). Churches throughout the Mediterranean world received life in "the communion of the blood of Christ . . . [and] the body of Christ" (I Cor. 10:16), and in the ministry of preaching, to "receive with meekness the engrafted word" (James 1:21). Worship was central to New Testament Christianity.

Principles of Evangelical Worship

Worship was commanded and conducted in the New Testament era. While the imperative is made clear, no detailed provisions are given for the conduct of public worship. This stands in marked contrast to the Old Testament, where divine decrees specify minutest details of liturgy, ceremony, hierarchy, and sanctuary. The spirit of Christ's covenant, in contrast to that of Moses, is one of liberty and creativity. While worship is mandatory, the manner in which one obeys the injunction is a matter of Christian freedom. Lutherans believe that there is no such thing in New Testament Christianity as one divinely ordained type of liturgy, ceremony, hierarchy, or sanctuary. While certain principles are prescribed, and worship is enjoined, believers are given freedom in the way in which they implement these commands.

It was the loss of this insight that, in the opinion of the reformers, led to certain of the corruptions of worship that occurred in the Middle Ages. A major task of the Protestant Reformation was the evaluation of the various ingredients of Christian worship to determine what elements were of divine institution. Certain guidelines were necessary in this process. From a careful reading of the New Testament, the Lutheran theologians established four principles that are now normative for evangelical worship.

Protestant worship involves participation. This was the expression of the evangelical principle of the universal priesthood of believers. It was based on the passage that spoke of Christians as "a chosen generation, a royal priesthood, an holy nation, a peculiar people; that ye should shew forth the praises of him who hath called you . . ." (I Peter 2:9). By virtue of baptism all disciples are of this priesthood. Biblical worship is the work of all, not the few. It is the solemn obligation and joyous responsibility of each Christian to be present in the assembly and to fulfill his function in this priesthood. Worship is a participatory event, not a spectator sport.

Protestant worship involves proclamation. This is the expression of the evangelical principle of *sola Scriptura*, or the primacy of the Word in all matters of faith and morals. Tradition, reason, experience, and private opinion, however valuable, are not to be given authority over the Word in the public worship of the people of God. Instruction is to be based on the Bible. This principle rests on such passages as Peter's statement, "We have also a more sure word of prophecy; whereunto ye do well that ye take heed, as unto a light that shineth in a dark place . . ." (II Peter 1:19). All that transpires in the Christian time of worship must be centered in the reading, teaching, and preaching of God's Word. Scripture is to be the source and norm for edification of the faithful. Worship is an occasion for the open proclamation of the Word, not the exercise of self-centered speculation.

Protestant worship involves celebration. This was the expression of the evangelical principle of *sola gratia*, or "grace alone," that man is saved apart from his works by the action of God. This divine initiative toward us involves baptism (our initiation into His church, incorporation into His body) and communion (our preservation in the true faith, feeding upon Christ). For the reformers, baptism and the Lord's Supper clearly taught and wrought salvation by grace alone through faith alone. Worship was to be sacramental, focusing on the divinely ordained means of grace. This drew on the Pauline literature, particuarly the apostle's counsel to the Corinthians, "But ye are washed, but ye are sanctified, but ye are justified in the name of the Lord Jesus, and by the Spirit of our God" (I Cor. 6:11). Worship stressed God's, not man's, contribution, for it was a celebration of His acts, not a recollection of man's works.

Protestant worship involves justification. This was the expression of the evangelical principle of *sola fides*, or "faith alone." The Lutheran confessors taught that man is made right with God by divine, not human, activity. According to the Apology of the Augsburg Confession, the cardinal doctrine of Christianity is that of "justification by grace alone received through faith."[2] This teaching is based on many proof passages, particularly the one through which the Holy Spirit enlightened Luther during his "tower experience." That passage reads, "For I am not ashamed of the gospel of Christ: for it is the power of God unto salvation to everyone that believeth; to the Jew first, and also to the Greek. For therein is the righteousness of God revealed from faith to faith: as it is written, The just shall live by faith" (Rom. 1:16–17).

Every evangelical service of worship must tell the story of salvation. A venerable Lutheran pastor, the late John O. Lang, told one of the authors in confirmation class, "Every sermon, no matter what its subject, must make clear at some point the way of salvation." Evangelical worship, to be worthy of its name, must teach the Good News. True worship is rooted and grounded in the doctrine of justification.

Utilizing the evangelical principles, the Lutheran reformers differentiated between the various elements involved in worship. Some are of the essence and being of evangelical worship, such as Word and sacrament. Some are not essential but are useful, contributing to the well-being of evangelical worship. These would include employing a liturgy and the church year and using a sanctuary. Some are absolutely harmful and contrary to the nature of Lutheran adoration, such as private masses, the invocation of saints, and prayers to the dead. Some, such as particular robes (the cope, for instance), chanting, or ceremonies, are nonessential, neither commanded by God nor forbidden, to be used at the discretion of the local church.

For practical purposes Lutheran scholars often made a simple twofold distinction. Some items have divine authorization. They are mandatory; for example, preaching, baptizing, and communing. Some items have a human origin. They are matters of Christian liberty, for they are *adiaphora*, "neutral things," which in and of themselves are neither for nor against the Word of God (candles and incense, for example). In the matters of adiaphora the Lutheran church has traditionally allowed considerable variety, for "it is not

2. Apology of the Augsburg Confession, article 4.

necessary for the true unity of the Christian church that ceremonies, instituted by men, should be observed uniformly in all places."[3]

The History of Lutheran Worship

Because of these evangelical principles and due to immigration of Lutherans from various parts of Europe, Lutheran worship in America has tended in the past to exhibit considerable diversity. Some sections of the church have been very free, others rather formal. Norwegian immigrants of the Haugean or pietistic tradition emphasized informality. "New Measures" Lutherans in the nineteenth century embraced revivalism. The Dutch Lutherans in the colonial New Netherlands were moderately liturgical, with a service similar to that of their Reformed neighbors. The Pennsylvania Germans stressed expository preaching and experiential worship. The Swedes of Delaware brought with them the vestments and customs of the High Mass as it was celebrated in Uppsala. As immigration to the United States from Europe continued, even more variety came to characterize Lutheran worship.

While there has been a movement toward uniformity in liturgy in the nineteenth and twentieth centuries, both authors have witnessed simple services in Lutheran churches where there were no robes, no ritual, and no elaborate sanctuary. But there was the primacy of the Word, the teaching of God's saving grace, and the administration of the sacraments. It was Lutheran worship. Both authors have also observed very elaborate services in Lutheran churches where there were the historic mass vestments, a high altar, considerable ceremony, elaborate texts, and much symbolism. But there also was the exaltation of the Scriptures, the celebration of the sacraments, and the proclamation of justification. It was Lutheran worship. Lutheranism can comprehend a wide variety of modes of worship as long as the fundamental principles of the Reformation are not compromised. The majority of America's Lutherans today are neither Low Church

3. The Augsburg Confession, article 7.

nor High Church. In their worship practices they follow a via media between the informality of evangelicalism and the formality of Anglo-Catholicism.

Luther's worship practices are known. Even before there was a Lutheran Confession, there was a Lutheran service. It was not until 1530 that Lutheranism produced the Augsburg Confession, yet already in 1523 it had prepared the first order of Lutheran worship. This initial experiment by Luther was known as the *Formula Missae* and was in Latin. Three years later the reformer introduced the German Mass (*die deutsche Messe*). What Luther did as a conservative reformer was to retain the Mass of the Catholic Church, with its two great sections inherited from earliest Christianity, the Service of the Word and the Service of the Altar. However, Luther did make some basic changes in order to eliminate those elements and emphases that he felt were incompatible with the gospel. The result was to be a service of worship that was Catholic in form and evangelical in content.

The Service of the Word was maintained with certain subtractions and additions. Luther eliminated all things that tended to detract from the primacy of the Scriptures, such as the legends, stories, and myths that often received so much attention in medieval piety. Prayers for the dead and to the saints were removed. To the service Luther added the singing of hymns. Since participatory worship was his goal, Luther translated the service into the vernacular, made provision for congregational responses in the various versicles of the liturgy, and added the singing of chorales, carols, and spiritual songs. In the absence of a suitable hymnody, Luther himself compiled the first Lutheran hymnal, the *Book of Eight Hymns* (*Achtliederbuch*). A poet, Luther was to write many hymns, including "A Mighty Fortress Is Our God," "Lord, Keep Us Steadfast in Thy Word," and "Dear Christians, One and All Rejoice." Luther insisted on the generous reading of the Scriptures in the service (soon to be done from his own German translation of the Bible). In much of this Luther seemed to anticipate many of the changes of Vatican II, 400 years later.

A lengthy sermon on a suitable text was delivered. Some

thought that length was almost mandatory. Sometimes Luther's peers preached for more than an hour. Since it became the custom to take an hourglass along into the pulpit, a preacher sometimes would stop at the end of sixty minutes, hold up the timepiece, and inquire of the congregation, "Shall we tip another glass?" Philip Melanchthon was more humane, as his hourglass timed only forty-five minutes. After preaching would come the prayer of the church, often with responsive portions for the congregation.

The Service of the Altar was also maintained, with certain subtractions and additions. Luther eradicated all notions of the Lord's Supper as a good work that man performed to merit favor. He eliminated the concept of a bloodless sacrifice and denied the doctrine of transubstantiation (see chapter 4). Luther also abolished such extrabiblical customs as the reservation apart from use and the procession of the consecrated host. The cup was restored to the laity. Luther's eucharistic reforms involved addition as well as subtraction. A strong emphasis was placed on the Lord's Supper as a proclamation of the death and resurrection of Jesus Christ for "us men and our salvation." For Luther the words of institution were not a magical formula, but a mighty affirmation directed to humanity, clearly stating the justification of the sinner by grace alone. Luther also stressed the communing, in both kinds (bread and wine), of all those adults in good standing in the parish. Emphasizing the real presence of Christ in the Supper, Luther insisted that communicants examine themselves, lest they receive unworthily and bring condemnation, not benediction, upon themselves. Luther encouraged frequent communion. This was in opposition to the medieval practice when often the laity received the elements only once a year, usually on Easter. All the changes made by Luther were to emphasize the proclamation of the Good News of salvation by "grace alone through faith."

The Lutheran Liturgy Today

Unlike Anglicanism, which has a uniform *Book of Common Prayer*, Lutheranism has never elevated Luther's service to a normative position. Undoubtedly its influence was formative to the literally hundreds of Lutheran church orders that were developed in Europe. Adaptation, however, was done in the spirit of liberty, not conformity. American settlers usually brought with them the orders of service of their native land. The patriarch of Colonial Lutheranism, Henry Melchior Muhlenberg, attempted to introduce a uniform service in 1748 during the first meeting of the United Pastors (or United Congregations; it later became the Pennsylvania Ministerium). Based on the Savoy Liturgy used by the expatriate Lutheran congregation in London, it was a composite of many of the finest Lutheran and Anglican liturgies of the time. Though Muhlenberg offered America's Lutherans a good model, it was not widely employed. After a century and a half of experimentation, a common service in the English language was commended to the American churches in 1888 by an intersynodical committee. This was to win almost universal acceptance by 1980. It was published in the *Service Book and Hymnal* of 1958 (used by more than two thirds of America's Lutherans), and in *The Lutheran Hymnal* of 1941 (used by the Synodical Conference, representing the remaining third of American Lutherans). In spite of the experimentation of the 1960s and 1970s, involving innovations and textual alterations, the common service remains the classic Lutheran liturgy in the English language.

Lutheran worship may be called by many names—"the Liturgy" (literally, "the work of the people"), "the Divine Liturgy," "the Service," or occasionally "the Mass." The Lutheran liturgy, as it exists in the common service, is composed of two parts. (Refer to Figure 5).

First is the Service of the Word, the ancient Mass of the Catechumens, which had its origin in the service in the Jewish synagogue. Open to all—members, inquirers, and visitors—this part of the liturgy is evangelistic and educational in orientation, climaxing in the exposition of the Scripture in the sermon.

The Service of the Word is preceded by a preparatory rite, the Office of Public Confession, which enables people to make the transition from the world to the Word. It is the textual equivalent to the narthex in church architecture. Confession

Figure 5 **A Lutheran Liturgy for Communion**

Preparation

Organ Prelude
Hymn
Invocation
The Confession of Sins
- Invitation
- Confession
- Absolution

Part One—The Service of the Word

The Introit
The Gloria Patri
The Kyrie
The Gloria in Excelsis
The Salutation
The Collect
The Readings
- The Lesson
- The Epistle
- (The Gradual)
- The Holy Gospel

The Creed (Apostles' or Nicene)
The Hymn of the Day
The Sermon
The Offertory
The Prayer of the Church

Part Two—The Service of the Altar

The Preface
- Salutation
- Versicles
- Proper Preface

Sanctus
(Eucharistic Prayer)
The Words of Institution
The Lord's Prayer
Salutation and Agnus Dei
Distribution of the Elements
The Post-Communion
- Nunc Dimittis
- Prayers

Benediction
Hymn
Organ Postlude

provides a time of transition from secular to sacred concerns. This rite places immediately, at the very start of the service, a proclamation of the central Lutheran doctrine of justification by grace alone. Lutheran Christians commence worship with an acknowledgment of sin, a declaration of pardon, a prayer for power, and a resolution for "the amendment of life."

A rite of prayer and praise comes next. Starting with an introit (Latin for "he enters"), a portion of a psalm either sung by the choir or spoken by the minister, it continues with the singing of the Gloria Patri, an ancient Christian hymn to the Trinity. The Kyrie, an intercessory prayer by pastor and people for the peace of the world and the welfare of the church, comes next. The name *Kyrie* is reminiscent of the cry of blind Bartimaeus, *Kyrie eleison*, "Lord have mercy" (see Mark 10:47). It also brings to mind the Greek origins of the church and thus the church's catholic quality.

Then the greater Gloria, or the Gloria in Excelsis, is chanted by minister and congregation: "Glory be to God on high . . . ." This venerable hymn was inspired by the song of the angel choir on the first Christmas Eve, for the "multitude of the heavenly host [was] praising God, and saying, Glory to God in the highest, and on earth, peace, good will toward men" (Luke 2:13–14). The rite of prayer and praise concludes with the salutation, a personal greeting by the minister to the people, and their response; and the collect, a concise prayer that literally "collects" the various themes of the service that day.

The Service of the Word climaxes in the reading and exposition of the sacred Scriptures. Traditionally three lections are read: a lesson, a promise of God from the Old Testament; an epistle, instruction from God through an apostle; and the holy Gospel (for which the people stand), a proclamation of the words and works of Jesus in the writings of an evangelist. To this recitation of the Word of God the congregation responds in affirmation, with the confession of faith, normally in the words of the Apostles' Creed, when communion does not follow. On eucharistic occasions, the Nicene Creed is used. After the hymn of the day, one sermon is delivered, which is often an exposition of some portion of the Scripture previously read.

The Service of the Word concludes in sharing. The offertory is sung, normally the prayer of David, "Create in me a clean heart, O God" (Psalm 51:10–12). The offering is received, as the faithful respond once more to the proclamation of the Word, this time not simply in words, as in the creed, but in deeds, with gifts. At this point there may be an offertory procession as the tithes and offerings are presented at the altar. All join in a general prayer, or the prayer of the church, which is liturgy, or "the work of the people," par excellence. Intercession is made for the church and its ministry, evangelists, and missionaries, the nation and its leaders, schools and shops, farms and factories, homes and offices, all those who suffer affliction of mind and body, and those who are persecuted for the faith; thanksgiving is offered for God's mercies in creation, redemption, and sanctification; and those who have died in the faith are remembered with affection. If there is no communion, the Lord's Prayer is spoken, a hymn of praise may be sung, the benediction is pronounced, and, usually, to the sound of a recessional hymn, the congregation departs.

In the ancient church, at the end of the general prayer the Mass of the Catechumens ended. Those under instruction (catechumens), those under age (children), those under discipline (for offense in faith or life), and those who were not members of the church were dismissed. What followed was regarded as uniquely Christian worship. This service is retained as the second part of the Lutheran liturgy.

This second part of the liturgy is the Service of the Altar, the ancient Mass of the Faithful. It had its origin in the upper room when Jesus celebrated the Last Supper with His disciples (Matt. 26:26–29; Mark 14:22–25; Luke 22:17–19). It has many names, including the Supper, the Last Supper, the Lord's Supper, the Sacrament, Holy or Blessed Sacrament, Sacrament of the Altar, the Eucharist or Thanksgiving, Communion or Holy Communion, the Breaking of Bread, the Service of the Table, and the Mass proper. Lutherans continue the early Christian tradition of "close communion," that is, of admitting to the sacrament only those who believe in Jesus Christ, who are baptized and of age, who are conscious of what they are about to do, who lament their sins and resolve to receive Christ in a worthy manner and to lead a life that glorifies God.

The Service of the Altar has three parts.

There is a service of preparation. This includes a salutation, or greeting by the presiding minister to the people, a series of versicles inviting the faithful to adoration, a proper preface (an appropriate sentence for the season), and the singing of the ancient hymn, the *Sanctus*, "Holy, holy, holy, Lord God of Sabaoth, Heaven and earth are full of thy glory . . . ," reminiscent of Isaiah's vision of God in the Temple (Isa. 6).

There is the service of consecration and distribution of the elements. This involves the *Verba*, or the words of institution ("Our Lord Jesus Christ, in the night in which he was betrayed . . ."), perhaps a prayer of thanksgiving (eucharistic prayer), the Lord's Prayer, the sharing of the peace of God, the singing of the *Agnus Dei* ("O Christ, Thou Lamb of God, that takest away the sin of the world, have mercy upon us . . ."), and the reception of the sacrament by the communicants. Among Lutherans it is customary for the faithful to come forward and receive at the communion rail, either standing or kneeling.

There is a service of dismissal. This contains the *Nunc Dimittis*, the song of Simeon (Luke 2:29–32), "Lord, now lettest thou they servant depart in peace, according to thy word: For mine eyes have seen thy salvation. . . ." Prayers of gratitude and versicles of praise are offered, the benediction is spoken, and the people depart, usually after singing a recessional hymn.

The liturgy is the most common form of worship. There also are occasional services, such as baptism, confirmation, ordination, marriage, public and private confession, burial of the dead, and the installation of clergy and elders, deacons, and other officers. These may occur either in the context of the liturgy or independently.

Reading Psalm 119:164, "Seven times a day do I praise thee," early Christians, adding to this, decided to establish eight hours of daily prayers—matins, lauds, prime, terce, sext, none, vespers, and compline. Of these, two—matins and vespers—are common in Lutheran congregations. Luther adapted all the offices to the needs of participatory evangelical worship (in contrast to the way in which the eight hours were often kept in monasteries). In Lutheran colleges, seminaries, and retreat centers, many or all of the eight hours are still observed. Lutherans also worship at home, both privately and as a family. To the Small Catechism, Luther appended "Morning and Evening Prayer" for domestic use as well as "Blessing and Thanksgiving" to be said at mealtimes. Informal prayer is always appropriate. Lutherans seek to be a worshiping people, trying in all times and places to obey the observation of Jesus "that men ought always to pray, and not to faint" (Luke 18:1).

Customs in Lutheran Churches

A custom is a practice followed as a matter of course. All worshiping communities have customs. These may be intentional or accidental. They may be useful or harmful. In any circumstance, customs are inevitable. Decency and good order require that public worship proceed according to a predictable pattern. While Christ Himself did not specifically establish many such customs, He did command His people to worship. During the centuries the church has devised certain practices that facilitate public worship. No one claims these were necessarily instituted by Jesus. But many feel that they are extremely beneficial to us as we seek to be faithful in our adoration of God. Space prohibits a discussion of all the customs that one might see observed in a Lutheran church. Let us, therefore, consider five types of customs that are fairly common—those pertaining to time, leadership, ceremonies, vestments, and places of worship.

In the old covenant God decreed that worship be held at certain times, especially on the Sabbath, the seventh day. In the new covenant, living under the liberty of Christ, believers are free to worship on any day they choose. One of the authors resided in Iran for a year. There the churches held their services on Friday because it was the day of rest in that Muslim nation. This was perfectly acceptable. Lutherans do not believe that there is a Christian Sabbath, for Paul wrote to the church at Colosse, "Let no man therefore judge you in meat, or in drink, or in respect to an holyday, or of the new moon, or of the sabbath days; Which are a shadow of things to come; but the body is of Christ" (Col. 2:16–17). While it is commanded that Christians ought to worship, no one day has been prescribed for that purpose.

The weight of Christian tradition, however, supports Sunday as the preferred day of worship. Certainly believers may worship on Friday (as do Christians in Iran) or on Saturday (as do Seventh-Day Adventists), but the majority of Christians have always met on Sunday. Sunday, the day on which God the Father began creation, God the Son rose from the dead, and God the Holy Spirit descended on Pentecost, has a trinitarian significance for the faithful. Every Sunday is a new creation, another Easter, another birthday of the church. Biblical evidence suggests that it was usual for the earliest Christians to worship on "the first day" (Acts 20:7). The Lord's Day, or Sunday, was not a Sabbath in the Jewish sense. The faithful met for worship, then went to work.

Through the centuries the Christian church developed its own calendar for the year. The church year attempts to present in systematic fashion the main events and teachings of the faith. Luther found this ordering of time to be useful. He reformed and then retained the church year. Today it is kept almost universally among Lutherans.

The Christian year (refer to Figure 6) has two parts.

The festival portion commemorates the life of Jesus Christ. It commences with Advent, a season emphasizing the four comings of Christ—in prophecy to the Hebrews, in history when Jesus was born of Mary, in the means of grace to the church today, and in the future, when "He shall come again, with glory, to judge both the quick and the dead. . . ."

Christmas honors the incarnation of Christ. Epiphany concentrates on the life and ministry of Jesus, how by word and deed He manifested the glory of God (The word *epiphany* means "shining forth" or "manifestation"). Lent, or Passiontide, is a season of forty days set aside to recall the cost of our salvation. Meditation on the suffering and death of Christ is in order. Beginning on Ash Wednesday, a day of penitence, Lent continues through the events of Holy Week—Palm Sunday, Maundy Thursday, Good Friday, and Holy Saturday. Easter begins a time of forty days of joy celebrating the resurrection of Christ (it is a counterpart to Lent). Pentecost,

Figure 6 **The Church Year**

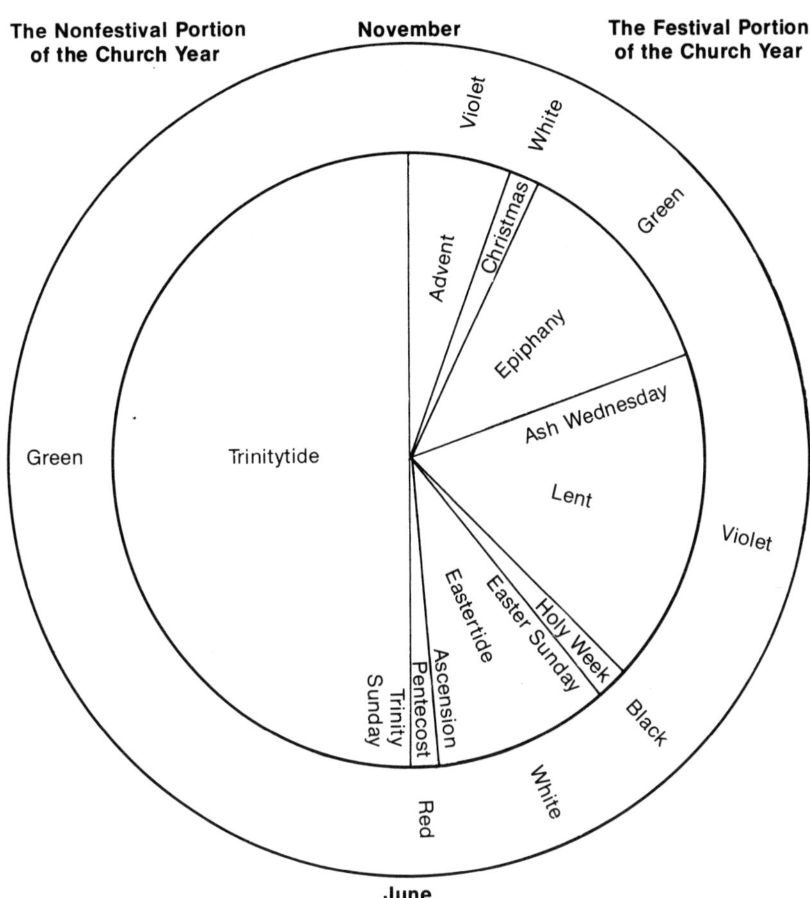

the Sunday fifty days after Easter, recalls how the ascended Christ sent the Holy Spirit upon His disciples and the Christian church was born. Ascension Day marks the coronation of Christ as Lord of heaven and earth. With it the festival half of the year draws within fifty days of its end.

The nonfestival portion of the church year celebrates the work of the Christian church. From Pentecost to Advent the emphasis is on the work of God through the means of grace in His church for the salvation of the world. Sometimes this lengthy season is called Kingdomtide—for it is about the growth of the kingdom of God. More customary is to name it Pentecost season or Trinitytide, if the season is reckoned from Trinity Sunday.

Lutherans have a strong sense of time. For that reason other events may be observed in a Lutheran congregation. These are of four types.

Great events of church history may be commemorated. Biblical saints—especially New Testament personalities such as apostles and evangelists—are often honored. Heroes and heroines of postbiblical church history may be remembered. Reformation Day, October 31, is set aside to recall the Reformation, through Luther, of the church in the sixteenth century. All Saints' Day, November 1, is retained as a time to give thanks for all, great and small, who have borne the name *Christian*. One day, Saint Michael and All Angels, September 29, is kept to remind us that we in the church militant are not alone in our struggle against evil, but live in a radically supernatural universe.

Great events of national history may be commemorated. Paul commanded prayer for those in authority. In Europe Lutherans often held worship on the birthday of the king or the emperor. In the United States Lutherans frequently worship on days set aside by this republic for prayer. Among the national holidays that may be observed in a Lutheran church are Thanksgiving Day, Independence Day, Memorial Day, and any other occasion set aside by the government (such as a presidential call for a day of prayer and penitence.) Though citizens of heaven, Lutherans realize they are also citizens of an earthly nation, and they seek in all ways, including worship of God, to fulfill their pledge of due respect to the state.

Great events within the year of nature may be commemorated. The historic church year includes several occasions when God is praised for the beauty and bounty of nature. Within the church special services are held to honor God for His work in creation, including harvest festivals, Rogation, or planting festivals. Like Paul, Lutherans confess in both word and worship that God "left not himself without witness, in that he did good, and gave us rain from heaven, and fruitful seasons, filling our hearts with food and gladness" (Acts 14:17).

Great events within the community may require commemoration. During times of social distress and natural calamity, Lutherans pray. Services during times of fire, flood, war, famine, and drought are known, as are services for peace, justice, and brotherhood. Happier occasions also call for special services—church convocations, synodical conventions, graduation at church-related educational institutions, or the installation of a minister and church officers. Services of dedication for church facilities, festivals of missions and evangelism, and celebrations of all sorts occur within the context of the congregation. With the psalmist of old, Lutherans can say, "I will bless the LORD at all times; his praise shall continually be in my mouth" (Ps. 34:1).

Another cluster of Lutheran customs concerns leadership in worship. The word *liturgy* means "ministry." This underscores a basic evangelical principle—the priesthood of all believers. Participation by all in public worship is an exercise of this priesthood of the laity. Certainly all Lutherans take part in worship through the responsive portions of the liturgy and in the singing of hymns. To further emphasize Lutheran worship as the worship of God by the people and for the people, the laity are encouraged to render "special service" during the service. Some share talents. Music is usually provided by an organist, choirs, and often by vocalists and instrumentalists. Some Lutheran churches have had chamber orchestras.

Other laity help in different ways. Acolytes light candles, receive the offering plates, and otherwise assist the clergy. Banner and flag bearers, as well as crucifers, are not unknown. Laymen as lectors may publicly read the Scriptures. Sometimes parts of the liturgy are led by a layman or a seminary student. Deacons and elders may serve in a variety of functions—seating members of the congregation, ushering people forward for communion, or assisting in the distribution of the Lord's Supper. On occasion a layman may deliver the sermon. Normally preaching and the consecration of the elements used in the Lord's Supper are reserved for ordained clergymen. Nearly all other duties within the liturgy are shared with the laity.

A number of ceremonies may accompany Lutheran worship. Some of these involve physical posture. During the long history of biblical religion, many modes of prayer have been employed. Prostration was known in the East; lifting the hands to heaven was common in the West. Normally in a Lutheran service three postures are observed, each with a different significance: standing for praise or respect, sitting for instruction, and kneeling for prayer is a helpful rule. A variety of other liturgical actions may be in evidence—processionals and recessionals, making the sign of the cross, veiling the crucifix for Lent, distributing palms on Palm Sunday, or marking with ashes on Ash Wednesday. In these and many other ways, Lutherans seek to worship God not only with words but also by the very movement of their bodies.

Vestments are normally worn during a Lutheran service. Robes are not mandatory in the church of the New Testament as they were in that of the old covenant. Furthermore, unlike the law of Moses, which specifies priestly attire in some detail, the New Testament allows complete liberty in this area. Traditionally, however, vestments are recommended to the minister. The gown becomes the symbol of the office. Once it is worn, one is able to differentiate between the person and the parson. Once vested for the service, the minister speaks no longer simply as an individual but as the spokesman of God and the representative of the community. This may be shown by the robe. Just as the uniforms of the doctor, nurse, policeman, and fireman indicate their duties, some Lutheran pastors wear a clerical collar (Anglican or Roman) and a black vest (rabat) so that they may be identified as clergy by those who may need their services. Most Lutheran ministers vest for the liturgy. Two types of vestments may be seen in a Lutheran church, depending on what aspect of the ministerial office the pastor wishes to represent.

Academic gowns were for a long time almost universal in American Lutheran churches. Representative of the highest earned degree (bachelor's, master's, or doctor's) of the clergyman, the university robe testified to the minister's educational qualifications and his competence to be a public expositor of the Word. The man was often quite literally a doctor of the church (the word *doctor* is Latin for "teacher").

Education has always been highly valued in the Lutheran

church and rightfully so, since the Reformation began in the university and was led by professors. The academic gown (refer to Figure 7) is usually black, though there are blue and red doctoral robes, and may be worn with velvet frontals, a collar and tabs, and a hood. The doctor's gown also has velvet bars on each sleeve. This robe is reminiscent of the philosopher's robe often worn by preachers in the early church and the doctor's gown used by Luther. The academic gown indicates the minister's role as teacher and preacher and identifies him as a servant of the Word, one in the prophetic tradition. The Geneva gown appears to be a descendent of this type of vestment. Academic robes, hoods, and colors are now standardized in the United States according to an academic code.

Communion vestments (see Figure 8) are now common within Lutheranism. They indicate the minister's role as president of the eucharistic assembly, the celebrant of the Lord's Supper. White, as with the vestments of the priests of Israel, is indicative of the pastor's place as a servant of the altar, one in the sacerdotal or priestly tradition. Communion vestments vary. One basic garment is the cassock, a black robe reaching from the neck to the ankles. Over this may be worn either a surplice or an alb. Both the surplice and the alb are white robes, but they differ in length, shape, and cut. A surplice reaches below the knees and has large, flowing sleeves. An alb always extends to the ankles and fits more closely than a surplice. Today some clergy wear an alba, a modification of the alb that makes the wearing of a cassock unnecessary. Over the surplice or alb a stole may be worn. Symbolic of the yoke of Christ, it varies in color according to the liturgical season. Cassock, surplice, and stole are undoubtedly the most commonly worn vestments in American Lutheranism today.

Full mass vestments are becoming more common (see Figure 9). Over the alb or alba, with its stole and cincture (a girdle or a belt), is placed a chausable, a poncholike vestment. It is worn only by the officiant at a communion service. Within Lutheranism one will find considerable diversity in vestments, sometimes within the same service. (The preacher may wear his doctor's robe, the celebrant may don his mass

Figure 7
Doctoral Robe and Hood

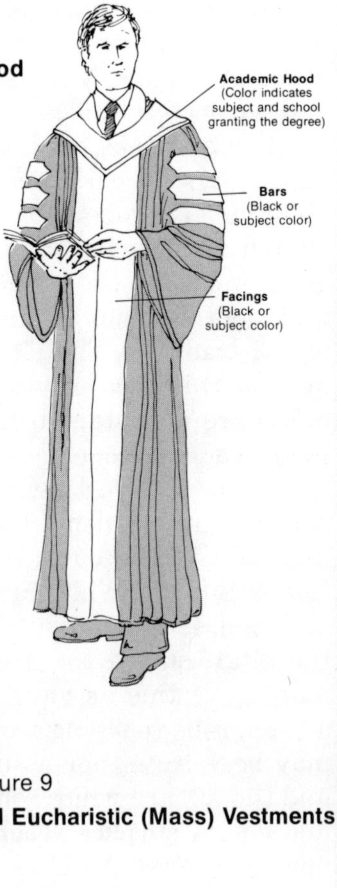

Academic Hood
(Color indicates subject and school granting the degree)

Bars
(Black or subject color)

Facings
(Black or subject color)

Figure 8
Communion and Preaching Vestments

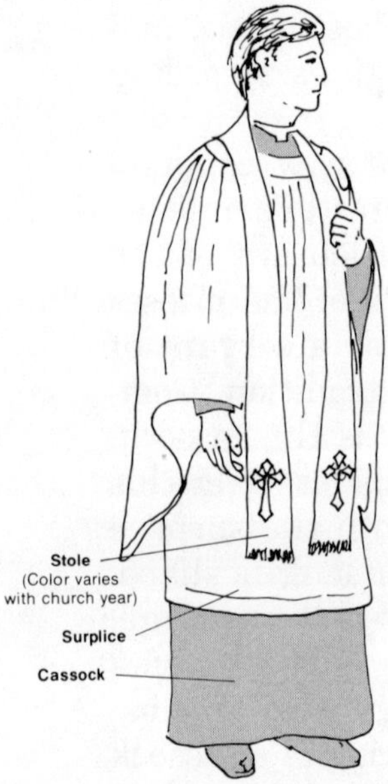

Stole
(Color varies with church year)

Surplice

Cassock

Figure 9
Full Eucharistic (Mass) Vestments

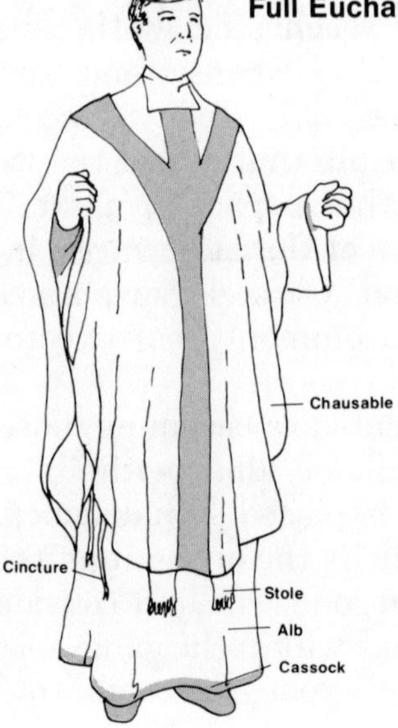

Chausable

Cincture

Stole

Alb

Cassock

vestments, the liturgist may be attired in cassock, surplice, and stole. Each uses what is symbolic of his function in the liturgy that day.) Within the confines of good taste Lutheranism rejoices in this liberty.

Symbolism is also reflected in the place of worship. The importance of architectual symbolism is evidenced by the elaborate plans revealed by God for the tabernacle and the temple. Within the New Testament liberty is allowed. Jesus preached not only in synagogues and the temple, but also on the mount, in the plain, by the seashore, the riverside, and the well, at the edge of the desert, in the marketplace, and on the highway. For several centuries Christians could not build churches and worshiped wherever they could—private homes, catacombs, and public halls. From the Roman basilica, or public hall, evolved the earliest patterns for the Christian church. Through the subsequent millennia believers have experimented with many forms. Lutherans in Europe inherited much Roman Catholic architecture. Lutherans in America worshiped wherever they could, in fields, homes, barns, courthouses, schools, and even butcher shops! As prosperity permitted, America's Lutherans built churches that normally reflected the fashion of the age. Among the multitude of architectural styles, the most prevalent are Georgian or Colonial, Romanesque and Gothic, and modern or contemporary. Contrary to much popular opinion, there is no such thing as Lutheran church architecture. Any style that is aesthetically pleasing, economically feasible, and functional in terms of the programs of the parish is acceptable. (For a sampling of typical floor plans, refer to the figures.)

Regardless of style employed, the floor plan of a Lutheran church frequently follows a threefold pattern that indicates a progression of the people of God from the world to the kingdom. A narthex or vestibule, a place of transition from the street to the sanctuary, corresponds to the rite of preparation and the introit in the text of the liturgy. A nave is a place for the gathering and seating of the congregation. A chancel is where the leaders of worship function.

Within the chancel there are often several pieces of furniture that are used for functions at different points during the service. There is a pulpit, reading desk, or ambo for

Unaisled Cruciform Plan

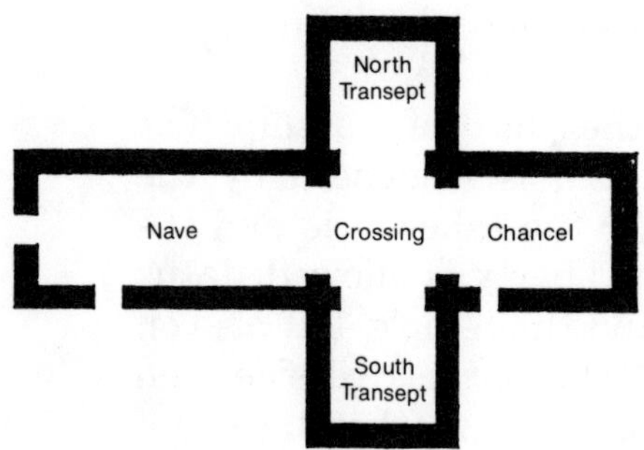

An Aisled Cruciform Plan

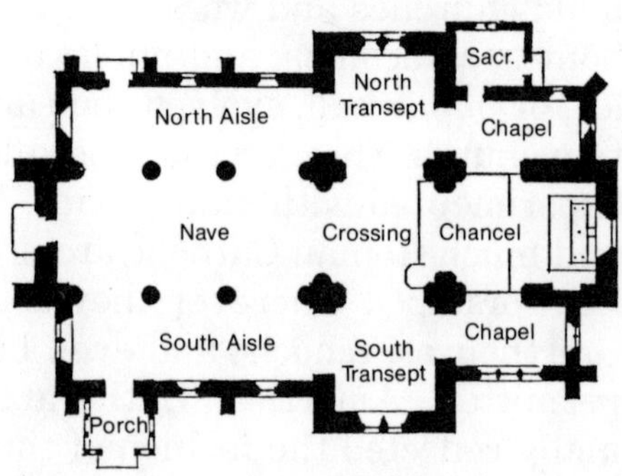

A Typical Post-war Plan

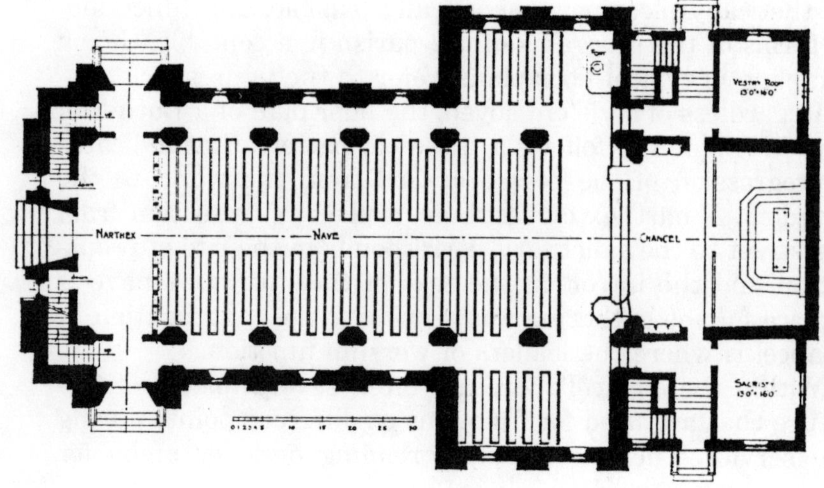

Muhlenberg College Chapel, Allentown, PA, The Plan
Frank R. Watson, Edkins & Thompson, Architects
Ruhe & Lange, Associated Architects

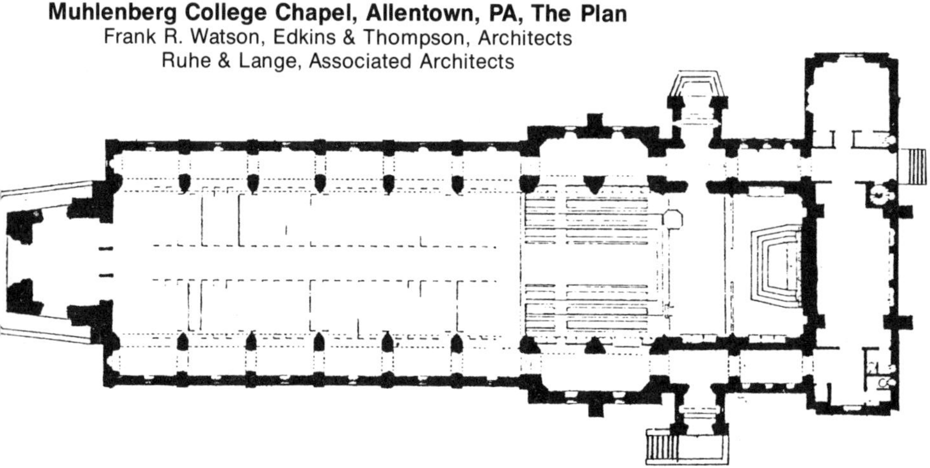

Saint Dominic's, Procter, VT
Maginnis & Walsh, Architects

A typical Catholic plan, with side altars and confessionals.

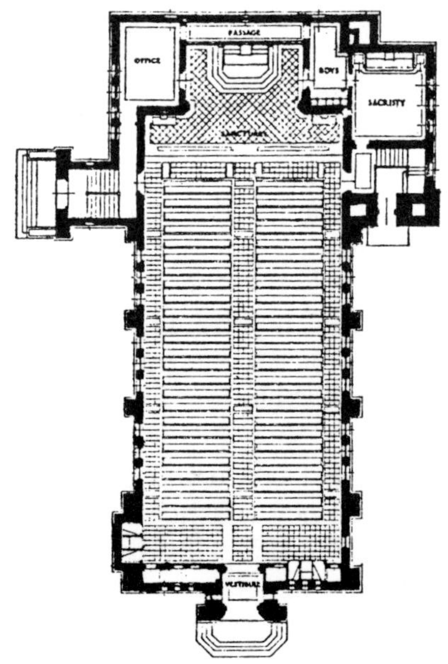

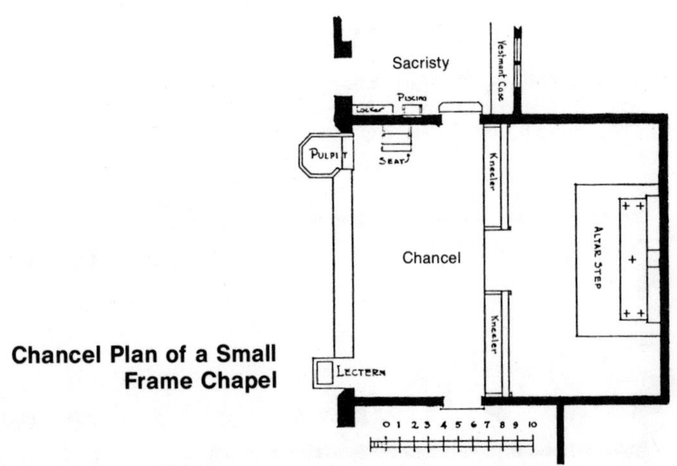

Chancel Plan of a Small Frame Chapel

preaching, and a lectern for the reading of the Scriptures. In a "divided chancel," pulpit and lectern are on opposite sides of the chancel so that attention may focus on the altar in the center.

Because Christians offer the sacrifice of prayer, praise and thanksgiving, and tithes and offerings, Lutherans have retained the term *altar*. The altar (shown in Figure 10) is the focus for the service of communion. A baptismal font is often evident, sometimes placed at the steps leading from the nave to the chancel, suggesting baptism's role as the initiatory sacrament into the Christian life. The four main items of furniture in a Lutheran chancel—pulpit, lectern, altar, and font—suggest in wood and stone what Lutherans teach in words: that God works in us through Word and sacrament. The very plan of the church and its appointments proclaim in symbols the theology that is taught there.

Many other items may be evident in a Lutheran church, such as pictures, statues, bells, candles, sanctuary lamps, a credence table for the offerings, kneeling benches, and pews for clergy and laity. Whatever is present must be both functional and beautiful. It ought not in any way detract from the primacy of the Word and the centrality of the sacraments. Traditionally Lutherans have not been fond of either cluttered sanctuaries filled with useless decorations or bare chapels that reduce a church to a mere auditorium with a speaker's stand in the front.

Christian faith is a response of the total person to the goodness of God in Christ. It involves words and deeds. When these are directed toward man, we have mission. When these are directed toward God, we have worship. Within the directives given us by the Scriptures, Christians have considerable freedom. Liturgy, ceremony, symbols, and vestments all are employed not because we must but because we may. Given the divine initiative of Word and sacrament, the Holy Spirit has allowed believers the opportunity to exercise sanctified reason in all other matters pertaining to worship. In one of the most beautiful and compelling passages in the New Testament, Jesus discussed worship with an outsider, the woman at the well. The Samaritan woman, like many novices in the faith, felt that religion must be a matter of many rules and much regulation. Surely God must have pre-

Figure 10 **An Altar and Its Paraments**
Showing the three coverings that lie at all times upon the properly vested altar.

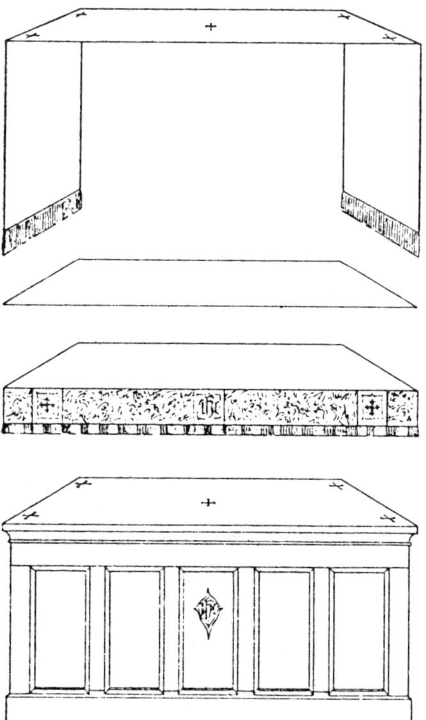

scribed in an elaborate manner all the details of worship. When the Master was asked about such matters, He predicted that "... the hour cometh, and now is, when the true worshippers shall worship the Father in spirit and in truth: for the Father seeketh such to worship him" (John 4:23). That hour is now. Let us honor it as Christ has suggested.

PART THREE

A Way of Becoming

Thou art the Life:
The rending tomb proclaims Thy conquering
  arm;
And those who put their trust in Thee
  Nor death nor hell shall harm.

George W. Doane

CHAPTER

7

The Calling of God

I believe . . . in one Lord Jesus Christ . . . whose kingdom shall have no end.

James, the brother of our Lord, asked a profound question in his general epistle: "What is your life?" (James 4:14). The saint did not inquire about believing or belonging, but about living. This is not to say that creed and church were insignificant for James, but his emphasis in this letter is on conduct—a life filled to overflowing with significance. To James, the challenge to the Christian is to fulfill the calling of God, showing, like Abraham, "how faith wrought . . . works, and by works was faith made perfect" (James 2:22).

Vocation, the doctrine of calling, is important for Lutherans. With James, Lutherans seek to find ways in which to live lives that are significant for God and man. This is done by faith. To Lutherans the calling of Christ involves a paradox. The Master normally does not call us out of the world. Occasionally, as in the case of the rich young ruler, Christ may command a person to "sell all that thou hast, and distribute unto the poor, . . . and come, follow me" (Luke 18:22). This is the exception, not the norm, even in the New Testament. To the healed Gadarene, who wished to forsake all to follow his Savior, Jesus said, "Return to thine own house, and shew how great things God hath done unto thee" (Luke 8:39). After his call, Peter remained married, paid taxes to Caesar, and plied the fishing trade. After his call, Paul stayed single, enjoyed Roman citizenship, continued to teach and make tents, and relaxed by watching athletic contests or reading classical literature. After their visitation, Lazarus,

Henry Melchior Muhlenberg

(1711–1787)
Patriarch of Colonial Lutheranism

Mary, and Martha still dwelt in their home in Bethany, obeyed the governor of Judaea, and retained the ordinary routine of life. For most of us, our faith is to be lived out in the world. Conversely, the calling of Christ changes everything. Paul confessed, "If any man be in Christ, he is a new creature," for "old things are passed away; behold, all things are become new" (II Cor. 5:17). Peter spoke of the Christian calling as a rebirth, comparing believers with "newborn babes" (I Peter 2:2). Saint John the Divine heard the ascended Christ promise, "Behold, I make all things new" (Rev. 21:5). While the external circumstances of our lives may not be altered, our interior condition is. As Paul testified to the Colossians, "Your life is hid with Christ in God" (Col. 3:3).

For Lutherans, the question of James, "What is your life?", is answered in this way: we live *in* the world *by* faith *for* Christ.

Since the Reformation, Lutheran theologians have identified four natural orders or estates in which we ordinarily live.[1] These distinct dimensions of life provide physical, social, intellectual, and spiritual benefits to all persons, regardless of race, creed, sex, or nationality. They are part of God's common grace in creation. While these orders were established before the fall, and continue to flourish in all societies, they have become distorted. The normal Christian vocation is to renovate these relationships so that God may be glorified and man may be edified through them. For that reason Lutherans have practiced their faith in these natural orders: the family, the state, work, and culture. (Figure 11 illustrates this principle.) It is the purpose of this chapter to explain how that calling is fulfilled. One of these orders, the family, is primary; the other three are derivatory. Let us consider both the family and the orders of society.

The Family

The Bible is many things. It is, among others, a love story. It starts with a couple, Adam and Eve, deeply in love, sur-

1. The church is sometimes added as a fifth natural order. As the "ark of salvation" and "the body of Christ," we believe the church is in a different category from the other natural orders. For that reason we have treated it in chapter 5, "The Congregation of Christ."

Figure 11 **Man and the Natural Orders**

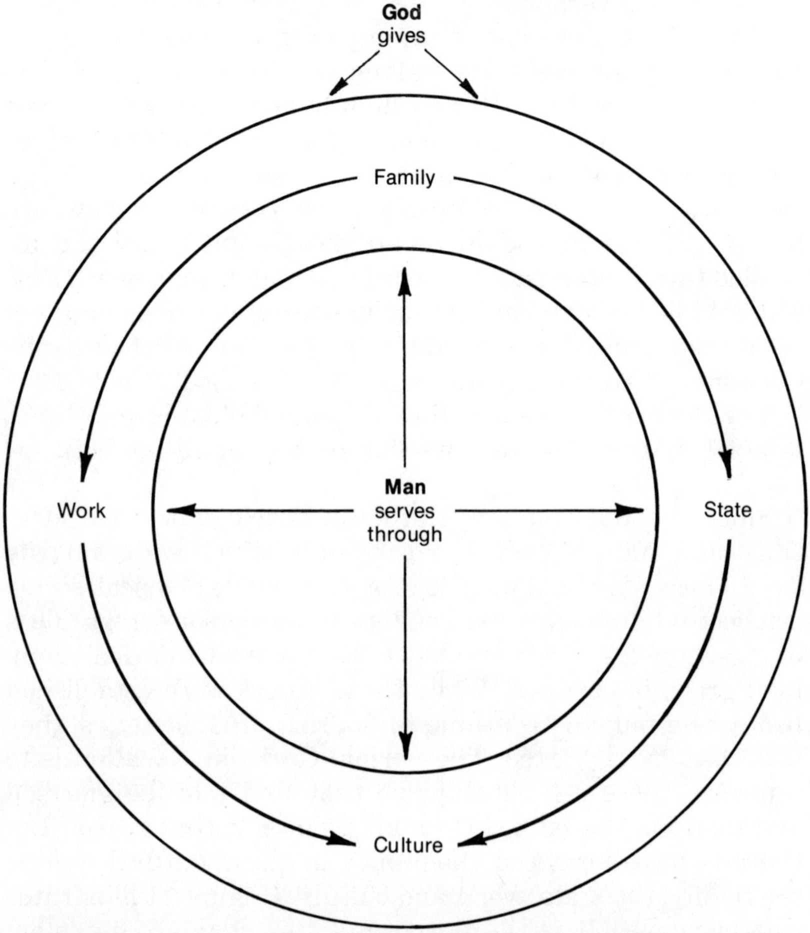

Through the natural orders, man receives blessings from God and returns service to God. The Christian brings the mind of Christ to these situations to realize the realm of right relationships.

rounded by idyllic conditions. Romances ever since reflect nostalgia for the love of this couple in Eden. Within the Pentateuch other love stories appear—that of Abraham and Sarah; Isaac and Rebekah, for "she became his wife: and he loved her" (Gen. 24:67); Jacob and Rachel, for whom he labored fourteen years, for "Jacob loved Rachel" (Gen. 29:18). The love of man and woman is celebrated throughout the Old Testament, in the Book of Ruth, the Song of Solomon, the story of Esther, the prophets (for example, Hosea), the Psalter, and the wisdom literature, where, in Proverbs, one learns that a good wife has a "price . . . far above rubies," that "the heart of her husband doth safely trust in her," and that "she will do him good . . . all the days of her life" (Prov. 31:10–12). Within the New Testament we learn of the affection of Joseph and Mary and that their home was honored by the special presence of God Himself, for Christ was born into their family. Our Lord performed His first miracle at a wedding in Cana. Jesus and Paul both compared the church to a bride, God to a groom. Though Christ was celibate and Paul was single (or perhaps widowed or divorced), many of the apostles appear to have been married. Peter's mother-in-law was healed by Christ (Matt. 8:14), and the apostle and his wife traveled together on missionary journeys (I Cor. 9:5). The New Testament closes with the vision of New Jerusalem "coming down from God out of heaven, prepared as a bride adorned for her husband" (Rev. 21:2). From Genesis to the Apocalypse the Bible celebrates the love of man and woman.

This love normally results in marriage and the founding of a home. Christian marriage ideally is a loving, lifelong union of a man and a woman. It has four component functions.

Marriage has a physical basis, the sexual union of male and female. Marriage is the sexual friendship of man and woman. This component of marriage is recognized in both Testaments. The second chapter of Genesis introduces marriage, saying, "a man [shall] leave his father and his mother, and shall cleave unto his wife: and they shall be one flesh" (Gen. 2:24). Both Jesus and Paul quote that Pentateuchal passage with approval. Sex within marriage serves many purposes. One of them is procreation, the incarnation of the love of man and woman in new life. The primordial imperative, "be fruitful and multiply, and replenish the earth" (Gen. 1:28), is written into the very flesh and soul of human beings. Procreation is not the only purpose of sexual activity. Physical love demonstrates the loyalty of man and woman; it shows the preference of one person for another; it enriches and seals friendship by a total communion of minds, souls, emotions, and bodies; it gives pleasure to body and soul. Sex is an act of beautiful self-surrender, and mutual giving. The

Song of Solomon celebrates sexual love, saying, "Let him kiss me with the kisses of his mouth: for thy love is better than wine" (Song of Sol. 1:2).

Marriage has a social basis, the companionship of male and female. Marriage is a lasting friendship of man and woman. For Erasmus of Rotterdam marriage was "friendship" intended to "double our joy and divide our grief." This friendship, according to Erich Fromm,

> [is an attitude] of responsibility, care, respect, and knowledge, and the wish for the other person to grow and develop. It is the expression of intimacy between two human beings under the condition of the preservation of each other's integrity.[2]

This component of marriage is recognized in both Testaments. The second chapter of Genesis introduces marriage when God says, "It is not good that the man should be alone" (Gen. 2:18). Paul compared the fellowship of Christ and the church with that of husband and wife (Eph. 5:22–33). This companionship may serve many purposes. In former times the couple was an economic unit (our word *economics* is from the Greek term for "law of the household"). Family firms—the Welsers, the Fuggers, and the Medici—were prominent in Martin Luther's time.

This companionship can be a political unit, providing security not only for the family, but sometimes for an entire nation. Who cannot be impressed by the power of couples such as William and Mary or Albert and Victoria? This companionship can be a cultural unit, producing aesthetic enrichment for both the children and the larger human family. Illustrative are Jonathan and Sarah Edwards or John and Abigail Adams. This companionship of man and woman can be socially enriching, affording intimacy with another self, as can be seen in the unions of Luther and Katrina von Bora or John Calvin and Idelette de Bure.

Marriage has an intellectual basis. It is a sharing of thought and sentiment. William Shakespeare spoke of marriage as a melding of kindred minds. This intellectual excitement often

2. Quoted by Vernon C. Grounds, "Therapist and Theologian Look at Love," *Christianity Today*, vol. 25, August 6, 1971, p. 32.

outlasts the sensual. It enriches the social fabric of matrimony. Luther quipped that the first love, founded on physical attraction and emotional infatuation, is drunken; but the second love, based on moral, intellectual, and spiritual values, is sober and enduring.

This component of marriage is recognized in both Testaments. With the inauguration of matrimony in Genesis, Eve is introduced as "an help meet" for the man (Gen. 2:18). The closeness of Abraham and Sarah, Isaac and Rebekah, Jacob and Rachel in the Old Testament, and that of Joseph and Mary and Aquila and Priscilla in the New, all testify to the matching of minds in good marriages. This ideal is reflected repeatedly in the Scriptures. In the Old Testament, wisdom is portrayed as a woman. The author of Proverbs says of a good wife, "She openeth her mouth with wisdom" (Prov. 31:26). This companionship of man and woman can be intellectually enriching, as evidenced in the history of civilization in creative couples such as Will and Ariel Durant, Calvin and Harriet Beecher Stowe, and Pierre and Marie Curie.

Marriage has a spiritual basis. For believers it is founded on a common faith. The union of man and woman mirrors the marriage of Christ and His church. This truth has been much discussed among Lutherans. Luther referred to marriage as "the school for character," while Philip Melanchthon called it "the first church." Scholars of the age of Lutheran orthodoxy often marveled that baptism was compared to birth and that the Eucharist was established in a home at suppertime. Other scholars have commented on the terminology so prevalent within Christianity—God is our Father, Jesus is our brother, the church is our mother, and we live in "the household of faith." Some Christians call their pastor "father" and some Christians address each other as "brother" and "sister." These practices reflect the origin of the church within the context of the family.

In New Testament times, church members met in homes. Paul writes, "Salute the brethren . . . and Nymphas, and the church which is in his house" (Col. 4:15). As the new Israel began, so did the old. The faith appeared first in families—that of Adam and Eve, Noah and his household, Abraham and his clan. The founders of the Jewish faith are called the patriarchs and the matriarchs. No wonder C. C. von Pheil, a hymn-writer in the eighteenth century, could say,

> O blest the house where faith ye find,
> And all within have set their mind
> To trust their God and serve Him still,
> And do in all His holy will.

As nature is designed to glorify God, so the natural orders are designed to fulfill His intentions. Through a good marriage God is honored, man and woman are edified, the human family is perpetuated, society is sustained, and the church is extended. God calls man and woman to live together as a couple, and in their union the two become more than each could have been alone. In the world of the Bible, marriage is a central reality.

While marriage, as a lifelong union of a man and a woman, is the norm for humanity, we must immediately admit, along with most classic Lutheran theologians, that there are exceptions to this norm. Let us consider some of these.

Not all persons marry. Through choice or chance many remain single. The Bible is aware of this reality. Christ was celibate. Paul was single. John the Baptist and many of the prophets were unmarried. Within the history of the church, celibacy has been common. Some have not married so that, like Paul, they may devote themselves entirely to the work of Christ. Celibacy has become the norm for the Roman Catholic clergy and for the hierarchy of Eastern Orthodoxy. Others would have married, but never had that opportunity. America's most famous preacher and bishop during the last century, Phillips Brooks, was single. Lutheran theology recognizes the status of being single as a valid and a God-pleasing vocation. Celibate orders of service are known within Lutheranism. A number of eminent Lutheran leaders have remained single, as did the late Edward C. Fendt. The Lutheran ethic is that of Paul, who wrote, "If thou marry, thou hast not sinned" (I Cor. 7:28) and "he that is unmarried careth for the things that belong to the Lord" (I Cor. 7:32).

Not all persons stay married. Marriage can be broken by death. This reality is also recognized in Scripture and in the church. Baby Jesus was greeted in the temple by Anna, "a widow of about fourscore and four years" (Luke 2:37). Ruth was a widow. Elijah the prophet was cared for by a widow. The early church had an order of widows. One of the main concerns of the Christian community in Jerusalem was the care of widows. The violent termination of marriage because of the death of a spouse is experienced in both the church and the world. Calvin was a widower. Lyman Beecher, the Congregationalist patriarch, outlived three wives; his father had five. After the death of a spouse, the survivor may remarry. Paul advised that "If [a woman's] husband be dead, she is at liberty to be married to whom she will" (I Cor. 7:39).

In addition, marriage can be broken by factors other than death. This is recognized in the institution of divorce. What is commonly called divorce does not break up a marriage; it is simply a public and a legal recognition that a marriage has failed. For the orthodox Lutheran theologians, divorce was an admission that the marriage contract had been broken. Every branch of the Christian church regards divorce as a tragedy and contrary to God's primordial intention; yet, with the exception of the Roman Catholic community, all make provision for divorce. (Even within the Roman Catholic Church allowance is made for the "annulment" of marriages under certain circumstances.)

The attitude of Lutheran theology toward divorce is paradoxical. As Melanchthon wrote, "Marriage is the legitimate and indissoluble union of one man and one woman"; it is a natural order intended to endure. God's desire is that marriages not be broken. However, Lutheran scholars have recognized the empirical fact, evident in a fallen world, that marriages do fail. Marriages malfunction. They become *dis*orderly, *ab*normal, *un*natural, and *de*structive. God's intention for man and woman cannot be fulfilled in such situations. There are four ways in which the fundamental purposes of marriage are not attained.

There may be a variety of physical malfunctions. Christ Himself referred to permanent impotence (and by implication, frigidity; see Matt. 19:12) and to adultery, by which He meant not a temporary liaison but repeated sexual union with other persons (Matt. 19:9). Other sexual impediments or preferences may preclude a heterosexual marriage. In any case, sexual fulfillment is denied one spouse. A major purpose of marriage is the orderly expression of sexuality. Paul advised that "it is better to marry than to burn" with desire (I Cor. 7:9). Paul also encouraged couples to enjoy sex, saying, "Defraud ye not one the other" (I Cor. 7:5) so that "Satan tempt you not for your incontinency" (I Cor. 7:5). Whenever the sexual expression of marriage is absent, through malicious intent, the marriage has been broken.

There may be a variety of social malfunctions. Paul referred to these collectively as "desertion," writing that if a spouse "depart, let him depart. A brother or a sister is not under bondage in such cases . . ." (I Cor. 7:15). This Pauline privilege is a public recognition that marriage can fail to provide the companionship for which it was designed. This may occur through faulty intention or willful action. Perhaps the union was like those misconceptions in the womb that nature must terminate through miscarriage. Perhaps the union was like a birth defect, as are two fingers grown together abnormally, needing separation by surgery. It must be admitted that desertion of mind and heart long precedes separation from bed and board. Divorce is a public confession that marriage as companionship has terminated.

There may be a variety of mental malfunctions. Marriage as a union of kindred minds can be disrupted. God Himself recognized this reality in the legislation given through Moses to the children of Israel (Deut. 24:1–4). Hardness of heart or hardship of circumstance may play havoc with a marriage. This was the admission of Christ to the Pharisees (Mark 10:2–12). In His own life, Jesus neither condemned nor condoned the divorced, but ministered to them as individuals. This is clear from Christ's encounter with the woman at the well (John 4:1–30), the woman taken in adultery (John 8:1–11), and the incident of the Gadarene separated from wife and family through mental incapacity (Luke 8:26–39). Whether desertion takes place through physical, mental, moral, or psychological absence, the marriage has malfunctioned. The ethic of love, wrought by Christ and taught by the apostles, impels the church to be evangelical, not legalistic, when serving such suffering individuals.

There may be a variety of spiritual malfunctions. Marriage between Christians and unbelievers is a reality. The church recognizes that in such marriages an important component of the good life is missing: spiritual unity. The Christian partner remains lonely at the most important and intimate level of his existence. Paul advised such couples to try to stay married (I Cor. 7:14–16). He also recognized that commitment to Christ could cause irreparable conflict between the spouses. In such instances, the believer is encouraged to try to maintain the marriage bond. This is the opinion of both Paul and Peter, who hope that the unbeliever may be saved and sanctified through closeness with a practicing Christian (I Cor. 7:16; I Peter 3:1–7). If such intimacy threatens to compromise the believer's loyalty to Christ, the believer must reorder his priorities, a painful process. The principle is that one must always obey God rather than man.

God placed Adam in a garden. But the Lord saw that man needed a mate. Together Adam and Eve became a couple and founded a family. While the home was the locus of the greatest tragedy to ever occur—the fall—it was also the source of the finest benefaction afforded our race—the incarnation of Christ. The marriage ceremony recognizes the mixture of delight and suffering in married life. The vows required of bride and groom express both realities:

> . . . to have and to hold from this day forward, for better for worse, for richer for poorer, in sickness and in health, to love and to cherish, till death us do part. . . .

For Lutherans, adversity and victory are both part of the benediction God can give to those who are married. For this reason the wedding service may conclude:

> O God, who hast so consecrated the state of Matrimony that in it is represented the spiritual marriage and unity betwixt Christ and his Church; look mercifully upon these thy servants, that they may love, honour, and cherish each other, and so live together in faithfulness and patience, in wisdom and true godliness, that their home may be a haven of blessing and of peace; through the same Jesus Christ our Lord, who

liveth and reigneth with thee and the Holy Spirit ever, one God, world without end. Amen.

Society

Derived from the family are three other natural orders: the state, work, and culture. Collectively these three institutions, together with the family and the church, constitute society. Let us now consider these essential natural estates.

The Bible is many things. It is, among others, a political document. So it was perceived by ancient personalities such as Eusebius of Caesarea and Augustine of Hippo and by emperors such as Constantine at Rome, Charlemagne at Aachen, and Justinian at Constantinople, as well as by modern figures such as Calvin and Melanchthon, Oliver Cromwell and the British Puritans, the authors of the Mayflower Compact, the signers of the Declaration of Independence, and many pivotal individuals in subsequent American political life (for example, John Adams, Abraham Lincoln, and Woodrow Wilson). These perceptions accurately reflect a scriptural reality: where two or three persons are present, politics is necessary. Politics is the process of the orderly conduct of all human relationships. God Himself ordained a government for Israel through Moses (Exod. 19:5–6) and through Christ enjoined obedience to Caesar (Matt. 22:21). Cyrus, emperor of Iran, is regarded as God's "shepherd" and "anointed one" (Isa. 44:28; 45:1) and a foretype of Christ.

In the Old Testament, from Genesis to the apocalyptical literature, prophets are portrayed as active participants in the political process: Joseph is prime minister to Pharaoh, Daniel is advisor to the shahs, Nathan is chaplain to King David, Ezra and Nehemiah are civil servants in the Persian Empire. The same situation is evident in the New Testament, where Christ praises Roman centurions; Paul preaches before governors, kings, and the emperor; and the apostle urges due regard for secular authority:

> I exhort therefore, that, first of all, supplications, prayers, intercessions, and giving of thanks, be made for all men; For

> kings, and for all that are in authority; that we may lead a quiet and peaceable life in all godliness and honesty.
>
> [I Tim. 2:1–2]

The state, which is the embodiment of the political process, has four component functions.

The state has a physical basis, for it should guarantee the survival, security, and prosperity of individuals and their institutions. Through the military the state affords protection against foreign oppression and domestic insurrection. Paul called this "the ministry of the sword."

> For he is the minister of God to thee for good. But if thou do that which is evil, be afraid; for he beareth not the sword in vain: for he is the minister of God, a revenger to execute wrath upon him that doeth evil.
>
> [Rom. 13:4]

God raised up judges (Joshua and Jeptha, Deborah and Gideon, Samson and Samuel) in Israel to give the people domestic tranquillity and national liberty. God also raised up great kings, such as David the warrior and Solomon the builder. The state not only protects life, but it also enhances life by providing facilities that are necessary but beyond the capability of the individual to provide. Through its agencies and offices the state nurtures life. Solomon, for example, the most glorious king of Israel, gave his people benefits such as a merchant marine and a dependable money supply, seaports and city police, royal highways, currency and culture, fair weights and measures, and much more (see I Kings 4–10). The state must combine the "sword" and the "trowel," the arts of war and the pursuits of peace, as did the Hebrews in the time of Nehemiah. We read,

> They which builded on the wall, and they that bare burdens, with those that laded, every one with one of his hands wrought in the work, and with the other hand held a weapon.
>
> [Neh. 4:17]

In such fashion the physical welfare of society is maintained.

The state has a social basis, for it should guarantee justice. Seeking to establish a realm of right relationships in society, the state exercises legislative, executive, and judicial power by making, enforcing, and interpreting laws. Through due process it arbitrates disputes concerning persons and property. Solomon was famed for his judicial wisdom: "And all Israel heard of the judgment which the king had judged; and they feared the king: for they saw that the wisdom of God was in him, to do judgment" (I Kings 3:28). The state, therefore, has not only the ministry of "sword and trowel," but also that of the scales of justice. Many a county courthouse in America is topped with a statue of Justice, blindfolded so that she will be no respecter of persons, holding in one hand the sword, in the other the scales. Such an image is eminently biblical and reflects a Lutheran understanding of the state.

The state has an intellectual basis, for it should guarantee freedom of expression and communication. Society is more than a marketplace, a courthouse, or a militia; it is a forum for the free give and take of opinions. The Greek city of Paul's day was often dominated by the agora, a place of exchange for goods and ideas. The Jerusalem of Christ's time was dominated by the temple, a place where the boy Jesus debated the doctors: "And it came to pass, that after three days they found him in the temple, sitting in the midst of the doctors, both hearing them, and asking them questions" (Luke 2:46). The New England town traditionally was built around a public square fronted by the courthouse and the meeting house, places of intense intellectual activity. The Germany of Luther's time was a country not only of territorial principalities but also of burgeoning universities. The Reformation was born in a college, fathered by a professor who engaged in public dispute, spread by the printed page, and protected by princes concerned with the rights of conscience.

Since then, sensitive souls have insisted upon the citizen's sacred right of dissent and upon the obligation of society to respect that prerogative. This is eminently biblical, for ancient Israel was a land filled with intellectual creativity and prophetic activity. The Christian era was born in dissent—within the temple, the synagogue, the school, and the forum.

Often Paul appealed to the Roman state to protect his right of free expression. If Christians are consistent with their sources, they will insist on a society that upholds full civil liberties for all.

The state has a spiritual basis, for it should guarantee freedom of religion. It not only promises security, promotes justice, and fosters civilization, but also ensures the free expression of religion. Like all natural orders, the state is to glorify God. Previous generations felt this was accomplished through a union of church and state. This was the conviction of Constantine, Justinian, and Charlemagne. Europe became a Christendom ("Christ's kingdom") presided over by pope and emperor. Some Lutherans, such as Ernst Hengstenberg, regarded such an arrangement as the fulfillment of millennial expectation. Other Lutherans preferred the "state church" system. To us, however, it appears that the best interpretation of Luther's life and thought is one that views him as a pioneer of the separation of church and state. The import of that doctrine for a religiously pluralistic society is obvious. Because persuasion is the only legitimate means of religious conversion, as stated by Augustine in his early career, the state must abstain from any form of the persecution or propagation of organized religion. The state today glorifies God and edifies man when it allows the free and open preaching of God's Word. This is suggested in a passage pregnant with meaning in the prophecy of Isaiah. God selected Cyrus, a secular prince, to prepare the nations to receive His message:

> . . . I girded thee, though thou hast not known me: That they may know from the rising of the sun, and from the west, that there is none beside me. I am the LORD, and there is none else.
>
> [Isa. 45:5–6]

Through the centuries God's people have lived under a variety of governments. Within biblical times the Hebrews passed through a tribality, slavery, a theocracy, a national monarchy, and a protectorate, and became a diaspora minority in empires as divergent as the Persian and the Roman. Within Christian times God's people have flourished under systems as divergent as imperial and national monarchies, secular republics, and dictatorial oligarchies. Today, politically, Lutherans live under systems as divergent as democracy (in the United States), monarchy (in Norway), and dictatorship (in East Germany). Lutherans do not believe any one form of government is divinely mandated. They contend, however, that both anarchy and tyranny are contrary to God's preferred purposes. Any government that provides for physical security, social fraternity, intellectual prosperity, and spiritual liberty is acceptable. We personally believe democracy to be the preferable form of government because it consistently strives to respect the dignity of the individual and to facilitate his responsible participation in the political process.

While the state is divinely ordained and merits due obedience, we admit that there are occasions when civil disobedience or even revolution is mandatory for Christians. This was recognized by the Reverend John Peter Gabriel Muhlenberg, son of the great Lutheran patriarch, who, at the start of hostilities with Britain, divested himself of his pulpit gown during a church service in Woodstock, Virginia, and subsequently served as a colonel in the Revolutionary Army. Revolution is justified when the state has malfunctioned, thus creating radical abnormalities within society that can be cured only by radical change. The fundamental purposes of the state are not attained in four instances.

There may be a variety of physical malfunctions. The security of the population may be imperiled by a state that is unable or unwilling to provide the basic necessities of everyday life. The central event of Old Testament history, the exodus, was a revolution. Moses was raised up by God to be both a provider and a liberator for a people suffering under oppression. Without his ministry, the people would have faced certain annihilation. Their government was insistent on the destruction, not the preservation, of life. God Himself not only inaugurated the Hebrew revolution but also preserved it by destroying Pharoah in the Red Sea.

There may be a variety of social malfunctions. The prosperity and the liberty of the population may be endangered by a state that is unable or unwilling to provide justice. God Himself sent prophets to condemn the tyranny of Assyria and to pronounce doom on Nineveh, to indict Babylon for its massive suppression of liberty:

> Go up against the land of Merathaim, even against it, and against the inhabitants of Pekod: waste and utterly destroy after them, saith the LORD, and do according to all that I have commanded thee. A sound of battle is in the land, and of great destruction. How is the hammer of the whole earth cut asunder and broken! how is Babylon become a desolation among the nations! I have laid a snare for thee, and thou art also taken, O Babylon, and thou wast not aware: thou art found, and also caught, because thou hast striven against the LORD. The LORD hath opened his armoury, and hath brought forth the weapons of his indignation: for this is the work of the Lord GOD of hosts in the land of the Chaldeans. Come against her from the utmost border, open her storehouses: cast her up as heaps, and destroy her utterly: let nothing of her be left. Slay all her bullocks; let them go down to the slaughter: woe unto them! for their day is come, the time of their visitation.
>
> [Jer. 50:21–27]

Even Israel, His chosen nation, became politically corrupt and inept. God sent prophets, such as Amos, to call for social justice. This simple spokesman of the people was a pioneer of the fundamental liberties of the person over against the oppression of the state. Finally God Himself willed the destruction of both the northern and southern kingdoms because of their incurable apostasy and injustice.

There may be a variety of intellectual malfunctions. Suppressing thought is surely murder of the mind, just as withholding bread is murder of the body. Governments that deny freedom of expression are themselves judged by the God of history in two ways. First, intellectual leaders flee, taking refuge in free societies, and a "brain drain" occurs that reduces the nation to mental mediocrity or fanaticism. Second, intellectual leaders remaining in the country conspire to facilitate the fall of such a government. Germany in the 1930s and 1940s is a classic example. Many of the elite of her universities fled, leaving the society that produced Goethe at the mercy of Goebbels. Those intellectuals who remained, such as Dietrich Bonhoeffer, became confessors of both Christ and civil liberty. Though unsuccessful in his effort to overthrow the Nazi regime, Bonhoeffer has become immortal to all who prize freedom.

There may be a variety of spiritual malfunctions. The state can commit idolatry, confusing itself with God. Though Paul and the early Christians prayed for the emperor, they could not pray to him or make sacrifices to him. The ancient church engaged in civil disobedience in a variety of ways. Christ and most of the apostles were killed as enemies of the Roman state because of their refusal to compromise conscience. This precedent has been normative for Christian history. Before Luther was excommunicated from the Roman church, he had defied and disobeyed the German emperor. Though the reformer feared social disorder, he himself was a model of what it means to be a religious revolutionary, standing before the Diet of Worms and saying,

> Should I recant at this point, I would open the door to more tyranny and impiety, and it will be all the worse should it appear that I had done so at the instance of the Holy Roman Empire. . . . When Christ stood before Annas, he said, 'Produce witnesses.' If our Lord, who could not err, made this demand, why may not a worm like me ask to be convicted of error from the prophets and the Gospels? If I am shown my error, I will be the first to throw my books into the fire. I have been reminded of the dissentions which my teaching engenders. I can answer only in the words of the Lord, 'I came not to bring peace but a sword.' If our God is so severe, let us beware lest we release a deluge of wars, lest the reign of this noble youth, Charles, be inauspicious. Take warning from the examples of Pharoah, the king of Babylon, and the kings of Israel. God it is who confounds the wise. I must walk in the fear of the Lord. I say this not to chide but because I cannot escape my duty to my Germans.[3]

3. Roland H. Bainton, *Here I Stand: A Life of Martin Luther* (New York: Abingdon-Cokesbury, 1950), pp. 184–185.

A sizable number of the German princes and people followed Luther in this great religious insurrection that is now commonly called the Lutheran Reformation.

The Bible is many things. It is, among others, a chronology of labor. It opens with God creating the universe. Adam and Eve were instructed to toil, for work existed both before and after the fall. It is even said that the creation of man was inspired by the need for labor.

> And every plant of the field before it was in the earth, and every herb of the field before it grew: for the LORD God had not caused it to rain upon the earth, and there was not a man to till the ground.
>
> And the LORD God took the man, and put him into the garden of Eden to dress it and to keep it.
>
> [Gen. 2:5, 15]

Throughout the Scriptures we are given vignettes of men and women at work: Moses is called while tending sheep (Exod. 3), Peter and John while fishing (Matt. 4:18, 20), Matthew while counting money (Matt. 9:9), Amos while farming (Amos 1:1), and Mary while keeping house (Luke 1:27). The saints are shown at work: Joseph and Daniel as statesmen, Paul as a teacher and tentmaker, David as a soldier-king, Solomon as a builder, Habakkuk as a priest, and our Lord Himself as a carpenter. From Genesis to the Apocalypse the Bible is a saga about labor, from Adam in the idyllic conditions of the oasis of Eden to Saint John the Divine in the oppressive environment of the salt mines of Patmos.

Work has four component functions.

Work has a physical basis. It is the production and distribution of goods and services for the preservation of human life. In the Bible the classic example is Joseph, appointed by God to sustain both Israel and Egypt in a time of economic hardship through the production, preservation, and distribution of goods. Moses and Jesus both fed the people. Our Lord took bread and wine, the fruit of both nature and labor, as the essential elements in the sacrament. At the altar each Lord's Day we are reminded of the work of Christ and of the dignity of the work of man.

Work has a social basis. It provides for the maintenance of society. Apart from labor there could be no culture. (It is revealing that the words *agriculture* and *culture* are from the same root.) The goal of a just society is not economic equality but equality of economic opportunity so that each person may have sufficient occasion to express his personality and to fulfill his duty. Both Plato and Paul compared society to a body, composed of many members, not all similar or equal, yet each part indispensable to the other. Medieval theologians, such as John of Salisbury, were fond of this analogy. When the great cathedrals of Europe, such as Chartres, were raised, priest and peasant, carpenter and prince, mason and musician, mechanic and sculptor, merchant and monk all cooperated to glorify God and to benefit society through shared activity.

Work has a mental basis. It is an expression of ingenuity and genius. This is recognized in great modern churches, as in the National Cathedral in Washington, D. C., where inventors are honored, in stained glass, alongside saints and statesmen. As God revealed Himself in the creation of the universe, so man expresses himself in the work of his hands. For this reason all work has dignity, for it grows out of man's spiritual energy. All centers of civilization—from the agricultural communities of Mesopotamia to the industrial complexes of middle America—are expressions and extensions of human personality through labor in work. This theme is admirably developed in the art of the Lutheran Reformation with its emphasis on the dignity and ingenuity inherent in daily tasks as varied as farming and cooking, printing and trading.

Work has a spiritual basis. Work is regarded in Lutheran theology as a vocation, a calling of God to witness through one's occupation to our salvation in Christ. This teaching is profoundly biblical. Paul wrote to the Colossians, "And whatsoever ye do in word or deed, do all in the name of the Lord Jesus, giving thanks to God and the Father by him" (Col. 3:17). To the Thessalonians, waiting for the coming of Christ, he commented,

> And that ye study to be quiet, and to do your own business, and to work with your own hands, as we commanded you; That ye may walk honestly toward them that are without, and that ye may have lack of nothing.
>
> [I Thess. 4:11–12]

This echoed the command of the Master, who said to those servants entrusted with goods, "Occupy till I come" (Luke 19:13).

The biblical attitude toward labor as a spiritual calling went contrary to the values of both Latin and Germanic society. However, Benedict, the father of Latin monasticism, prized labor. Part of the ordinary routine for monks was the daily alternation of prayer and labor, reading and resting. This ethic came to permeate Western Catholicism. A millennium later Luther established principles that have pervaded Protestantism ever since. Luther, for instance, commenting on the value of the work of teaching school, said,

> Workers with brawn are prone to despise workers with brain, such as city secretaries and schoolteachers. The soldier boasts that it is hard work to ride in armor and endure heat, frost, dust, and thirst. But I'd like to see a horseman who could sit the whole day and look into a book. It is no great trick to hang two legs over a horse. They say writing is just pushing a feather, but I notice that they hang swords on their hips and feathers in high honor on their hats. Writing occupies not just the fist or the foot while the rest of the body can be singing or jesting, but the whole man. As for schoolteaching, it is so strenuous that no one ought to be bound to it for more than ten years.[4]

Yet Luther in no way despised manual toil. With Erasmus he could say, "The world was made by a Carpenter; by a Carpenter it was redeemed." For Luther, Christ was a worker:

> I can just imagine the people of Nazareth at the judgment day. They will come up to the Master and say, 'Lord, didn't you build my house? How did you come to this honor?'[5]

4. *Ibid.*, pp. 234–235.
5. *Ibid.*, pp. 233–234.

Work, like the state and the family, has been affected by the fall. This natural order also malfunctions. As divorce and revolution are sometimes tragic necessities in their realms, so within the order of labor correctives are sometimes required.

There may be a variety of physical malfunctions. The production and distribution of goods and services may break down. Intellectual or individual incentive may falter. Poor management or inefficient labor may cripple the economy. Vested interests may seek monopolies that are contrary to the common good. Certainly the medieval sin of sloth covers a multitude of modern inequities. Adaptation is a law of physical survival. If gradual adaptation fails, sudden and violent change is inevitable.

There may be a variety of social malfunctions. The social organism may become diseased, in part or in its entirety. Extremes of wealth and poverty may occur. Deception and fraud can infect the economy. Unjust or inept government can prevent the good life for many. The Bible is replete with stories of social injustice and its consequences. After the death of Solomon, for instance, his son Rehoboam ascended the throne of an undivided Israel. Because of Solomon's building projects, the people had been heavily taxed and belabored. Economic advisers urged the young king to change his father's policies. Instead of allowing for peaceful transition, the king unwittingly caused revolution by telling his counselors,

> . . . Thus shalt thou answer the people that spake unto thee, saying, Thy father made our yoke heavy, but make thou it somewhat lighter for us; thus shalt thou say unto them, My little finger shall be thicker than my father's loins. For whereas my father put a heavy yoke upon you, I will put more to your yoke: my father chastised you with whips, but I will chastise you with scorpions.
>
> [II Chron. 10:10–11]

The result of this policy was rebellion and irreparable division of the kingdom.

There may be a variety of intellectual malfunctions. Lack of vision can paralyze an economy as surely as it can kill a congregation. Innovation is essential for economic progress. The loss of inventive genius results in centuries of agricultural and industrial stagnation. At such times only an unprecedented acceleration of applied imagination, as in the Neolithic and Industrial revolutions, can redeem the situation. Prior to the revolution wrought by James Watt in the eighteenth century, England could support 8 million people. Today, due to the inventive genius of several generations, Britain can provide a home for more than 60 million inhabitants. The biblical imperative, "be fruitful and multiply," is directly related to the other injunction to have dominion over the earth and subdue it (Gen. 1:28).

There may be a variety of spiritual malfunctions. The economy, like every other dimension of nature, is intended to glorify God. When it fails to do this, as in the case of contemporary materialism (be it the consumerism of the West or the communism of the East), there is disjuncture in the social and spiritual fabric of a nation. Violent changes may take place in the spiritual realm as well as in the social order. Monasticism was the Christian protest against the materialism of the ancient world. Today in Marxist Europe the protest against materialism expresses itself in a return to traditional Christian values and practices. In the West, Christians are struggling to find conscientious and responsible ways in which to be good stewards of affluence. They are well aware of our Lord's condemnation of rampant consumerism.

> And he said unto them, Take heed, and beware of covetousness: for a man's life consisteth not in the abundance of the things which he possesseth. And he spake a parable unto them, saying, The ground of a certain rich man brought forth plentifully: And he thought within himself, saying, What shall I do, because I have no room where to bestow my fruits? And he said, This will I do: I will pull down my barns, and build greater; and there will I bestow all my fruits and my goods. And I will say to my soul, Soul, thou hast much goods laid up for many years; take thine ease, eat, drink, and be merry. But God said unto him, Thou fool, this night thy soul shall be required of thee: then whose shall those things be, which thou

> hast provided? So is he that layeth up treasure for himself, and is not rich toward God.
>
> [Luke 12:15–21]

Throughout history God's people have experienced a variety of economic systems:

the pastoralism of the Book of Genesis
the communalism of the Book of Acts
the manorialism of the *Book of Hours*
the capitalism of *The Wealth of Nations*
the Marxism of *The Communist Manifesto*
the socialism of the Peoples' Charter

Today the world's Lutherans live under capitalism in North America, socialism in Scandinavia, and Marxism in Eastern Europe. For Lutherans no one system of economics is of divine institution. That philosophy seems best which serves God and man most.

The Bible is many things. It is, among others, a story of civilization. The Scriptures open with a vision of a garden; they close with a picture of a city. From Genesis to the Apocalypse man is portrayed as a cultural being. Early in the Pentateuch we learn that Cain "builded a city" (Gen. 4:17), that Jubal "was the father of all such as handle the harp and organ" (Gen. 4:21), that Tubal-cain was "an instructor of every artificer in brass and iron" (Gen. 4:22). In the middle of the Old Testament we read about the building of the temple with its furnishings and its finery (see II Chron. 3–5). At the conclusion of the canon we find "the holy Jerusalem" where "the length and the breadth and the height of it are equal" (Rev. 21:10, 16). It is clear that the biblical understanding of man is this: he was made for the garden, not the jungle; for the city, not the wilderness. For man to be civilized is natural or normal. That is why Lutherans refer to culture as one of the natural orders.

Culture, the manmade part of the environment, has four component functions.

Culture has a physical basis. Civilization is the extension

of man's spirit into the environment. Human personality is writ large upon the planet. That is the meaning of the phrase *the garden*. A garden, be it Persian or English, Chinese or French, has been a symbol of civilization throughout the earth. It is a place where man and nature exist in mutual ministry and harmony, creating beauty that delights the eye and products that nourish both body and soul. Beauty and utility, the labor of artist and artisan, indicate the material basis of culture.

Culture has a social basis. Civilization is a communal expression of the people. Certainly the artist, like David, works in "splendid isolation." That withdrawal from society, however, is only for the purpose of enriching the community. The poetry of Prince David was finally enjoyed by the public in the Hebrew prayer book, the Psalter, in the forum of temple, synagogue, and church. Poet and people, artist and community, author and audience, exist in creative symbiosis. Together they provide three things by which the community survives history: an interpretation of the present, a preservation of the past, and an anticipation of the future. Culture has a social function to fulfill.

Culture has an intellectual basis. Civilization is a unique manifestation of the mind of man. It reflects the human capacity for "imaging." Made in the "image of God," man can also image—the past, through recollection; the future, by expectation; alternative worlds, through imagination; and options not immediately available, through reinterpretation. Whether the images are electronic on a television screen, sculpted in a Pietà, spoken in a recitation of poetry, or enacted in a ballet is irrelevant. Man can image or envision, a trait that makes the artist strangely akin to the prophet and raises him above mere utilitarianism.

Culture has a spiritual basis. Civilization is a way in which the community offers adoration to God. Society should glorify the Creator through its creations. The psalmist recalled the worship of God in a symphony of praise in the temple:

> Praise ye the LORD. Praise God in his sanctuary: praise him in the firmament of his power. Praise him for his mighty acts: praise him according to his excellent greatness. Praise him

> with the sound of the trumpet: praise him with the psaltery and harp. Praise him with the timbrel and dance: praise him with stringed instruments and organs. Praise him upon the loud cymbals: praise him upon the high sounding cymbals. Let every thing that hath breath praise the LORD. Praise ye the LORD.
>
> [Ps. 150]

This is a paradigm of the orchestra of culture glorifying God.

Lutheran philosophers as divergent as Albert Schweitzer and Christopher Ernst Luthardt have puzzled over the character of civilization. It appears that in order to have a community, a people must have someone or something in common. The quality of that commonality determines the character and destiny of the community. For us, the biblical portrait of community is this: its core is found in the common glorification of God. This is the only fully adequate basis for civilization. Only faith can found a civilization that will be intellectually honest, emotionally and aesthetically satisfying, socially significant, and spiritually rewarding.

All the natural orders, including culture, exist after the fall. Like the other orders, culture has been infected by evil. This means that there will be malfunctions of civilization that call for intervention and correction. Sometimes these are of a gradual nature, sometimes of a radical nature.

There may be a variety of physical malfunctions. For example, society may be overwhelmed by the spirit of nature. This has occurred in cultures dominated by materialism (the worship of matter) or vitalism (the worship of life). Personality, the highest reality in the universe under God, is prostituted to things. To Paul, Greece and Rome, in spite of their venerable art and ancient literature, were capitulating to the world, not mastering it. Luke tells us that "while Paul waited . . . at Athens, his spirit was stirred in him, when he saw the city wholly given to idolatry" (Acts 17:16). Or again, society may be overwhelmed by the spirit of the natural man. This has occurred in cultures that have reverted to barbarism, where physical and mental skills are lost, or to a demonic paganism, where the achievements of art and science are employed to destroy nature (in ecological disasters) or to harm humanity (in sociological disasters, such as the Holocaust). In such instances civilization is no longer an extension of the spirit of man. It has become demonized and is in need of restoration.

There may be a variety of social malfunctions. For example, intellectual leaders may provide a misinterpretation of the past, a distortion of present reality, or false expectations for the future. Such misconceptions can doom a society. The Bible presents this as the dilemma of the later kingdom of Israel. Prophecy abounded, but it was mostly false. Another problem can be the alienation of the seers from the people, the estrangement of the artist and the masses. Then the nation is without soul and voice, the poet without support and sustenance. Articulation falters, and "where there is no vision, the people perish" (Prov. 29:18). Another problem can be the obsession of a civilization with itself. It confuses its accomplishments with God. The Book of Genesis contains the startling story of the tower of Babel. The people said, "Let us make a name" (Gen. 11:4). Such civilizations are in need of reformation through a return to the common roots of the people in God.

There may be a variety of intellectual malfunctions. For example, there may be a termination of the imaging process. Society is left without adequate symbols. The imaging may instead become obsessed with the past, so that instead of innovation there is only repristination. Or imaging can become diseased, a hallucination offering sick or inadequate models of meaning. As individuals can be crazed, so societies can go mad. A brilliant intellectual heritage is no guarantee against a corporate insanity. This was tragically illustrated in the German Third Reich and the Cambodia of the Pol Pot regime. Such cultures need rebirth, a renaissance. It is strangely appropriate that the word *renaissance*, first applied to Europe's rebirth between 1300 and 1648 when there was a revival of the classics and Christianity (the two component parts of Western culture), is derived from the sacrament of baptism. A Latin term for baptismal regeneration has become historical shorthand for the renewal of societies.

There may be a variety of spiritual malfunctions. Instead of glorifying God, the culture may exist for other ends. Lutheran philosopher Paul Tillich discussed three possible orientations for civilizations. There is autonomy, or the serving of self. This makes the civilization ultimate, a law unto itself. According to the prophets of Israel, this was the predicament of Assyria and Babylon, obsessed with the arrogance of power. There is heteronomy, or the serving of another; this makes another civilization ultimate. The law by which our ways are ordered is borrowed from a neighbor. This was the predicament of the Sadducees of the time of Christ. They attempted to make Jewish culture into an imitation of Roman civilization. Imitative and alien, such efforts pervert the spirit of man and raise idols in the place of God. There is theonomy, or the serving of God. This makes God the ultimate.

An entire community aspires in its art and music, its literature and living, to glorify the Deity. This was Christ's intention for His people. An amazing aspect of Christ's ministry was His severe condemnation of the temple. The place set aside to show the centrality of God had become a shrine for the honor of man. Before Israel could be restored, the temple had to be violently destroyed. Its veil was rent when Jesus died on the cross. Its walls were torn down when Rome took the city. It is revealing that in the perfect civilization, New Jerusalem, there will be no temple (Rev. 21:22), for God will permeate everything. In the history of all cultures sometimes only revolutionary reconstruction and revision can suffice.

Margaret Mead once lectured at the Iran-America Society. She suggested that one tragedy of the late twentieth century is the disappearance of many local cultures. "They are being replaced by a monotonous, monochrome world civilization," she said. For her this was a disaster for the human spirit. Man is capable of an almost infinite variety of cultural expressions. These are as varied as the Incan culture of Peru and the Chou Dynasty of China, the Florentine Renaissance and the achievements of Zimbabwe. Pluralism of cultural expression is compatible with God's will for human civilization.

Lutherans agree with that analysis. For them there is no one ideal civilization, be it the culture of Greece and Rome, the civilization of Byzantium, or the accomplishments of the

Figure 12 **The Components of the Natural Orders**

	Family	State	Work	Culture
Physical	Sexual union—procreation	Survival Security Prosperity	Production Distribution	Extension of man's spirit into the environment
Social	Companionship Economic unit Political unit	Justice	Maintenance of society	Communal expression
Intellectual	Sharing of thought and sentiment	Freedom of expression	Expression of ingenuity and genius	Imagination
Spiritual	Common faith	Freedom of religion	Vocation	Adoration to God
Malfunction	Death or alienation	Oppression	Deprivation of resources and opportunities	Limitation or distortion of reality
Disruption results in	Widowhood Divorce	Revolution Referendum Re-formation	Redistribution Transition Adaptation	Revision Reconstruction Renaissance

German Reformation. No mood—Gothic or Georgian, Baroque or Romanesque—is ultimate. All cultures can become fit vehicles for the proclamation of the gospel, the salvation of man, and the glorification of God. Today Lutheranism lives and thrives in a variety of cultures—Anglo-Saxon in North America, Germanic in Central Europe, Latin in South America, Islamic in Jordan, Chinese in Taiwan, and African in Nigeria. To each culture Christ brings liberation from sin and the opportunity and impetus for new creative expression. (Figure 12 summarizes the points made in our discussion of the natural orders.)

The Christian movement embraced the natural orders, filled them with new vitality, and redeemed them for the realm of right relationships. Christians "live and move and have their being" in them. The church recognizes this liturgically. Crucial family events, such as marriage and baptism, occur in the context of the sanctuary. From altars around the earth, prayers are offered each Lord's Day for national and global leaders. Offerings, the expression of human labor, are received. Music, art and architecture, poetry and drama, enhance the worship of God. The church obeys the Great Commission of its Master, going into all the world—not only geographically but also socially. An anonymous Christian, writing in the second century, said,

The difference between Christians and the rest of men is neither in country, nor in language, nor in customs. . . . They dwell in their own fatherlands, but as temporary inhabitants. They take part in all things as citizens, while enduring the hardships of foreigners. Every foreign place is their fatherland, and every fatherland is to them a foreign place. Like all others, they marry and beget children; but they do not expose their offspring. Their board they set for all, but not their bed. Their lot is cast in the flesh; but they do not live for the flesh. They pass their time on earth; but their citizenship is in heaven. They obey the established laws, and in their private lives they surpass the laws.

They love all men; and by all they are persecuted. They are unknown, and they are condemned. They are put to death, and they gain life. They are poor, but make many rich; they are destitute, but have an abundance of everything. They are dishonored, and in their dishonor they are made glorious. They are defamed, but they are vindicated. They are reviled, and they bless; they are insulted, and they pay homage. When they do good, they are punished as evil-doers; and when they are punished they rejoice as if brought to life. They are made war upon as foreigners by the Jews, and they are persecuted by the Greeks; and yet, those who hate them are at a loss to state the cause of their hostility.

To put it briefly, what the soul is in the body, that the Christians are in the world. The soul is spread through all parts of the body, and Christians through all the cities of the world. The soul dwells in the body, but it is not of the body; and Christians dwell in the world, though they are not of the world.[6]

---

6. Letter to Diognetus, in *The Faith of the Early Fathers*, vol. 1, trans. William A. Jurgens (Collegeville, MN: The Liturgical Press, 1970), pp. 40–41.

CHAPTER

The Heroes of Faith

I believe . . .

The Bible celebrates heroes of faith. Both Testaments praise the saints of the Lord. The Psalter reports,

> The steps of a good man are ordered by the LORD: and he delighteth in his way.
>
> For the LORD loveth judgment, and forsaketh not his saints; they are preserved for ever. . . .
>
> [Ps. 37:23, 28]

The Book of Hebrews, the consolation of the new Israel, provides a holy necrology, a roll call of the heroes of faith, those

> who through faith subdued kingdoms, wrought righteousness, obtained promises, stopped the mouths of lions, Quenched the violence of fire, escaped the edge of the sword, out of weakness were made strong, waxed valiant in fight, turned to flight the armies of the aliens. Women received their dead raised to life again: and others were tortured, not accepting deliverance; that they might obtain a better resurrection: And others had trial of cruel mockings and scourgings, yea, moreover of bonds and imprisonment: They were stoned, they were sawn asunder, were tempted, were slain with the sword: they wandered about in sheepskins and goatskins; being destitute, afflicted, tormented; (Of whom the world was not worthy:) they wandered in deserts, and in mountains, and in dens and caves of the earth. And these all . . . obtained a good report through faith. . . .
>
> [Heb. 11:33–39]

C. F. W. Walther

(1811–1887)
Churchman and Theologian

Between the covenants stands the Apocrypha, containing the Wisdom of Joshua, the Son of Sirach, or Ecclesiasticus, which includes these memorable lines:

> Let us now praise famous men, and our fathers that begot us. The Lord hath wrought great glory by them through his great power from the beginning. Such as did bear rule in their kingdoms, men renowned for their power, giving counsel by their understanding, and declaring prophecies: leaders of the people by their counsels, and by their knowledge of learning meet for the people, wise and eloquent in their instructions: such as found out musical tunes, and recited verses in writing: rich men furnished with ability, living peaceably in their habitations: all these were honored in their generations, and were the glory of their times. There be of them, that have left a name behind them, that their praises might be reported.
>
> The people will tell of their wisdom, and the congregation will show forth their praise.
>
> [Ecclesiasticus 44:1–8, 15]

From the rapture of Enoch in Genesis to the vision of the saints in the Apocalypse, the sacred Scriptures resound with the praise of "the servants of the Lord."

The same sentiment is evident in the Christian community. Both in the liturgy and on the calendar of the church, the heroes of faith are honored. In the office of matins is found the ancient and venerable hymn, the "Te Deum Laudamus," proclaiming that

> The glorious company of the Apostles praise Thee;
> The goodly fellowship of the prophets praise Thee;
> The noble army of martyrs praise Thee;
> The holy Church throughout all the world doth acknowledge Thee:
> The Father of an infinite majesty; Thine adorable true and only Son;
> Also the Holy Ghost, the Comforter.

Within the church year, days have been set aside to commemorate the twelve apostles, the blessed Virgin Mary, the evangelists, and many others. All Saints' Day, on whose eve the Reformation commenced, recalls the vast company of the baptized who lived and died in faith. From the shrines of first-century martyrs to the cenotaphs of the anonymous thousands who perished in the persecutions of our era, the elect of God "being dead yet speaketh" (Heb. 11:4).

Lutherans, as part of "the communion of saints," also revere and respect the heroes of faith. One of the central affirmations of the Reformation was the doctrine of the universal priesthood of believers. It was a providential coincidence that the Reformation and All Saints' Day coincided in history, as they do on the ecclesiastical calendar. Lutherans believe that there are two sorts of saints: the great saints, who have rendered extraordinary service to God and man, and the lesser saints, who have proven faithful in the ordinary routines of life. The service offered is conditioned by the situation into which God calls. As Jesus taught in the parable of the talents, the Master "unto one . . . gave five talents, to another two, and to another one; to every man according to his several ability" (Matt. 25:15). Each was differently productive. To all who bore fruit the Lord said, "Thou hast been faithful over a few things, I will make thee ruler over many . . ." (Matt. 25:23). Whether the saints are commemorated in the stained-glass window or whether they sit in the pew matters not. What counts is that they share one common quality: faith.

This was made clear in a history class at Ohio State University. Harold J. Grimm was discussing the art of the Renaissance. Donatello's "David" was introduced. The story of David was retold to provide the biblical context for this bronze. Then Grimm inquired, "How did little David slay the giant Goliath?" A student answered, "With a slingshot." But Grimm asked again, "How did little David slay the giant Goliath?" There was silence. Finally the instructor offered his answer. It was a theological one—one implicit in the biblical account, one explicit in the Donatello statue. David overcame not by strength or reason (as suggested in Michaelangelo's "David"), but by faith. Grimm then quoted a New Testament text to serve as a commentary on the story and the art: "This is the victory that overcometh the world, even our faith" (I John 5:4).

We live by faith.

Harry Emerson Fosdick, long-time minister of Riverside Church in New York City, once remarked that there are two ways in which our faith changes the world: by our speaking and by our working. In this chapter we want to consider these two expressions of "faith active in love," as we study speaking to God and man, the former as prayer, the latter as witnessing; and working in love to serve others. For the sake of convenience we will call these categories of active faith piety and morality.

Piety

Piety has always been important to Lutherans. Martin Luther's "Morning Prayer" petitions God for it, for "I pray Thee that Thou wouldst keep me this day also from sin and every evil, that all my doings and life may please Thee." A major movement in the history of Lutheranism was called Pietism. Lutheran hymnals traditionally have been replete with exhortations about Christian "walking" and "watching." One of these hymns admonishes,

Let us ever walk with Jesus,
Follow His example pure,
Flee the world with all its pleasures
That to sin the soul allure.
Onward let us move as pilgrims,
Sojourn here, yet dwell above,
That by faith and hope and love,
We may prove our heav'nly calling,
Saviour mine, abide with me;
Still lead on, I follow Thee.

[S. V. Birken, 1652]

Another hymn advises,

With thy watching mingle prayer;
Grace but rids from slumber.
God rids thee from slothful care
And the weights that cumber;

Else will still
Mind and will
Lukewarm praises tender,
And cold service render.

[Johann Burchard Freystein, 1687]

Evangelist George Whitefield, while preaching the Great Awakening in colonial America, remarked of the Pennsylvania German Lutherans that they "are holy souls; they keep up a close walk with God and are remarkable for their sweetness and simplicity of behavior." Lutheran piety also impressed young John Wesley while he was a missionary in Georgia and had opportunity to observe Salzburger immigrants at Ebenezer. Or again, during the 1950s a popular television serial (based on Kathryn Forbes's novel of the same name) was "I Remember Mama." The saga of a Norwegian immigrant family in San Francisco at the turn of this century, it gave insight into Lutheran life. One reviewer's lasting impression of the program was that "it provides an accurate and moving portrayal of Lutheran piety."

The word *piety* is derived from a Latin root meaning "devotion to God and man." Piety has been an important concept for Western Christianity in general and for Lutheranism in particular. Lutherans have referred to piety as "the walk with God," recalling the righteous Enoch of old who "walked with God" (Gen. 5:24). Walking in biblical times was an occasion for talking. According to Genesis, the Lord God was accustomed to "walking in the garden" to converse with Adam and Eve (Gen. 3:8). Jesus, God incarnate, often walked and talked with His disciples, as He did on the road to Emmaus. Then, as often since, believers have confessed that in the presence of the risen Lord "their eyes were opened, and they knew him" for "did not our heart burn within us, while he talked with us by the way . . . ?" (Luke 24:31, 32). Today this kind of walking means "talking." Lutherans, as people of the Word, understand piety in this conversational sense. A pious person is one who talks with God in prayer, and one who talks about God to his neighbors.

Prayer is the source, norm, and substance of piety. The late Roy A. Burkhart, for many years senior minister of the

First Community Church in Columbus, Ohio, explained the Christian way by comparing the abundant life with a key ring, a golden circle on which there are seven keys. What are the seven keys?

> The master key is *prayer.* As you use this key, you come into a more vital *faith* and your *love* grows. Using the key of love, you come into a greater capacity for *acceptance* and are prepared not only for greater *commitment* but you also come to know the grace of *forgiveness* and the reality of *healing.* The key ring is a symbol of *eternal life within.*[1]

The first key is prayer. That is the start of piety, devotion to God and man. Prayer is "the first cause." That is the considered opinion of the saints. The English preacher, William Law, said, "He who has learned to pray has learned the greatest secret of a holy and happy life." The greatest female theologian of the ages, Teresa of Avila, a doctor of the church, wrote the same thing. When the Bishop of Osma asked her why his spiritual life was weak, Teresa answered,

> . . . you still want that which is the foundation of every virtue, and without which the whole superstructure dissolves and falls in ruins. You want prayer. You want believing, persevering, courageous prayer. And the want of that prayer causes all that drought and disunion from which you say your soul suffers.[2]

Teresa's German contemporary, Luther, felt the same way. A section about prayer was one of the "Five Principal Parts" of the Small Catechism, to which was appended a section on "How the Head of the Family Should Teach His Household to Pray Morning and Evening." Prayer matters, as Jesus admonished His followers: "That men ought always to pray, and not to faint" (Luke 18:1).

People in the Bible prayed. These include the patriarchs, Abraham ("Abraham prayed . . . and God healed Abimelech,"

1. Quoted in "Youth Emphasizes Seven Keys," *First Community Church News*, (January 9–15, 1972), p. 4. Italics in the original.

2. Quoted by Arthur John Gossip, *In the Secret Place of the Most High* (New York: Charles Scribner and Sons, 1947), p. 91.

Gen. 20:17), Isaac ("And Isaac went out to meditate in the field at the eventide," Gen. 24:63), and Jacob ("I have seen God face to face . . . ," Gen. 32:30); the lawgivers, Moses ("I prayed therefore unto the LORD . . . ," Deut. 9:26) and Ezra ("Now when Ezra had prayed . . . ," Ezra 10:1); the prophets, Samuel ("I will pray for you unto the LORD," I Sam. 7:5), Elijah (who was a "prayer warrior" on Mount Carmel, see I Kings 18:36), Elisha (who prayed for Gehazi, II Kings 4:33), Isaiah (II Chron. 32:20), and Jeremiah (who received this promise, "Then shall ye call upon me, and ye shall go and pray unto me, and I will hearken unto you. And ye shall seek me, and find me, when ye shall search for me with all your heart," Jer. 29:12–13); the kings, David (whose prayers grace the Psalter, the hymnal of the old and new Israel; who said, "Evening, and morning, and at noon, will I pray, and cry aloud: and he shall hear my voice," Ps. 55:17), and Solomon (see I Kings 8 for his prayer at the dedication of the temple), and Hezekiah (whose prayer for healing is in II Kings 20:2–3); the blessed Virgin Mary (in the immortal words of the Magnificat, still sung in the church (Luke 1:46–55); and the apostles, Peter and John (who prayed for the Samaritan church, Acts 8:15) and Paul (who with the elders at Miletus "kneeled down, and prayed with them all," Acts 20:36). The Bible is a book of prayers and pray-ers. It begins with sabbath worship in the garden (Gen. 2:2–3) and it ends with the vision of Saint John the Divine "in the Spirit on the Lord's day" (Rev. 1:10).

All of this is certainly in the spirit of Jesus, who is central to both Testaments. Our Lord prayed. Christ began His ministry with forty days of prayer in the wilderness and concluded it with three hours of prayer on Calvary. In between, the Gospels describe the Master at prayer "at all times and in all places," ranging from the upper room to the Mount of Olives. Twice it is reported that Jesus taught His disciples to pray, saying, "Our Father, who art in heaven." In this phrase the Master defined prayer. It is conversation with God. No wonder this is the key to the life of piety. For if we want the house key, we had better be on speaking terms with the householder. Prayer is the key that unlocks the door to God.

Without prayer, we are distant from God. When we do not share our concerns, cares, and hopes with our Father, we inherit a silent and lonely world. We lack spiritual power. An absence of conversation creates an absence of community, and an absence of community leads to personal impoverishment.

Prayer, as communion with the Divine, can take many forms, both public and private (see chapter 6 on worship). Paul, for example, writing to Timothy, admonished that "supplications, prayers, intercessions, and giving of thanks, be made for all men" (I Tim. 2:1). Prayers, as suggested by *The Worship Supplement* to the 1941 *Lutheran Hymnal*, are normally of four types: adoration, confession, thanksgiving, and supplication.[3] These varieties, remembered through the acrostic *acts*, include most of the moods and needs of our conversations with God.

Let us consider each of these types of prayer.

One type of prayer is adoration. This is the expression of a sense of wonder, awe, and majesty at being in the presence of God. Adoration also implies loving deeply. Sentiments of joy and admiration are evident in the liturgy and in the Scriptures. During the "Gloria in Excelsis" the congregation sings to God:

> We praise Thee,
> We bless Thee,
> We worship Thee,
> We glorify Thee,
> We give thanks to Thee,
> For Thy great glory.

Such prayer is akin to the adoration of angels, for Isaiah the prophet, while at worship, experienced the following:

> In the year that king Uzziah died I saw also the Lord sitting upon a throne, high and lifted up, and his train filled the temple. Above it stood the seraphims: each one had six wings; with twain he covered his face, and with twain he covered his feet, and with twain he did fly. And one cried unto another, and said, Holy, holy, holy, is the LORD of hosts: the whole

3. Commission on Worship, The Lutheran Church-Missouri Synod, *The Worship Supplement* (Saint Louis: Concordia, 1969), p. 106.

> earth is full of his glory. And the posts of the door moved at the voice of him that cried, and the house was filled with smoke.
>
> Then I said, Woe is me! for I am undone; because I am a man of unclean lips, and I dwell in the midst of a people of unclean lips: for mine eyes have seen the King, the LORD of hosts.
>
> [Isa. 6:1–5]

Another type of prayer is confession. This is the admission of our sins to God. Having come into the presence of the Holy One of Israel, we fear, like Isaiah, "Woe is me! for I am undone; because I am a man of unclean lips" (Isa. 6:5) or Peter, who cried out, "Depart from me; for I am a sinful man, O Lord" (Luke 5:8). God's intention, however, is not that we should know permanent separation from Him because of our sin, but that we should experience reconciliation to Him. This occurs in prayers of confession.

Prayers of confession are important in the Lutheran liturgy. The common service employed by most of America's Lutherans opens with the confession of sins. This preparatory office (based on the *Confiteor*, the once-private prayer of the priest in the Roman rite), involves contrition. The minister invites the congregation, saying, "Let us draw near with a true heart and confess our sins unto God our Father. . . ." It continues with the oral confession of sin, for we "are by nature sinful and unclean, and that we have sinned against Thee by thought, word, and deed." Then the rite concludes with an absolution, spoken by the pastor:

> Almighty God, our Heavenly Father, hath had mercy upon us, and hath given His only Son to die for us, and for His sake forgiveth us all our sins. To them that believe on His Name, He giveth power to become the sons of God, and bestoweth on them His Holy Spirit. He that believeth, and is baptized, shall be saved.

A similar though longer confessional service often preceeds the celebration of Holy Communion.

Another Lutheran liturgical expression of confession is found in the Office of the Keys. For a time, Luther believed that the Roman Catholic sacrament of penance (or absolution) should be retained as an evangelical sacrament. After much thought, he decided that it lacked a physical element like water, wine, or the loaf to make it comparable to baptism and the Eucharist. Resting on a command of Christ and conveying His promises, absolution or penance was kept by Luther as a peculiar church power. Appended to the Small Catechism is a section on confession. For some it is the sixth part of the Lutheran enchiridion. The name *Office of the Keys* not only is reminiscent of Burkhart's description (given earlier in this chapter) of prayer as the master key, but also is a recollection of an act of Christ in His ministry. To the apostles, represented by Peter, Jesus said, "And I will give unto thee the keys of the kingdom of heaven: and whatsoever thou shalt bind on earth shall be bound in heaven; and whatsoever thou shalt loose on earth shall be loosed in heaven" (Matt. 16:19). Luther explained the Office of the Keys in his Small Catechism, saying, " . . . Christ has given to His Church on earth [power] to forgive the sins of penitent sinners, but to retain the sins of the impenitent as long as they do not repent."

Within the Lutheran tradition, the Office of the Keys may be administered in one of two ways. There is the rite of private confession, whereby one may seek out a pastor for counsel and absolution; in this connection, Lutheran practice is identical with the Anglican, as described by Bishop Stephen Neill—"none must; all may; some ought." There is the rite of public confession, whereby the congregation and pastor together approach God at the start of Sunday service to hear again the good news that "God so loved the world, that he gave his only begotten Son, that whosoever believeth in him should not perish, but have everlasting life" (John 3:16).

Yet another type of prayer is thanksgiving. This is the expression of gratitude to God for all of His blessings, both temporal and spiritual. It is significant that the central sacrament of the Christian life is called the Eucharist, or Thanksgiving. It is not surprising that the Lutheran liturgy for communion begins with the minister saying, "Let us give thanks unto the Lord our God," and the congregation responding, "It is meet and right so to do." The celebrant then continues,

> It is truly meet, right, and salutary, that we should at all times, and in all places, give thanks unto Thee, O Lord, Holy Father, Almighty Everlasting God. . . .

For Lutherans, every Sunday is a thanksgiving day.

Thanksgiving is essential to the Christian life. Paul Gerhardt, a seventeenth-century German hymnist, sang,

> O Lord, I sing with voice and heart,
> Joy of my soul! to Thee;
> To earth Thy knowledge I impart,
> As it is known to me. . . .

This affirmation was echoed by Martin Rinkart, who wrote,

> Now thank we all our God
> With heart and hands and voices,
> Who wondrous things hath done,
> In whom His world rejoices;
> Who from our mothers' arms
> Hath blessed us on our way
> With countless gifts of love,
> And still is ours today.

A final type of prayer is supplication. This is the expression of need and desire to God for both spiritual and physical blessings—for ourselves and others. Jesus taught us to pray, "Our Father . . . Hallowed be thy name." That is adoration. "Our Father . . . forgive us our trespasses. . . ." That is confession."Our Father . . . for thine is the kingdom, the power, and glory, forever and ever." That is thanksgiving. But He also taught us to pray, asking, "Our Father . . . thy kingdom come, thy will be done . . . give us this day our daily bread . . . and . . . deliver us from evil. . . ." That is supplication. Supplication has an important place in the Lutheran liturgy. Following the offering, a general prayer is spoken. Sometimes known as the pastoral prayer, the prayer of the church, or the common prayer, it normally includes petitions for the church universal, for all clergy and leaders of the Christian community, for missionaries and evangelists, for the nation and its elected officers, as well as state, county, and local officials, for peace and justice throughout the earth, for schools and universities and centers of research, for homes and parents and children, for those sick in body or soul, for seedtime and harvest, and for ". . . whatever else thou seest that we need. . . ." There is nothing too personal or too public, too small or too large, that we cannot bring to our heavenly Father.

Much more could be written concerning prayer. Space, in a volume of this scope, prohibits further elaboration. James Montgomery, a celebrated poet, taught us the prayer of every pious disciple:

> Lord, teach us how to pray aright
> With reverence and with fear;
> Though dust and ashes in thy sight,
> We may, we must draw near.

He continued, addressing Christ,

> O thou by whom we come to God,
> The Life, the Truth, the Way,
> The path of prayer thyself hast trod,
> Lord, teach us how to pray.

A person of piety not only talks with God in prayer; he also talks about God to his neighbors. At His ascension, Christ Himself connected prayer and proclamation:

> But ye shall receive power, after that the Holy Ghost is come upon you: and ye shall be witnesses unto me both in Jerusalem, and in all Judaea, and in Samaria, and unto the uttermost part of the earth.
>
> [Acts 1:8]

Ten days later, on Pentecost, both realities were present: the disciples in the upper room, praying; the disciples in the street, preaching. The dialectical tension of adoration and proclamation permeates the entire Book of Acts.

This tension has been present in the church ever since Pentecost. It can be a creative tension, enabling men like

Augustine, Francis, and Luther to exhibit a vital piety in both prayer and work. It also can be a destructive tension, disabling men, causing them to become casualties in the quest for piety. Prayer, without the discipline of witnessing and working, can degenerate into the luxuriant monasticism so condemned by the Cluniac reform. Witnessing, without the liturgical discipline of prayer, can degenerate into the aberrant fanaticism exemplified by the Muenster Saints—condemned by both Roman Catholic and Lutheran authorities. Together prayer and proclamation produce a model form of Christian piety, as exemplified by Bernard of Clairvaux, both popular preacher and devotional genius; or by Luther, both teacher of the people and reformer of the liturgy; or by John Wesley, who advocated both daily communion and "open field preaching," who was equally at home before the high altar and before the unchurched masses in the Highlands of Scotland.

These two aspects of piety—prayer and proclamation—are united in a beautiful way in the rite of confirmation, a memorable part of the spiritual pilgrimage of most Lutherans. Confirmation is two things.

Confirmation is the last act of the baptismal liturgy, for in it the confirmed makes his own the promises spoken for him by his sponsors. At the institution of baptism, Jesus connected both prayer and proclamation, for it occurs in the context of the Great Commission. The liturgy of baptism includes both a prayer for regeneration and a recitation of the creed of the church. At confirmation the pastor lays on hands and prays for the child, now come of age. He beseeches that "the Father in Heaven, for Jesus' sake, renew and increase in thee the gift of the Holy Ghost," thus connecting this event to that of Pentecost. The child confesses the Apostles' Creed, proclaiming before family and congregation his intention to live and die by this faith.

Traditionally in Lutheranism confirmation also has been the first act of the communion liturgy, for in it the confirmand declares his desire to be part of the communion of saints. The presiding minister, having heard the child's witness, states, in the words of the *Service Book and Hymnal*,

> For as much as you have made confession of your faith and have received Holy Baptism, I do now, in the Name of the Lord Jesus Christ, the great King and Head of the Church, admit you to the fellowship of the Lord's Table, and to participation in all the spiritual privileges of the Church.

This venerable rite of the church, confirmation, serves as a paradigm of the entire Christian life—rooted in baptism, nourished by prayer, explicated by confession, celebrated in the Eucharist, and resulting in a life of good works. So piety becomes morality. (Refer to Figure 13.)

Morality

Morality has always been important to Lutherans. Luther's conversion in the tower occurred while he was seeking righteousness. A major movement in the history of Lutheranism was called Pietism, defined by a poetry professor at the University of Leipzig:

> What is a Pietist? He's one who
> hears the Word
> And lives a holy life in terms of
> what he's heard.

Lutheran hymnals traditionally have been replete with exhortations to Christian morality. Representative of this longing for ethical living is a hymn composed by Matthias Loy, nineteenth-century theologian and president of the Ohio Synod, who wrote,

> O Lord, who hast my place assigned,
> And made my duties plain,
> Grant for my work a ready mind,
> My wayward tho'ts restrain:
>
> Let me in Thy most holy name,
> My daily task pursue;
> Thy glory be my only aim
> For all I think or do.

Figure 13 **The Cross of Piety and Morality**

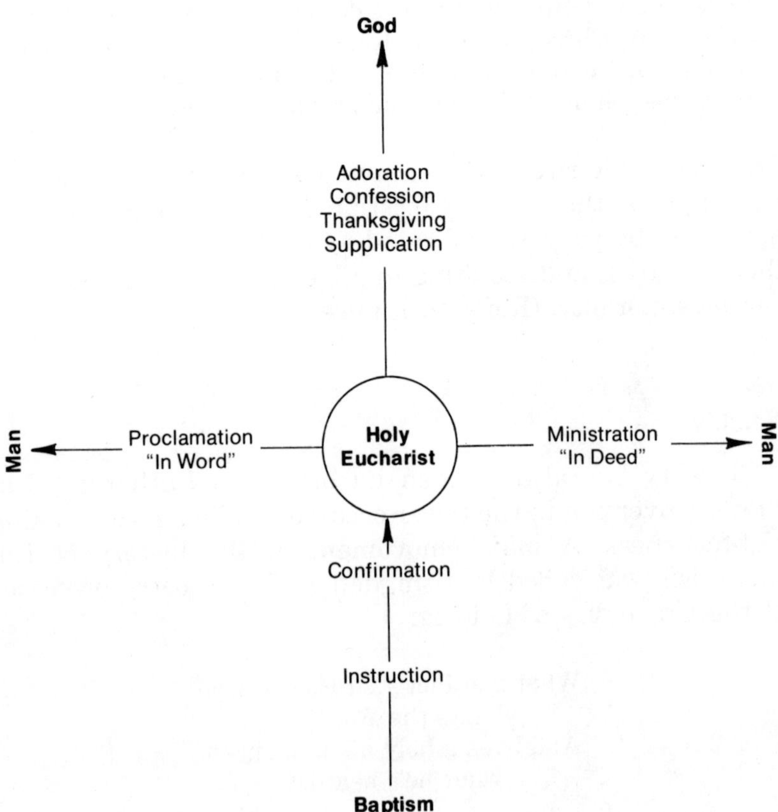

Classical Lutheranism has interpreted morality as realizing the realm of right relationships in both personal and social living. Luther divided the Ten Commandments into two tables: the first three are piety, our duty to God; the last seven are morality, our obligation to our neighbor. This morality is exhibited in both personal relationships, as in the family, and matters of public trust, as in respect for life, liberty, and property within society. For Lutherans, morality is not normally found through a permanent and total rejection of life in society. Instead, it is usually expressed by responsible and joyful participation in the natural orders of creation.

In the previous chapter we have discussed these natural orders—the family, the state, culture, and work. We did not, however, focus upon the issue of motivation. We have made clear the location for godly living; we have yet to explain the inspiration for such a lifestyle. Historically Lutherans have identified four basic motivations for moral living.

One of these is the imitation of Christ. This is an ancient motivation for godly living. Peter exhorted the dispersed Christians of his day, "For even hereunto were ye called: because Christ also suffered for us, leaving us an example, that ye should follow his steps" (I Peter 2:21). Paul admonished the Corinthians, "Be ye followers of me, even as I also am of Christ" (I Cor. 11:1). Both apostles reflected the mind of Christ on this matter, for Jesus said, "Take my yoke upon you, and learn of me; for I am meek and lowly in heart: and ye shall find rest unto your souls" (Matt. 11:29).

This is also a modern motivation for godly living, as reflected in hymnody. Horatius Bonar, conservative Scottish churchman, could sing,

> I long to be like Jesus,
> Meek, loving, lowly, mild;
> I long to be like Jesus,
> The Father's holy Child.

Washington Gladden, liberal American churchman, father of the social gospel, could sing,

> O Master, let me walk with Thee
> In lowly paths of service free;
> Tell me Thy secret, help me bear,
> The strain of toil, the fret of care.

Between ancient and modern times there have been others who were expositors of this motivation for ethical living. One of these was the author of *The Imitation of Christ*, a book praised by Lutheran philosopher Gottfried Wilhelm Leibniz, who said, "Blessed is he who lives according to this book, and is not merely content with admiring it." Tradition ascribes this book to Thomas à Kempis, born near Duesseldorf, Germany, about 1380. An Augustinian monk who took holy orders in 1413, Thomas, before his death at the age of ninety-one, wrote this volume which next to the Bible has become the most widely read devotional classic in the Christian world. His influence on Lutheran Johann Arndt (1555–1621), "the father of German Pietism," is beyond calculation. Called "a second Luther and a third Elijah," Arndt was to pen the most popular book in Lutheranism since the Small Catechism, *True Christianity*, which first appeared in 1605. Arndt, a pastor in Luther's hometown of Eisleben (and then general superintendent of Celle), pioneered this approach to Lutheran morality prior to his death in 1621. It was the way of radical spirituality in the imitation of Jesus. For Arndt, piety was expressed in morality, with Christ as the source and norm for all behavior—interior (aspiration) or exterior (action).

Another motivation for ethical action is the spirit of gratitude. Thanksgiving becomes the origin of morality. This is literally the case in the Eucharist. Holy Communion, as it is observed in most Lutheran churches, involves a dialectical motion. Christ comes to us "in, with and under" the elements of the Supper, so that we encounter Him in all the reality of His death and resurrection. Concurrently, the people come to Christ at the altar. There is an offertory procession of lay leaders presenting gifts before the communion table (often including the bread and wine), and the "coming forward" of the communicants to the holy supper, rededicating themselves to the way of Christ. The liturgy concludes with a recessional from the altar through the portals to the world. In everyday life Lutherans are to live a eucharistic (thankful) existence.

This attitude of gratitude is firmly rooted in both the biblical and the Lutheran traditions. Paul, corresponding with the Romans on knotty ethical issues, advised, "He that eateth, eateth to the Lord, for he giveth God thanks; and he that eateth not, to the Lord he eateth not, and giveth God thanks" (Rom. 14:6). This is one illustration of the apostle's attitude toward God-pleasing behavior. Paul urged the Colossians to be "stablished in the faith" and "abounding therein with thanksgiving" (Col. 2:7). The church in Corinth Paul urged to be "abundant also by many thanksgivings unto God" (II Cor. 9:12). He spoke for the entire ancient church when he taught the Ephesians to be "giving thanks always for all things unto God and the Father in the name of our Lord Jesus Christ" (Eph. 5:20).

This attitude of thanksgiving is also very evident within the classical Lutheran heritage in both hymnody and biography. Rinkart, who lived through the terrors of the Thirty Years' War, could sing,

> O may this bounteous God
> Through all our life be near us,
> With ever joyful hearts
> And blessed peace to cheer us;
> And keep us in his grace,
> And guide us when perplexed,
> And free us from all ills
> In this world and the next.

Another thankful saint was the missionary pastor Hans Egede (1686–1758). The apostle of Greenland, Egede was born in 1686 in Norway to a Danish father. A minister, Egede felt such a sense of gratitude to God that he wanted to share the gospel with those in America who had not heard it. These were the inhabitants of Greenland, earth's largest island. Ravaged by disease, mistreated by European traders, the Eskimos lacked both physical comfort in this world and eternal assurance for the next. In 1721 Egede sailed on the ship *Good Hope* for Greenland, where he ministered for more than fifteen years to the people of the far north. His life was one of "persevering kindness" that won the hearts of the people to Jesus. In this missionary bishop one finds an embodiment of the Lutheran ethic of gratitude.

Yet another motivation for ethical action is the spirit of "fear and obedience" before the Lord. A sense of wonder results in work. Those saved seek to serve. For believers the law can be a tutor in holiness. This moral mood is one that permeates the Bible. The Lord told the old Israel through Moses, "Ye shall be unto me a kingdom of priests, and an holy nation" (Exod. 19:6). Peter reaffirmed this calling, informing the new Israel that "ye are a chosen generation, a royal priesthood, an holy nation, a peculiar people; that ye should shew forth the praises of him who hath called you out of darkness . . ." (I Peter 2:9). That passage provided Luther with one of the four cardinal convictions of the Reformation: the universal priesthood of believers. All the baptized are, like Aaron of old, under obligation to re-present God to men and men to God.

This ethic of obedience has been especially strong within German Lutheranism. The attitude, however, is not alien to Anglo-Saxon Christianity, which produced the gospel song, "Trust and obey, for there's no other way/To be happy in Jesus but to trust and obey." Illustrative of this ethic is a German Lutheran who ministered in America, eventually becoming a leader of the Missouri Synod. Born in 1810 in the kingdom of Hanover, F. C. D. Wyneken was reared with an incomplete knowledge of Christ. After working as a tutor he started to explore biblical lore, musing on the Book of Maccabees. A series of conversions occurred, causing Wyneken to become obedient to God's purpose for his life. Wyneken professed Christ, entered the ministry, and served in America. In spite of himself, Wyneken went first to Baltimore, then to Fort Wayne, Indiana, becoming a patriarch of Lutheranism in the lower Midwest. Wyneken admitted,

> With deep regret I must confess that as far as I know myself, neither love for the Lord nor for the orphaned brethren drove me to America nor a natural desire. Rather I went contrary to my will and after great conflicts, from *a sense of duty*, driven in, and by, my conscience. As much as it saddens me that I did not have and still do not have more love for the Lord and that he had to drive me like a slave, still at times of spiritual trials and temptations, doubts and tribulations, which came over my soul during my ministry, this was my comfort that I could say: I had to come to America. Thou, O Lord, knowest how gladly I would have remained at home, but had I done this, I should not have been able to look up to Thee and pray to Thee; so I simply had to come.[4]

Surely here is a man whose motto could have been "trust and obey."

4. Quoted by Walter A. Baepler, *A Century of Grace: A History of the Missouri Synod, 1847–1947* (Saint Louis: Concordia, 1947), p. 54.

The last motivation for ethical action is love for Christ and one's neighbor. Paul, in a chapter many regard as his most splendid writing, said,

> Though I speak with the tongues of men and of angels, and have not charity, I am become as sounding brass, or a tinkling cymbal. And though I have the gift of prophecy, and understand all mysteries, and all knowledge; and though I have all faith, so that I could remove mountains, and have not charity, I am nothing. And though I bestow all my goods to feed the poor, and though I give my body to be burned, and have not charity, it profiteth me nothing.
>
> And now abideth faith, hope, charity, these three; but the greatest of these is charity.
>
> [I Cor. 13:1–3, 13]

To the apostle, charity or love, expressed in liturgy before God and in philanthropy to one's neighbor, is the ultimate expression of Christian morality.

After the Second World War, Lutheran World Action (LWA) worked to alleviate the suffering of millions of refugees. Soon LWA was nicknamed "Love's Working Arm." This is the highest articulation of the Lutheran ethic we know. Saved by grace, not works, the evangelical Christian need not live a self-centered life, one obsessed with his own salvation. Since salvation is the gift of God in Christ, love is liberated to minister to the neighbor. This I do, not because I *must* in order to please God. This I do because I *want* to serve my suffering neighbor. This "Good Samaritan ethic," taught by Jesus in His most famous parable, celebrated by Paul in his most famous passage, is the apex of Lutheran morality.

The love ethic is embodied in hymnody and Lutheran biography. Charles Wesley, profoundly influenced by Lutheran and Moravian piety, wrote,

> Love divine, all loves excelling,
> Joy of heaven, to earth come down:
> Fix in us thy humble dwelling,
> All thy faithful mercies crown:
> Jesus, thou art all compassion,
> Pure, unbounded love thou art;

Visit us with thy salvation,
Enter every trembling heart.

For the Wesleys, their generation's incarnation of love was found in the city of Halle. In this German community had lived the remarkable Lutheran pastor August Hermann Francke (1663–1727). Converted while contemplating the love of Christ, Francke observed, "When I knelt down I did not believe that there was a God; but when I stood up again I would no doubt have given my life for him." He did. Francke was a renewer of the church. Halle had replaced Wittenberg as the theological center of Lutheranism. Its university enrolled more than one thousand ministerial students. Halle was a publications center; it produced literature for Lutherans everywhere. Halle sent missionaries to points as remote as Philadelphia and India's Malabar Coast. Halle excelled in philanthropy—caring for orphans and widows, the aged and the infirm, providing jobs for the unemployed and sanctuary for the oppressed. Countless thousands benefited from these institutions of mercy. All of these agencies were funded entirely by freewill offerings. Here was born the doctrine of stewardship as understood by America's Lutherans. For Francke, the proof text for his high adventure in love was Paul's promise: ". . . God is able to make all grace abound toward you: that ye, always having all sufficiency in all things, may abound in every good work" (II Cor. 9:8). One visitor to Halle exclaimed, "Compassion, thy name is Francke; love, thy home is Saxony; Christ, thy people are the pious Lutherans."

To many observers Lutheranism is synonymous with theology. Yet a survey conducted in Fort Wayne, Indiana, a citadel of conservative Lutheranism, suggests otherwise. There Lutheranism was understood as being synonymous with charity. Though Fort Wayne has been the home of a Lutheran junior and senior college, a major theological seminary, more than forty congregations, a district office, and a number of other institutions, these were not the images of Lutheranism perceived by the people. The images of Lutheranism remembered by the public were those of philanthropy and charity—a Lutheran hospital, a home for the aged, the service of deaconesses, and outreach among the unemployed and the poor. One Hoosier said, "Lutherans care—a lot."

Piety (devotion to God and man) embodied in morality is Lutheran theology translated into life. Christ becomes real, a truth who is able to live in us, as we follow His way through the world. This way of piety and morality has been followed by countless Lutheran heroes of faith through the centuries, including:

Martin Luther, reformer

Philip Melanchthon, preceptor

Martin Chemnitz and Jacob Andreae, confessors

Albrecht Duerer, Franz Hals, Hans Holbein, and Lucas Cranach, artists

Johann Arndt, seer

Phillipp Jacob Spener and August Hermann Francke, pastors

Father Johann Campanius, evangelist

Claus Harms and Wilhelm Loehe, C. F. W. Walther and Hans Hauge, renewers of the church

Johann Sebastian Bach and George Frederick Handel, musicians

Hans Egede, Henry Melchior Muhlenberg, Christian Frederick Schwartz, missionaries

Frederick the Wise, Christian III, Haakon VII, sovereigns

Gottfried Wilhelm Leibniz, Immanuel Kant, and G. W. F. Hegel, philosophers

Louise Rathke, deaconess

Mother Basilea Schlink, sister

Gustavus Adolphus and Dietrich Bonhoeffer, martyrs

Nicolai Grundtvig, poet and bishop

Hanns Lilje, bishop

Albert Schweitzer, physician

Martin Niemoeller, witness

Like those of old, "all these obtained a good report through faith."

CHAPTER

The People of Victory

> I believe . . . He shall come again, with glory, to judge both the quick and the dead; whose kingdom shall have no end.
>
> And I believe in . . . the resurrection of the dead, and the life of the world to come. Amen.

To outward appearances, Maria Klein had led a tragic life. Born before the turn of the century to a German-speaking family in a predominantly Rumanian region of Austria-Hungary, she knew what it meant to be a minority person. Her mother died early. Her father, an officer in the Imperial Army, tried as best he could to rear his daughters. Hard times followed. When Maria was eighteen, her father asked her to go to America to "earn some money to build a house." She left, a bird of passage, coming to Columbus, Ohio, where she worked in a series of sweatshops, saving, through much sacrifice, dollars to send home. World War I meant that Maria was stranded in the United States. What was to be a place of temporary employment became a place of permanent residence. She never saw the house her money built in Europe. In the 1920s she married, a marriage that proved to be childless. Her husband was soon injured in an industrial accident and was an invalid many of the years they were together. The prosperity of the twenties by-passed the Kleins. The austerity of the thirties visited them. It was a struggle for Maria to make ends meet—to keep and furnish their small brick house, to pay the mortgage, to meet medical bills, and to find a surplus from which to help relatives in Europe. Somehow

Charles Porterfield Krauth

(1823–1883)
Churchman and Theologian

Maria managed. Following World War II, when many of her family were refugees in Germany, she was able to provide for their resettlement in Ohio. When one of the authors met Maria she was a widow, living on Social Security. She was in church every Sunday. "Oh, how I love the services of God's house," she told me. I'm sure she meant it. When money was raised to build a parish house, Maria, out of her poverty, gave more than fifty dollars. In spite of affliction, Maria was a woman of deep conviction. One Sunday she shared her faith with me. It was the last Sunday of the church year, Memorial Sunday (*Todtenfest* on the German agenda). I had preached about heaven. That sermon moved Maria. She asked, "Pastor, when will God let me go home?" Shortly afterward she fell, broke her hip, and died. At her funeral, the church was filled to capacity with mourners. All of us knew that for Maria death was a victory. By God's grace she had overcome all kinds of tragedy. Maria believed she had an eternal destiny. When she recited the creed, it was more than a theological affirmation. It was a personal aspiration: "I believe in . . . the resurrection of the dead, and the life of the world to come."

It is appropriate in this last chapter of a book on Lutheranism to speak of "the last things." Theologians call these matters eschatology. They are chronologically last, in the life of the individual and in the history of the world. They are logically last, for they are the termination point for persons and institutions. They are axiologically last, for they are the lasting things, the ends by which we order our lives, the values centered in the future, which, like powerful magnets, draw us forward through time toward our rendezvous with destiny.

In this chapter let us consider our personal and our social destiny.

Personal Destiny

At first glance, we do not appear to have a very desirable destiny. Death seems to be the goal of life. It is an empirical fact that life terminates. The Bible reports stories of a few individuals who escaped death, such as Enoch (Gen. 5:24) and

Elijah (II Kings 2:11). Christian tradition—accepted by the Orthodox and Roman Catholic churches, as well as some Anglicans and Lutherans—states that Mary, the mother of Jesus, was also spared, through dormition or assumption. But both biological fact and biblical narrative insist that death is the end of all living beings. According to the Scriptures even Jesus, the Son of God, tasted death on the cross and rested in the tomb.

Death has been defined many ways. Medical science explains it as the termination of bodily functions or the cessation of brain activity. Clinicians dispute the actual time of death or how to determine it. The traditional theological definition of the word *death* is twofold: physical death is the violent separation of body and soul, the two component parts of human personality; spiritual death is the eternal separation of the soul from God, its author and owner. The Bible presents death, in either form, as something unnatural, the result of the fall. Man was made for life; that is the witness of the opening chapters of Genesis. "Be fruitful, and multiply," stated the Deity. Men and women were to rejoice in life, to celebrate and share it, to enhance and extend it, to possess it eternally. Within the garden, however, was the potential for death. God said, "But of the tree of knowledge of good and evil, thou shalt not eat . . . for in the day that thou eatest thereof thou shalt surely die" (Gen. 2:17). The act of disobedience, whereby the primordial parents ate of the fruit, caused them to enter into a sacramental relationship with evil. Sin and death became part of their very natures. This caused them to know the power of anti-God (or Satan). As the force of anarchy and chaos in the universe, Satan stands for disintegration. Once in communion with such demonic forces, human life began to deteriorate. The final disintegration of personality is the divorce of body and soul. The body then returns to the elements out of which it is composed, for, as Genesis states, "dust thou art, and unto dust shalt thou return" (Gen. 3:19). Of the billions who have lived, little remains. Their physical elements have returned to nature. No wonder the burial service of *The Book of Common Prayer* says,

> Man that is born of a woman hath but a short time to live, and is full of misery. He cometh up, and is cut down, like a flower; he fleeth as it were a shadow, and never continueth in one stay.

Death destroys the body, but what of the soul?

The soul does not perish at death. That is the common conviction of both natural and revealed theology. The American poet, Henry Wadsworth Longfellow, writing in "A Psalm of Life," said,

> Life is real! Life is earnest!
> And the grave is not its goal;
> Dust thou art, to dust returnest,
> Was not spoken of the soul.

This echoes the sentiment of Scripture, where the Preacher states, "Then shall the dust return to the earth as it was: and the spirit shall return unto God who gave it "(Eccles. 12:7). This is the doctrine of the immortality of the soul. This doctrine teaches that the soul is indestructable; that it is capable of life apart from the physical body; that it can exist, following death, under circumstances and conditions which we can only dimly imagine.

The belief in immortality, while older and more universal than Christianity, rests on five major arguments.

There are the metaphysical proofs. The soul of man by definition is not physical, but is derived from the immortal and eternal Spirit, God. The Book of Genesis reports, "The LORD God formed man of the dust of the ground, *and breathed into his nostrils the breath of life*" (Gen. 2:7; italics added). The body is of earth; the soul is of heaven. While the body is composed of physical elements, which can decompose, the soul is a unit, incapable of destruction, capable of fellowship with God. Religion, the longing of man for God, is proof that there is something in man that is immortal, for else there would be no common ground for contact between the human and the divine. Evidence of this is seen in the capacity of the human spirit to transcend physical existence. The mind can imagine the future, remember the past, contemplate alternative worlds, and aspire to perfection. The heart can love, without limits of history or geography. The will longs for permanence and righteousness. Even the author of Ecclesiastes, for all his lamentation about life, can admit God "has also set eternity in their heart" (Eccles. 3:11, NASB).

There are the historical proofs. Immortality is one of the most universally held beliefs in the history of humanity. Monuments to faith in personal immortality abound. Neanderthals buried their dead. The pyramids of ancient Egypt testify to an expectation of life after death. Tombs from the Tiber to the Tigris reflect this longing. Cemeteries from Chicago to Chang'An, from the Stone Age to the High Renaissance, for the rich and the poor all reflect the appeal of this conviction. Furthermore, belief in immortality has been held by some of the most sophisticated members of the human community, from Socrates, Aristotle, Plato, and Zeno through Anselm and Thomas Aquinas to William James, Josiah Royce, and Alfred North Whitehead. Immortality commends itself to the highest intellect as a feasible option after physical death. Because immortality has been the conviction of "the brightest and the best," it commends itself to us.

There are the analogical proofs. Analogy compares things or ideas to find similarities between them. It is one way of learning. Sometimes analogy is helpful in religious matters. In the history of thought, spiritual realities often have been explained by physical analogies. By comparing the known with the unknown we grow in understanding. This method applies to the doctrine of immortality. Among the many analogies employed, two are especially helpful—those of the seasons and of the seed.

From time immemorial men have compared life to the succession of seasons. A kinship between human existence and nature has been perceived. Man, like the year, experiences spring (childhood), summer (youth), autumn (maturity), and winter (old age and death). Spring rests in the womb of winter. Death is mother to rebirth. Though life dies in the winter, it is reborn in the spring. As nature contains the cycle of death and rebirth, so it is felt that human life can survive the tomb. It is noteworthy that Easter, the Christian festival of resurrection, corresponds, in the northern hemisphere, to the return of spring. Venatius Fortunatus, Latin hymnist, compared the two, saying,

> Earth with joy confesses, clothing her for spring,
> All good gifts return with her returning King:
> Bloom in every meadow, leaves on every bough,
> Speak his sorrows ended, hail his triumph now.

Equally ancient is the analogy of the seed. Bodies, from early times, have been buried in the earth as seed is sown in the soil. Often the corpse has been laid to rest in a posture comparable to that of the fetus in the womb. The hope expressed by this action is obvious—rebirth will follow. Both Jesus and Paul employed this venerable analogy. Christ said, anticipating His own death, "Except a corn of wheat fall into the ground and die, it abideth alone; but if it die, it bringeth forth much fruit" (John 12:24). Paul wrote concerning these matters to the Corinthian church. About burial, he said,

> . . . thou sowest not that body that shall be, but bare grain, it may chance of wheat, or of some other grain: But God giveth it a body as it hath pleased him, and to every seed his own body.
>
> So also is the resurrection of the dead. It is sown in corruption: it is raised in incorruption. . . . It is sown a natural body; it is raised a spiritual body. There is a natural body, and there is a spiritual body.
>
> [I Cor. 15:37–38, 42, 44]

Death, understood in such analogies, is not annihilation but transformation.

There are psychological proofs. These are many. To begin with, we feel immortal. Furthermore, most of us desire immortality. Some lives demand immortality. The noble army of martyrs—Jeremiah and Abraham Lincoln, John Huss and Thomas Cranmer, Joan of Arc and John the Baptist—like Abel, their biblical prototype, "being dead yet speaketh" (Heb. 11:4). Their sacrificial deaths cry out for life abundant. Still other lives also demand immortality—those of the brave and the true. Extinction simply could not be the fate of an Isaiah, a Michaelangelo, a Frédéric Chopin, a Saint John the Divine, a Johann Sabastian Bach, or an Isaac Newton. There is something immortal about such genius. Yet other lives demand immortality—those who have not attained fulfillment in their earthly pilgrimage, women and men of magnificent potential, who were cut down before their course was run. Imagine what Wolfgang Amadeus Mozart would have been had he attained even more maturity, or Dietrich Bonhoeffer, or Gustavus Adolphus. The question is as haunting as Thomas Gray's "Elegy Written in a Country Church-Yard," where the poet mused,

> Perhaps in this neglected spot is laid
>   Some heart once pregnant with celestial fire;
> Hands, that the rod of empire might have sway'd,
>   Or wak'd to ecstasy the living lyre.

And even yet other lives demand immortality—those of the oppressed and the deprived, denied "the furniture of fortune," unable to fulfill their potential for living within the confines of history. Conscience calls for gracious recompense for such persons. Of them Isaac Watts thought, when he wrote,

> They go from strength to strength,
> Through this dark vale of tears,
> Till each arrives at length,
> Till each in heaven appears.

There are the biblical proofs. For Lutherans the compelling argument for life after death comes from the sacred Scriptures. Even the patriarchs, when they died, were said to have been "gathered to [their] people" (Gen. 25:8). When Moses encountered the living God, He introduced Himself as the God of the patriarchs, for "I am the God of thy father, the God of Abraham, the God of Isaac, and the God of Jacob" (Exod. 3:6). Christ commented on that passage, showing how it testified to the immortality of these men, saying, "God is not the God of the dead, but of the living" (Matt. 22:32). Jesus saw Abraham in paradise, as was illustrated in His story of

Lazarus and Dives (Luke 16:22–23). David, king of Judah, upon the death of his firstborn child by Bathsheba, "... arose from the earth, and washed, and anointed himself, and changed his apparel, and came into the house of the LORD, and worshipped. ..." (II Sam. 12:20). When asked by his servants how he could mourn while the lad was ill and rejoice now that he was dead, David said,

> ... while the child was yet alive, I fasted and wept: for I said, Who can tell whether God will be gracious to me, that the child may live? But now he is dead, wherefore should I fast? can I bring him back again? *I shall go to him*, but he shall not return to me.
>
> [II Sam. 12:22–23; italics added]

David knew his son was not lost, but found in God, and that in due season he would rejoin him. This conviction is evident throughout the Scriptures. When Moses (who died) and Elijah (who was translated, like Enoch) appeared to Christ on the Mount of Transfiguration, the Master was not at all surprised (Matt. 17:1–9). Christ had taught that while men can kill the body, they cannot destroy the soul (Matt. 10:28). Jesus could later promise the penitent thief on the cross, "Today shalt thou be with me in paradise" (Luke 23:43). Christ had earlier warned, "What is a man profited, if he shall gain the whole world, and lose his own soul?" (Matt. 16:26). The belief of Christ in the immortality of the soul was communicated to his followers. Paul, who met the living Christ on the Damascus Road, spoke of death not as extinction but as communication with Christ. Paul wrote, "Whilst we are at home in the body, we are absent from the Lord" (II Cor. 5:6), but he longed "to be absent from the body, and to be present with the Lord" (II Cor. 5:8). Or again, the apostle told the Philippians of his "having a desire to depart, and to be with Christ" (Phil. 1:23). Saint John the Divine, presumably the disciple Jesus especially loved, had visions not only of the ascended Christ, but also of the dead saints, living in victory in paradise, "... a great multitude, which no man could number, of all nations, and kindreds, and peoples, and tongues, ... [who] cried with a loud voice, saying, Salvation to our God, which sitteth upon the throne, and unto the Lamb" (Rev.

7:9–10). From the Pentateuch to the Apocalypse, the biblical literature testifies to personal survival following death.

What happens to the soul after death?

Lutherans believe that there is an interim state, a period between personal death and public judgment of all people at the end of history. During this time the body rests in the tomb. The soul returns to God. At death a private judgment is rendered. Saved souls enter into rest, called heaven or paradise. Lost souls enter into torment, called hell or the inferno. On the last day all bodies will be raised and reunited with their souls, and a public judgment will be rendered for each person. The just will enjoy the immediate presence of God in a new heaven and a new earth. The condemned will be separated eternally from the fellowship of God.

Our knowledge of the interim state is scanty. We do well to follow Reinhold Niebuhr's advice and not offer too much speculation concerning "the furniture of heaven" or "the temperature of hell." On the basis of the biblical witness, however, some things can be said with certainty concerning heaven and hell.

One of these is that Jesus believed that heaven exists. On the cross He commended His soul to God, assuring the penitent thief that they would be together in paradise (Luke 23:46; 23:43). Christ promised His followers prior to His death that He was going to heaven to prepare a place for them (John 14:3). Jesus taught his friends that He would bring them to heaven (John 14:3), which He compared with a house filled with many rooms (John 14:2). The Master also informed the saints that this kingdom had been prepared for them from the very foundation of the world (Matt. 25:34). In heaven the elect, Christ said, are with Him (John 17:24) and they will behold God and enjoy His blessing (Matt. 5:8). This is called the beatific vision.

Paul also believed that heaven exists. This was a corollary of his belief in Christ. The apostle was converted amidst light and a voice from heaven, that of Jesus Christ inviting him to discipleship (Acts 9:1–9). Following his instruction in the faith, Paul taught much concerning paradise. To the Romans he wrote that the tribulations of the present life are negligible compared with the glories of heaven (Rom. 8:18). Those in heaven behold God. Paradise, for Paul, was a place of light, forgiveness, love, peace, justice, and joy (see Col. 1:12–15). The apostle spoke not simply on the authority of instruction, but on the basis of personal revelation, for he wrote that he himself had been exalted to the third heaven (II Cor. 12:2–4). What Paul taught others, he desired for himself. Writing to the Philippians, people he loved dearly, Paul admitted he would rather depart and be with the Lord (Phil. 1:23). For Paul, paradise was a reality, even on earth.

The faith wrought by Christ and taught by Paul was accepted by the early church. Stephen, protomartyr, at the hour of his death, said, "Behold, I see the heavens opened, and the Son of man standing on the right hand of God" (Acts 7:56). Peter, prince of the apostles, exhorted the diaspora church to persevere in the faith, for we have "an inheritance incorruptible, and undefiled, and that fadeth not away, reserved in heaven" (I Peter 1:4). The author of Hebrews shared this conviction, writing of heaven as an eternal sabbath, for "there remaineth therefore a rest to the people of God" (Heb. 4:9). In that place, which he called "the city of the living God, the heavenly Jerusalem" (Heb. 12:22), filled with "an innumerable company of angels," we will come "to the general assembly and church of the firstborn, which are written in heaven, and to God the Judge of all, and to the spirits of just men made perfect" (Heb. 12:23). Saint John the Divine experienced heaven more fully than many others in the early church. While in the Spirit he wrote,

> After this I beheld, and, lo, a great multitude, which no man could number, of all nations, and kindreds, and people, and tongues, stood before the throne, and before the Lamb, clothed with white robes, and palms in their hands; And cried with a loud voice, saying, Salvation to our God which sitteth upon the throne and unto the Lamb.
>
> [Rev. 7:9–10]

No wonder this seer closed the Apocalypse and the canon and the witness of the apostolic church with the cry, "Even so, come, Lord Jesus" (Rev. 22:20).

Christians through the centuries have believed in heaven. Let us cite but three examples. Bernard of Clairvaux, a renewer of the medieval church, spoke of paradise:

The home of fadeless splendor,
  Of flowers that fear no thorn,
Where they shall dwell as children
  Who here as exiles mourn;
The peace of all the faithful,
  The calm of all the blest,
Inviolate, unvaried,
  Divinest, sweetest, best.

Bernard's contemporary, Peter Abelard, professor at Paris and critic of abuses in the church, confessed his faith in heaven in these words:

O what their joy and their glory must be,
Those endless Sabbaths the blessed ones see!
Crown for the valiant; to weary ones rest;
God shall be all, and in all ever blest.

Martin Luther, the reformer, had his faith in heaven tested at the time of the death of his fourteen-year-old daughter, Magdalena. As she was on her deathbed, Luther prayed, "O God, I love her so, but thy will be done." Then Luther asked his daughter, "*Magdalenchen*, my little girl, you would like to stay with your father here and you would be glad to go to your Father in heaven?" To this the child answered, "Yes, dear father, as God wills." Luther was amazed at Magdalena's simple faith. Later, following her death, Luther said, "*Du liebes Lenchen*, you will rise and shine like the stars and the sun. How strange it is to know that she is at peace and all is well, and yet to be so sorrowful!"[1]

Lutherans believe that heaven exists. Most would agree with Luther when he wrote,

> It is a divine truth that Abraham lives with God, serves him, and rules with him. But what kind of life that is . . . is a different question. How the soul rests we cannot know: but it is certain that it lives.[2]

1. Quoted by Roland H. Bainton, *Here I Stand: A Life of Martin Luther* (New York: Abingdon-Cokesbury, 1950), p. 227.

2. Quoted by John Theodore Mueller, *Christian Dogmatics* (Saint Louis: Concordia, 1955), p. 617.

Most would also agree with Johann Gerhard when he confessed,

> Scripture, by a general appellation, speaks of a place.... Not that it is a corporeal and physical place, properly so called, but because it is a 'where' into which souls, separated from their bodies, are brought together. Scripture enumerates only two such receptacles, or habitations, of the souls, one of which, prepared for the souls of the godly, is called by the most ordinary appellation *heaven*, and the other, intended for the souls of the wicked, is called *hell*.[3]

Lutherans also believe hell exists. This belief is held for many reasons.

One of these reasons is that Jesus believed hell exists. In one of His most famous stories, the parable of Lazarus and Dives, Christ described the lost "in hell . . . being in torments" (Luke 16:23) and crying out, "I am tormented in this flame" (Luke 16:24). On another occasion Jesus warned His disciples to take care so as not "to go into hell, into the fire that never shall be quenched" (Mark 9:43). In a different context Christ admonished those who felt spiritually secure to beware, lest they "be cast out into outer darkness: there shall be weeping and gnashing of teeth" (Matt. 8:12). The master predicted that the angels shall "... sever the wicked from among the just, And shall cast them into the furnace of fire: there shall be wailing and gnashing of teeth" (Matt. 13:49–50). The Scriptures also report that the Savior, following His death, visited hell (see I Peter 3:19). David Hollaz, seventeenth-century theologian, offered the traditional Lutheran interpretation of this text, writing, "Christ descended into hell, not for the purpose of suffering ... but to triumph over the devils." In both word and deed, Christ demonstrated that hell is a reality to be feared, a punishment to be avoided.

Paul also believed hell exists. In his letter to the Romans Paul referred to the "tribulation and anguish" set aside for the evil (Rom. 2:9). That was not a mere passing opinion. Writing to the Thessalonians much earlier in his ministry Paul had said,

3. Quoted, *ibid.*

> And to you who are troubled rest with us, when the Lord Jesus shall be revealed from heaven with his mighty angels. In flaming fire taking vengeance on them that know not God, and that obey not the gospel of our Lord Jesus Christ: Who shall be punished with everlasting destruction from the presence of the Lord, and from the glory of his power. . . .
>
> [II Thess. 1:7–9]

To the Galatians Paul sent a serious admonition, for he felt they were denying the faith not only in their words but also by their deeds. In that epistle the apostle listed "the works of the flesh" that invite eternal damnation:

> . . . Adultery, fornication, uncleanness, lasciviousness, Idolatry, witchcraft, hatred, variance, emulations, wrath, strife, seditions, heresies, Envyings, murders, drunkenness, revellings, and such like: of the which I tell you before, as I have also told you in time past, that they which do such things shall not inherit the kingdom of God.
>
> [Gal. 5:19–21]

The witness of the New Testament reveals that belief in the existence of hell was widespread in the early church. Peter wrote of Christ's descent into hell (I Peter 3:19–20) and Saint John the Divine, who enjoyed the beatific vision of paradise, also experienced the dreadful vision of the inferno. Inspired of God, John saw Satan and those who follow him suffering, for

> the same shall drink of the wine of the wrath of God, which is poured out without mixture into the cup of his indignation; and he shall be tormented with fire and brimstone in the presence of the holy angels, and in the presence of the Lamb: And the smoke of their torment ascendeth up for ever and ever: and they have no rest day or night. . . .
>
> [Rev. 14:10–11]

Or again the author of the Apocalypse could write,

> And the devil that deceived them was cast into the lake of fire and brimstone, where the beast and the false prophet are, and shall be tormented day and night for ever and ever.

> And whosoever was not found written in the book of life was cast into the lake of fire.
>
> [Rev. 20:10, 15]

Because of the teaching of Christ, the testimony of the apostles, and the heartrending vision of the seer, most Christians through the centuries have believed in hell. To them, however, it is a source of eternal comfort to know that on Good Friday, on the cross, Jesus Christ endured the pangs of hell for them, that they might be declared righteous before the Father, and enter into the bliss of paradise. Both the Catholic mystic, Bernard of Clairvaux, and the Lutheran hymnist, Paul Gerhardt (who translated the prayer), took consolation in this, praying to Jesus:

> Be near when I am dying
> O show thy cross to me;
> And for my succor flying,
> Come, Lord, to set me free:
> These eyes, new faith receiving,
> From thee shall never move;
> For he who dies believing,
> Dies safely, through thy love.

Social Destiny

Christian expectations, however, are not merely personal; they are also social. Eschatology, the doctrine of the last things, includes much that is corporate, concerning the collective fate of the human family. These teachings center in the Christian belief that history will climax in the second coming of Christ. Variously called the second advent, the parousia, or the eschaton, the return of Jesus to earth is the great hope of the church. Each Sunday Christians confess, "He shall come again with glory. . . ."

This affirmation is the most ancient confession of the church. Paul's earliest known writing, his first letter to the Thessalonians, concerns this subject. The last book of the New Testament, the Revelation, closes with the promise of Christ, "Surely I come quickly" (Rev. 22:20) and the prayer of the church, "Even so, come, Lord Jesus" (Rev. 22:20). Matthew, a book believed by many scholars to have been composed as a catechism for the apostolic church, contains the five great discourses of Christ. The last of these is about the second coming (Matt. 24–25). This same Gospel concludes with the Master's promise to be present "unto the end of the world" (Matt. 28:20). The final Gospel, John, concludes with a discussion of the Savior's return (John 21:22–23). To further confirm this hope, the story of the church literally begins with the proclamation of the second coming. At the ascension angels inform the disciples that ". . . this same Jesus, which is taken up from you into heaven, shall so come in like manner as ye have seen him go into heaven" (Acts 1:11).

What do we know about the second coming of Christ?

One thing we do not know is the time. Jesus told the disciples, "Of that day and hour knoweth no man, no, not the angels of heaven, but my Father only" (Matt. 24:36). The Master's return will come as a surprise, like a thief in the night (see Luke 12:39) or like the flood in the time of Noah (Matt. 24:38). All efforts to predict the exact year, day, and hour of the Lord's advent are doomed to failure. While His reappearance on earth is certain, the time is not. Jesus admonished His followers, "Be ye therefore ready also: for the Son of Man cometh at an hour when ye think not" (Luke 12:40).

We do know, however, the signs that will accompany His return. These signs will be of a paradoxical nature. In many ways, amazing normality will be observed. Life will continue with its regular routine. Christ foresaw that there would be "eating and drinking, marrying and giving in marriage" right until the last moment (Matt. 24:38). A superficial calm, like the quiet before a summer thunderstorm, will prevail. To those caught up in the web of daily existence, life will seem to go on, business as usual. However, some amazing abnormalities will be observable. But as with the star of Bethlehem (see Matt. 2), which greeted Messiah's first advent, so the signs that will foretell His second coming will be seen only by the discerning. One of the astounding facts of Christmas was the ability of people in Judaea to ignore the celestial sign of Savior's birth. We have no record in the New Testament that the scribes or the doctors, the Pharisees or the

Sadducees, King Herod or his court, the citizens of Jerusalem or the shepherds of Judaea beheld (at least with understanding) the

> . . . star of wonder, star of might,
> Star with royal beauty bright. . . .

So it will be with the signs that will herald the return of Christ to earth; they will be obvious to all, yet most people will be oblivious to them. Even though sky and sea, earth and heaven, culture and conscience all will have given testimony to what is about to transpire, the vast majority of humankind will be taken by surprise.

What are these signs of the return of Christ?

According to the sacred Scriptures extraordinary events will occur on the eve of Christ's second advent. These signs can be clustered into four categories.

There will be signs in the physical world. Nature itself "groaneth and travaileth in pain" (Rom. 8:22) as never before. Earthquakes, floods and fires, and disturbances in the heavens will transpire. Jesus predicted,

> And there shall be signs in the sun, and in the moon, and in the stars; and upon the earth distress of nations, with perplexity; the sea and the waves roaring; Men's hearts failing them for fear, and for looking after those things which are coming on the earth: for the powers of heaven shall be shaken.
>
> [Luke 21:25–26]

There will be signs in the biological world. Life itself will cry out to "be delivered from the bondage of corruption" (Rom. 8:21). Disease and famine will sweep the earth, as life enters into mortal combat with death. Christ, the Lord of life, foresaw this time when "there shall be famines, and pestilences" (Matt. 24:7) and all manner of manifestations of Satan, the lord of death.

There will be signs in the social world. Human community itself will be radically disrupted. Cancers, as old as the age of the Caesars, described by Paul in the opening passages of his Letter to the Romans (Rom. 1:21–32), will finally take their toll on the fabric of civilization. Christ the King anticipated “wars and rumors of wars” (Matt. 24:6) and that “nation shall rise against nation” (Matt. 24:7), while within states the rights of believers will be denied, and “then shall they deliver you up to be afflicted . . . and ye shall be hated of all nations for my name’s sake” (Matt. 24:9). The saints will recognize, as did Paul, that “. . . the sufferings of this present time are not worthy to be compared with the glory which shall be revealed in us” (Rom. 8:18). Before the glory of the elect can be manifested, the persecution of the church must occur.

There will be signs in the spiritual world. The souls of the saints will cry out to God, and “the Spirit itself maketh intercession for us with groaning which cannot be uttered” (Rom. 8:26). Christ and anti-Christ will come to full combat. Within the church there will be contradictory signs—both apostasy, as “the love of many shall wax cold” (Matt. 24:12), and apostolicity, as the planet is evangelized, for “this gospel of the kingdom shall be preached in all the world for a witness unto all nations . . .” (Matt. 24:14). Contradictory signs will include iniquity and sanctity, heresy and orthodoxy, false prophets and faithful preachers, the desertion of Jesus by many and the preservation of the elect until the end. Persecution, as never before known, will transpire; yet proclamation of the gospel, in unprecendented scope and power, will also occur. Then, as Luther quipped, when “the Egyptian darkness is full, the Sun of Righteousness will rise.”

What will Christ do when He returns?

According to the faith of the church, three events will conclude the drama of human history.

The first event will be the resurrection of the dead. Bodies and souls will be reunited. The billions resting in the earth will rise. Jesus said,

> Marvel not at this: for the hour is coming, in the which all that are in the graves shall hear his voice, And shall come forth; they that have done good, unto the resurrection of life; and they that have done evil, unto the resurrection of damnation.
>
> [John 5:28–29]

The second event will be the final judgment of men and nations. All who have lived will be gathered before the Master to give account of their lives. Jesus said,

> When the Son of man shall come in his glory, and all the holy angels with him, then shall he sit upon the throne of his glory: And before him shall be gathered all nations: and he shall separate them one from another, as a shepherd divideth his sheep from the goats. . . .
>
> [Matt. 25:31–32]

In this grand assize, those who believed in Christ will be declared righteous for the sake of His cross. Because of their faith they have been filled with the love of the Master and, like Him and the first disciples, all their lives they "went about doing good" (Acts 10:38). Believers will be surprised to know that their faith, active in love, served Jesus in the form of the woman or the man most in need. These righteous, in genuine astonishment, will inquire,

> . . . Lord, when saw we thee an hungered, and fed thee? or thirsty, and gave thee drink? When saw we thee a stranger, and took thee in? or naked, and clothed thee? Or when saw we thee sick, or in prison, and came unto thee?
>
> [Matt. 25:37–39]

These persons by baptism and belief, have been in Christ already. For that reason Luther could write,

> The judgment pertains to the believers as little as it does to the holy angels. All believers enter out of this life into the kingdom of heaven without judgment and are even the judges of others.[4]

It is the criterion of the Christian life, one of faith, love, and hope, that is applied to the lost. They are condemned, not primarily because the fruits of a good life are missing, but because the roots of such an existence, planted only by faith in Jesus, are totally absent. Their departure from the presence of God merely makes permanent what has been the

4. Quoted, *ibid*, p. 631.

pattern of their lives prior to the parousia—a self-serving and self-centered existence.

The third event will be the revelation of the new heaven and the new earth. The existing universe will "pass away" (Luke 21:33) to be replaced by God's new creation. As one changes clothes, so the world will be transformed. John caught a glimpse of "a new heaven and a new earth," for "the first heaven and the first earth were passed away" (Rev. 21:1). He "saw the holy city, new Jerusalem, coming down from God out of heaven, prepared as a bride adorned for her husband" (Rev. 21:2). In a chapter of pure rhapsody, John described what he saw, concluding,

> And I saw no temple therein; for the Lord God Almighty and the Lamb are the temple of it. And the city had no need of the sun, neither of the moon, to shine in it; for the glory of God did lighten it, and the Lamb is the light thereof. And the nations of them which are saved shall walk in the light of it: and the kings of the earth do bring their glory and honour into it.
>
> [Rev. 21:22–24]

Our imaginations strain and our aspirations soar, but the vision of what will be is far beyond our capacity to know. Suffice it to say that the world will end as it began, in creation by God and in praise by man, and all theology will be doxology,

> Saints robed in white before the shining throne
> Their joyful anthems raise,
> Till heaven's glad halls are echoing with the tone
> Of that great hymn of praise,
> And all its host rejoices,
> And all its blessed throng
> Unite their myriad voices
> In one eternal song.

Questions for Discussion

Introduction: The Lutheran Way

1. What images come to mind when you think of Lutheranism?
2. How does contemporary Lutheranism express itself in terms of community, theology, and liberty?
3. How do Christians of various traditions (including Lutherans) view Martin Luther today?
4. Has Lutheranism succeeded as a church-renewal movement within Western Christianity? In what ways?
5. Considering the various ages through which Lutheranism has passed, can Lutherans discuss theology and doctrine with an open mind? Discuss.

Chapter 1: The God of Creation

1. In what ways can we know God?
2. Is a definitive knowledge of God possible? Why or why not?
3. How do the attributes of God affect the everyday life of the believer? In what ways?
4. How is the fall experienced in the realms of church, state, and personal life?
5. Man is a unique personality. What are some of the ways in which man expresses his uniqueness?

Chapter 2: The Lord of Salvation

1. How does the question of Christ, "Whom do men say that I am?", affect modern man?
2. In what ways has the incarnation of Christ altered man and human history?
3. What is the significance of the ancient creeds of the church for contemporary Lutherans?
4. In your reflection upon the person of Christ, what takes precedence, His humanity or His divinity?
5. How do the ministries of Christ as prophet, priest, and king affect your local church? How is this expressed in the worship service?

Chapter 3: The Spirit of Conviction

1. Do Lutherans in general emphasize or avoid the subject of the Holy Spirit and His work?
2. In what ways has the Holy Spirit influenced your life through the offices and ministries of the church?
3. From your reading of the Scriptures, what role do you perceive the Holy Spirit playing in today's church?
4. What assurance is given you by the Scriptures concerning saving faith in Christ?
5. How would you attempt to explain the holy Trinity to a nonbeliever?

Chapter 4: The Means of Grace

1. List some of the ways in which we can use the Bible to a greater extent in church and personal life.
2. Discuss how Christ comes to us through the means of grace.
3. In what ways has your baptism enriched your individual life in Christ and your corporate life in the church?
4. Is there a relationship between peaceful congregational existence and participation in the Lord's Supper? Discuss.
5. Why is it important to recognize the real presence of Christ's body and blood in the Eucharist?

Chapter 5: The Congregation of Christ

1. Discuss the marks of the church (one, holy, catholic, apostolic) in terms of their impact upon your community.
2. What are the duties of the individual Christian as a member of the priesthood of all believers?
3. What do you consider to be the qualifications and the duties of a parish pastor?
4. What is the purpose of the Lutheran confessions?
5. What is the preeminent concern of your local church?

Chapter 6: The Worship of God

1. What do you perceive to be the focal point of your church's Sunday morning worship service? Why?
2. In what ways should the laity participate in public worship?
3. Which parts of worship do you consider adiaphora ("neutral things") and which parts do you consider essential?
4. Describe and discuss the various types of Lutheran worship services you have attended.
5. In what way does the church year influence and shape your life in Christ?

Chapter 7: The Calling of God

1. How do we serve God through the natural orders of the family, the state, work, and culture? Be specific.

2. In what particular ways can a couple glorify God through their marriage and family? What about the single person?
3. Should Christians strive for or expect a Christian government? Why or why not?
4. What is the Christian reaction to economic success or financial failure in both society and personal circumstances?
5. What is the role of the Christian artist? How do we reflect art and culture in church and home?

Chapter 8: The Heroes of Faith

1. Describe someone you have known whom you would designate as a hero of faith.
2. What would you identify as marks of Lutheran piety?
3. Describe the similarities and the differences between private and public prayer.
4. What does Luther's phrase *pray and work* indicate to you concerning the Christian life?
5. What is the place of morality and good works in the life of one who is saved by faith apart from works?

Chapter 9: The People of Victory

1. What is your attitude as a Lutheran toward death?
2. How does the church view those who have gone before us in the faith?
3. How does a belief in the existence of heaven and hell affect your day to day perspective on life?
4. Do you anticipate Christ's return in your lifetime? Why or why not?
5. How does the church look forward to Christ's return in glory in its worship?

A Bibliographic Essay

The corpus of literature concerning Lutheranism is immense. The entries in this section are meant to be suggestions for reading about the subject at hand, rather than an exhaustive bibliography. We have not mentioned many fine scholarly volumes, for lack of space. Those that are listed are books we have found especially helpful on our pilgrimage. For those desiring more detailed or abundant references on any particular subject, we recommend the bibliographies and articles contained in *The Encyclopedia of the Lutheran Church,* edited by Julius H. Bodensieck (Minneapolis: Augsburg, 1965) and the *Lutheran Cyclopedia*, edited by Erwin L. Lueker (Saint Louis: Concordia, 1975).

History

Harold J. Grimm, professor emeritus of history at Ohio State University, has written a definitive text about *The Reformation Era, 1500–1650* (New York: Macmillan, 1973). Insightful is Lewis W. Spitz's *The Renaissance and Reformation Movements* (Chicago: Rand McNally, 1971). British scholar Owen Chadwick has contributed to the general knowledge of this era with *The Reformation* (New York: Penguin, 1972).

Among biographical studies of Martin Luther, the popularity and reliability of Roland H. Bainton's *Here I Stand: A Life of Martin Luther* (New York: Abingdon-Cokesbury, 1950) remains unchallenged after a generation of use. The approach of Bainton, an American Quaker/ Congregationalist, is to be supplemented by that of the British Anglican and canon theologian, James Atkinson, in *Martin Luther and the Birth of Protestantism* (Baltimore: Penguin, 1968). The reformer's later years are given special attention in H. G. Haile's *Luther: An Experiment in Biography* (Garden City, NY: Doubleday, 1980).

Useful studies of Luther's thought include those by Paul Althaus, *The Theology of Martin Luther*, translated by Robert C. Schultz (Philadelphia: Fortress, 1966); John Dillenberger, *God Hidden and Revealed: The Interpretation of Luther's Deus Absconditus* (Philadelphia: Muhlenberg, 1953); Gerhard Ebeling, *Luther: An Introduction to His Thought*, translated by

R. A. Wilson (Philadelphia: Fortress, 1970); B. A. Gerrish, *Grace and Reason: A Study in the Theology of Luther* (Oxford: Clarendon Press, 1962); Ernest G. Schwiebert, *Luther and His Times (* Saint Louis: Concordia, 1950); and Philip S. Watson, *Let God Be God: An Interpretation of the Theology of Martin Luther* (Philadelphia: Muhlenberg, 1950).

The works of Martin Luther are available to the American reader in a number of forms. Two highly recommended sets are the six-volume *Works of Martin Luther, with Introductions and Notes—The Philadelphia Edition* (1915–1932; reprint ed., Grand Rapids: Baker, 1982) and the monumental fifty-five-volume *Luther's Works—The American Edition*, edited by Jaroslav Pelikan (Saint Louis: Concordia, 1955–).

The life and contributions of Philip Melanchthon have been skillfully presented to the modern mind by Clyde L. Manschreck in *Melanchthon: The Quiet Reformer* (Nashville: Abingdon, 1958), still the standard biography, and in *Loci Communes* (1965; reprint ed., Grand Rapids: Baker, 1982).

Surveys of Lutheranism since the Reformation include those of C. George Fry et al., *The Age of Lutheran Orthodoxy* (Fort Wayne, IN: Concordia Theological Seminary Press, 1979); *Christian Social Responsibility*, volume 2, *The Lutheran Heritage*, edited by Harold C. Letts (Philadelphia: Muhlenberg, 1957); Conrad Bergendoff, *The Church of the Lutheran Reformation: A Historical Survey of Lutheranism* (Saint Louis: Concordia, 1967); and Andrew L. Drummond, *German Protestantism Since Luther* (London: Epworth, 1951). Helpful, though now dated, is the Lutheran World Federation's publication, *Lutheran Churches of the World* (Minneapolis: Augsburg, 1957).

Studies of Lutheranism in America include those by C. George Fry and John M. Drickamer, *A History of Lutheranism in America, 1619–1930* (Fort Wayne, IN: Concordia Theological Seminary Press, 1979); A. R. Wentz, *A Basic History of Lutheranism in America* (Philadelphia: Muhlenberg, 1955); and *The Lutherans in North America* (Philadelphia: Fortress, 1975), edited by E. Clifford Nelson et al. Two useful volumes about the "separate history" of the Lutheran Church-Missouri Synod are the revised edition of Walter A. Baepler's *A Century of Grace: A History of the Missouri Synod, 1847–1947* (Saint Louis: Concordia, 1963) and *Moving Frontiers: Readings in the History of the Lutheran Church-Missouri Synod* (Saint Louis: Concordia, 1964), edited by Carl S. Meyer.

Theology

The average Lutheran's introduction to theology is provided by Martin Luther's Small Catechism (1529). Perhaps the most widely used interpretation of the catechism has been *A Short Explanation of Dr. Martin Luther's Small Catechism: A Handbook of Christian Doctrine* (Saint Louis: Concordia, 1943). Most Lutheran congregregations, by their constitutions, are committed to *The Book of Concord* (1580). Among the various editions available, two have been extensively employed by America's Lutherans: *The Concordia Triglotta* (Saint Louis: Concordia, 1921) and *The Book of Concord: A Handbook of the Evangelical Lutheran Church* (Philadelphia: Muhlenberg, 1959), edited and translated by Theodore G. Tappert. A useful anthology of Lutheran thought from the age of orthodoxy is Heinrich Schmid's *The Doctrinal Theology of the Evangelical Lutheran Church*, the third revised edition, translated by Charles A. Hay and Henry E. Jacobs (Minneapolis: Augsburg, 1961).

Among the classic expositions of Lutheran theology are Victor Beck's *Why I Am a Lutheran* (New York: Thomas Nelson and Sons, 1956); A. L. Graebner's *Outlines of Doctrinal Theology* (Saint Louis: Concordia, 1898); W. Q. Hove's *Christian Doctrine* (Minneapolis: Augsburg, 1930); Theodore Huggenvik's *We Believe* (Minneapolis: Augsburg, 1950); Henry Eyster Jacobs's *Summary of the Christian Faith* (Philadelphia: The United Lutheran Publication House, 1905); Christopher Ernst Luthardt's *Apologetic Lectures on The Fundamental Truths of Christianity*, translated by Sophia Taylor (Edinburgh: T. and T. Clark, 1909); P. L. Mellenbruch's *The Doctrines of Christianity* (New York: Revell, 1931); Hans Martensen's *Christian Dogmatics*, translated by William Urwick (Edinburgh: T. and T. Clark, 1866); John Theodore Mueller's *Christian Dogmatics* (Saint Louis: Concordia, 1955); Franz Pieper's *Christian Dogmatics*, four volumes, translated by Theodore Engelder and Walter W. F. Albrecht (Saint Louis: Concordia, 1957); J. A. Singmaster's *Handbook of Christian Theology* (Philadelphia: The United Lutheran Publication House, 1927); Joseph Stump's *The Christian Faith: A System of Christian Dogmatics* (Philadelphia: Muhlenberg, 1942); M. Valentine's *Christian Theology*, two volumes (Philadelphia: Muhlenberg, 1906); A. G. Voigt's *Biblical Dogmatics* (Columbia, SC: The Lutheran Board of Publication, 1917); and R. F. Weidner's *Dogmatic Theology: Based on Luthardt and Krauth* (Chicago: Wartburg, 1915).

There are also a large number of excellent dogmatic texts that are not yet (to our knowledge) translated from the German. A few of the more popular and beneficial texts are K. F. A. Kahnis, *Die lutherische Dogmatik historisch-genetische dargelstellt*, second edition, two volumes (Leipzig: Doerffling, 1874); Christopher Ernst Luthardt, *Kompendium Der Dogmatik* (Heidelberg: Jedermann Verlag, 1948); F. A. Philippi, *Kirchliche Glaubenslehre*, six volumes (Stuttgart: S. G. Liesching, 1883); and A. F. C. Vilmar, *Dogmatik* (Guetersloh: C. Bertelsmann, 1874).

Among the contemporary expositions of Lutheran theology, attention should be given to Gustaf Aulen, *The Faith of the Christian Church*, translated by Eric H. Wahlstrom and G. Everett Arden (Philadelphia: Fortress, 1961); Werner Elert, *An Outline of Christian Doctrine*, translated by Charles M. Jacobs (Philadelphia: The United Lutheran Publication House, 1927), and *The Structure of Lutheranism*, translated by Walter A. Hansen (Saint Louis: Concordia, 1962); Martin J. Heinecken, *Christian Teachings: Affirmations of Faith for Lay People* (Philadelphia: Fortress, 1967); Regin Prenter, *The Church's Faith: A Primer of Christian Beliefs*, translated by

Theodor I. Jensen (Philadelphia: Fortress, 1968); Helmut Thielicke, *I Believe: The Christian's Creed*, translated by John W. Doberstein and H. George Anderson (Philadelphia: Fortress, 1968), and *The Evangelical Faith*, translated by Geoffrey Bromiley (Grand Rapids: Eerdmans, 1974).

In more specialized areas of study we commend to the reader the classic work of Charles Porterfield Krauth, *The Conservative Reformation and Its Theology* (Minneapolis: Augsburg, 1963) and the major recent contribution of Robert D. Preus, *The Theology of Post-Reformation Lutheranism*, volume 2, *God and His Creation* (Saint Louis: Concordia, 1972). For early Christian perceptions, G. L. Prestige, *God in Patristic Thought* (London: SPCK, 1975) is unsurpassed.

In the realm of Christology and the church's confession of faith some standard works include Aloys Grillmeier, *Christ in Christian Tradition: From the Apostolic Age to Chalcedon* (Atlanta: John Knox, 1975); Martin Chemnitz, *The Two Natures in Christ*, translated by J. A. O. Preus (Saint Louis: Concordia, 1970); the still-valuable Philip Schaff, *The Creeds of Christendom*, in three volumes (1877; reprint ed., Grand Rapids: Baker, 1977); J. N. D. Kelly, *Early Christian Doctrines*, the revised edition (New York: Harper and Row, 1978); Gustaf Aulen, *Christus Victor* (London: SPCK, 1931); and Regin Prenter, *Creation and Redemption*, translated by Theodor I. Jensen (Philadelphia: Fortress, 1967).

Concerning the Holy Spirit, and the holy Trinity, we have found modern as well as ancient volumes enlightening. The premier ancient works are *The Library of Nicene and Post Nicene Fathers*, second series, volume 8, Basil, *On the Holy Spirit*, translated by Bloomfield Jackson (Grand Rapids: Eerdmans, 1975); and *The Fathers of the Church*, volume 45, Augustine, *The Trinity*, translated by Stephen McKenna (Washington, DC: Catholic University of America Press, 1963). Helpful modern volumes include Fredrik Wisloff, *I Believe in the Holy Spirit*, translated by Ingvald Baehlin (Minneapolis: Augsburg, 1947); Regin Prenter, *Spiritus Creator*, translated by John M. Jensen (Philadelphia: Fortress, 1953); and a new scholarly volume by William C. Weinrich, *Spirit and Martyrdom: A Study of the Work of the Holy Spirit in Contexts of Persecution and Martyrdom in the New Testament and Early Christian Literature* (Washington, DC: University Press of America, 1981).

For competent and penetrating discussions on the nature of sacred Scripture and the means of grace we suggest John K. S. Reid, *The Authority of Scripture: A Study of the Reformation and Post-Reformation Understanding of the Bible* (New York: Harper and Brothers, 1957); Regin Prenter, *The Word and the Spirit: Essays on the Inspiration of the Scriptures*, translated by Harris E. Kaas (Minneapolis: Augsburg, 1965); Werner Elert, *Eucharist and Church Fellowship in the First Four Centuries*, translated by N. E. Nagel (Saint Louis: Concordia, 1966); Herman Sasse, *This Is My Body* (Minneapolis: Augsburg, 1959); Carl J. F. Wisløff, *The Gift of Communion*, translated by Joseph M. Shaw (Minneapolis: Augsburg, 1964); and J. E. L. Oulton, *Holy Communion and Holy Spirit* (London: SPCK, 1954).

Liturgy

Since World War II, the most popular hymnals among North American Lutherans have been *The Lutheran Hymnal* (Saint Louis: Concordia, 1941), authorized for use in the Evangelical Lutheran Synodical Conference of North America; *Worship Supplement* (Saint Louis: Concordia, 1969), authorized by the Commission on Worship of the Lutheran Church-Missouri Synod and the Synod of Evangelical Lutheran Churches; *The Service Book and Hymnal of the Lutheran Church in America* (Minneapolis: Fortress, 1958), used by the American Evangelical Lutheran Church, the American Lutheran Church, the Augustana Evangelical Lutheran Church, the Evangelical Lutheran Church, the Finnish Evangelical Lutheran Church in America, The Lutheran Free Church, the United Evangelical Lutheran Church, and the United Lutheran Church in America (later the Lutheran Church in America); *Lutheran Book of Worship* (Minneapolis: Augsburg, 1978), prepared by the Inter-Lutheran Commission on Worship, now used in the Lutheran Church in America, the American Lutheran Church, the Evangelical Lutheran Church of Canada, the Lutheran Church-Missouri Synod, and the Association of Evangelical Lutheran Churches; and *Lutheran Worship* (Saint Louis: Concordia, 1981), prepared for use in the Lutheran Church-Missouri Synod.

Luther D. Reed, long-time professor at the Lutheran Seminary, Mount Airy, Pennsylvania, has written two excellent works on worship—*Worship: A Study of Corporate Devotion* (Philadelphia: Muhlenberg, 1959) and *The Lutheran Liturgy* (Philadelphia: Muhlenberg, 1947). Recent thinking on Lutheran worship is found in Eugene Brand, *The Rite Thing* (Minneapolis: Augsburg, 1970) and Herbert F. Lindemann, *The New Mood in Lutheran Worship* (Minneapolis: Augsburg, 1971). Two long-standing landmarks in the study of liturgy are Evelyn Underhill's *Worship* (New York: Harper and Row, 1936) and Paul Z. Strodach's *Manual on Worship*, the revised edition (Philadelphia: Muhlenberg, 1946). Among the many studies of the Christian year, we commend Edward T. Horn's *The Christian Year* (Philadelphia: Muhlenberg, 1957) and Theodore J. Kleinhans's *The Year of the Lord* (Saint Louis: Concordia, 1967). More specialized and useful studies include those by Ralph P. Martin, *Worship in the Early Church*, the revised edition (Grand Rapids: Eerdmans, 1975); Vilmos Vajta, *Luther on Worship* (Philadelphia: Muhlenberg, 1958); Arthur Carl Piepkorn, *What the Symbolic Books of the Lutheran Church Have to Say about Worship and the Sacraments* (Saint Louis: Concordia, 1952); the new standard reference work on pan-Christian worship, *The Study of Liturgy*, edited by Cheslyn Jones and Geoffrey Wainwright (New York: Oxford University Press, 1978); and the helpful reference work, *The Westminster Dictionary of Worship*, edited by J. G. Davies (1972; reprint ed., Philadelphia: Westminster, 1979).

Community

Very good material on the place of Lutheranism within the context of the broader Christian community is available as the result of the many formal dialogues with other traditions. Among these we recommend *Anglican-Lutheran International Conversations: The Report of the Conversations 1970–1972 Authorized by the Lambeth Conference and the Lutheran World Federation* (London: SPCK, 1973); *Lutherans and Catholics in Dialogue IV*, edited by Paul C. Empie et al. (Minneapolis: Augsburg, 1965–1974) in four volumes, and *A Reexamination of Lutheran and Reformed Traditions* (Geneva: Lutheran World Federation, 1964). A good synopsis of this material is provided by Warren A. Quanbeck, *Search for Understanding: Lutheran Conversations with Reformed, Anglican, and Roman Catholic Churches* (Minneapolis: Augsburg, 1972); and Myron A. Marty, *Lutherans and Roman Catholicism: The Changing Conflict, 1917–1963* (Notre Dame: University of Notre Dame Press, 1968).

The concern for ecclesiastical identity, both historically and denominationally, is well documented by Werner Elert in *The Structure of Lutheranism* (Saint Louis: Concordia, 1962); and Dietrich Bonhoeffer in *Life Together* (New York: Harper and Row, 1976) and *The Communion of Saints* (New York: Harper and Row, 1963). An excellent study of the ancient church in this regard is Robert F. Evans's *One and Holy, The Church in Latin Patristic Thought* (London: SPCK, 1972).

The ethics of the Christian community are explored by Dietrich Bonhoeffer in *Ethics* (London SCM Press, 1955); Werner Elert, *The Christian Ethos*, translated by Carl J. Schindler (Philadelphia: Muhlenberg, 1957); Adolf Koeberle, *The Quest for Holiness*, translated by John C. Mattes (Minneapolis: Augsburg, 1938); Christopher Ernst Luthardt, *Apologetic Lectures on the Moral Truths of Christianity*, translated by Sophia Taylor (Edinburgh: T. and T. Clark, 1881); Helmut Thielicke, *The Ethics of Sex*, translated by John W. Doberstein (1964; reprint ed., Grand Rapids: Baker, 1975); R. F. Weidner, *Christian Ethics* (New York: Revell, 1897); Gustaf F. Wingren, *Luther on Vocation* (Philadelphia: Muhlenberg, 1957); and John A. Hutchinson, *The Two Cities* (New York: Doubleday, 1957). More specialized studies and interpretations may be found in Carl F. H. Henry, *Christian Personal Ethics* (Grand Rapids: Eerdmans, 1957); Os Guiness, *The Dust of Death* (Downers Grove, IL: Inter-Varsity, 1973); and Jacques Ellul, *The Meaning of the City* (Grand Rapids: Eerdmans, 1970).

For the individual Christian, and his life in the community of faith, a great number of volumes are produced each year. It would be impossible to select even a cross section of what is available. In light of this we recommend three devotional classics, proven through time, and one modern addition. The oldest and most timeless of the three is *The Imitation of Christ* (Grand Rapids: Zondervan, 1969) by, it is supposed, Thomas à

Kempis, a Brother of the Common Life. The second volume, which has been presented in a new translation and format, is Johann Arndt's *True Christianity* (New York: Paulist Press, 1980). All traditions recognize the value of François Fénelon's *Christian Perfection* (New York: Harper, 1947). To these we add the name of C. S. Lewis, an author who is increasingly recognized by Christians worldwide. We especially commend *Letters to Malcolm: Chiefly on Prayer* (New York: Harcourt, Brace and World, 1964).

Subject Index

Scripture Index